Homeward Bound

RABBI MICHOEL GROS

Homeward Bound

Inspiring Stories of Return

DISTRIBUTED BY FELDHEIM

Unless indicated with an asterisk, all names and personal details are real.

ISBN 978-1-68025-283-5

For comments or to receive information on upcoming books from the author and dedication opportunities, please email: grospublishing@gmail.com.

Page layout by E. Chachamtzedek

DISTRIBUTED BY:
Feldheim Publishers
POB 43163 / Jerusalem, Israel

208 Airport Executive Park
Nanuet, NY 10954
www.feldheim.com

DISTRIBUTED IN EUROPE BY:
Lehmanns
+44-0-191-430-0333
info@lehmanns.co.uk
www.lehmanns.co.uk

DISTRIBUTED IN AUSTRALIA BY:
Golds World of Judaica
+613 95278775
info@golds.com.au
www.golds.com.au

Printed in Israel

Dedicated to my dear wife

Shoshana

There are insufficient words
to express my love, gratitude, and
admiration for my beloved *Eishes Chayil*,
who is the foundation of all the goodness
in my life. As the Gemara so poignantly
acknowledges: "One's wife is the source
of all of the blessings in his home"
(*Bava Metzia* 59a).

And to the members of the

Atlanta Scholars Kollel

who noticed my potential and helped me to
bring it out, and who then paid me the
ultimate honor by permitting me
to join their hallowed ranks.

Rabbi Reuven Feinstein
1880 Drumgoole Road East
Staten Island, New York 10309

שלו' ראובן פיינשטיין
ראש הישיבה
ישיבה ד'סטעטן איילענד

After reading some of the inspirational stories and well-explained *divrei Torah* in Rabbi Michoel Gros's inspiring *sefer*, it is my pleasure to write this letter of recommendation. This *sefer* will serve to enhance the appreciation of the guidance of the *Yad Hashem* in our everyday lives, specifically along the journey of *teshuvah* upon which so many of our brothers and sisters are embarking.

I hope this *sefer* will serve to inspire and encourage those who are giving of themselves to help our brethren along their paths back to the roots of our tradition. In it, Rabbi Gros has collected many examples of how Hashem guides us every step of the way, as well as providing insightful ways to understand this guidance through the eyes of the Torah.

It is important to share these stories, which can serve as encouragement in a confusing world. Rabbi Gros has done this with great skill, care, and effort. He is clearly a *talmid chacham* and a *yarei Shamayim*. *Yehi ratzon* that through his efforts, we will come closer to the time when all of *Klal Yisrael* join together in knowledge of Hashem and His Torah, with the coming of Mashiach.

Hatzlachah Rabbah,

שמואל קמנצקי
Rabbi S. Kamenetsky

2018 Upland Way
Philadelphia, PA 19131

Home: 215-473-2798
Study: 215-473-1212

בס"ד ה' תשרי תשע"ז

למע"כ הרב ר' מיכאל גראס שליט"א

ספרו הנכבד "האומווערד באונד" אודות כמה סיפורים שהיו
כמה יהודים ונעשו בעלי תשובה שנתעורר בהם נקודת
קדושתם שהם בשורשם בני עלי' בקדושה ושואפים וקשורים אל מקורם
ובסייעתא דשמיא חזרו אל מקורם.

ובודאי כל הסיפורים כאלו יהי' לתועלת גדולה לכל
מיני בעלי תשובה. גם להרבה שכל העוסק בענין קירוב
לתורה ויהדות ימצאו בספרו ענינים שמועילים בעסק
של קירוב לתורה ויהדות.

תקותי שיזכה כבודו להמנות ממקרבי בני ישראל
לבוראם ויהי' לזכות לו ולמשפחתו יחיו.

בברכת גמר חתימה טובה

שמואל קמנצקי

---

5 Tishrei 5777 בס"ד

Dear Rav R' Michoel Gros, *shlita*

This important *sefer* "Homeward Bound" includes many stories of Jews who have become *ba'alei teshuvah*. Their innate holiness was awakened within them, because at their root they are Jews who are inherently holy and strive for growth. They are connected to their source and they returned with *siyatta diShamaya*.

There is no doubt that these stories will be a great aid for all *ba'alei teshuvah*. In addition, anyone involved in *kiruv l'Torah v'yahadus* will find *inyanim* in this *sefer* that will assist them in that work.

It is my hope that the author will merit to be counted among those who bring Jews to their Creator, and this book will be a merit to him and his family.

Gmar chasimah tovah,

Rabbi Shmuel Kamenetsky

בס"ד

בית הכנסת
הגר"א
רמת בית שמש

Rabbi Elimelech Kornfeld Shlita
Rav of Kehillas Hagra
Ramat Beit Shemesh

הרב אלימלך קורנפלד שליט"א
רב קהילת הגר"א
רמת בית שמש

September 19, 2016
ט"ז אלול תשע"ו

I have had the *zechus* to know Rav Michoel Gros for quite a few years. He is an outstanding example of a *talmid chacham* who is overflowing with tremendous *ahavas haTorah* and *yiras Shamayim*. He learns in Beis Medrash HaGra and his great *hasmadah*, and the energy that he puts into his learning and into the *shiurim*, are *mechazek* all of us. His writing on Torah subjects also reveal a clarity and an ability to elucidate difficult subjects.

He is now publishing a *sefer* of *hashgachah pratis* stories of people who have returned to their Jewish roots. He has spoken to me about the *sefer* and I have seen portions of it. I am sure that everyone who reads it will be inspired by the *Yad Hashem* revealed in its stories and by the personal strength of the *ba'alei teshuvah* profiled within it. The book will enhance people's *avodas Hashem* and help them to gain a greater appreciation for Hashem and His ways.

May Michoel be able to continue to learn Torah and to spread its light throughout the world. He should have much *nachas* from all his children, and may they continue to follow in his path of pure *avodas Hashem mitoch ahavah*.

Contents

Acknowledgments

FIRST AND FOREMOST I am grateful to **Hashem** for His ceaseless blessings for my family and me. In particular, we have tremendous appreciation for being able to live in Eretz Yisrael in good health as observant Jews and to be able to learn His holy Torah. Thank You Hashem for guiding me at every stage of writing this book.

Thank you to my *Eishes Chayil*, **Shoshana**. She is the cause of the blessings and goodness of our home. I am forever amazed at her ability to juggle everything with nobility and warmth. She was the force behind this book and she is the reason that I am able to sit and learn. I look up to her and am honored to accompany her on our joint mission in life.

Thank you to our wonderful **children** for the ceaseless *nachas* they give us and for inspiring us with their own excitement for their learning and for their service of Hashem.

Thank you to my dear parents, **Jacques and Bonnie Gros,** for countless reasons, but especially for their love, for the strong foundation of Judaism they instilled in me, and for their continuous support throughout my journey.

Thank you to my grandmother **Isabel Gros** for her warmth, love, and laughs, and for continuing to visit us in Israel even though she is already into her ninth decade of life.

Thank you my wonderful in-laws, **Alan and Elaine Rashes,** for raising a beautiful, special daughter and for always showering me with love and encouragement.

I have gratitude to many people and organizations, without whom my family and I would be in a very different place today and this book may not have come into existence.

Thank you to the members of the **Atlanta Scholars Kollel** with whom I worked with: **Rabbis Doniel Pransky, Menachem Deutsch, David Silverman, Yaakov Fleshel, Binyamin Friedman, Michoel Friedman, Shlomo Gelbtuch, Menashe Goldberger, Ahron Golding, Moshe Hiller, Michoel Lipschutz, Daniel Freitag,** and **Jeremy Posen** and their families. Many of them helped to guide me on my initial journey home while I was a student in Atlanta, and then they continued to help shape the direction of my family and I while I was part of the Kollel. In addition, the professional and women's outreach staff of the Kollel with whom I worked: **Mrs. Miriam Cole, Mrs. Rivkie Freundlich, Mrs. Randy Goldberger, Mrs. Leah Pollock, Mrs. Julie Silverman, Ms. Marcia Sternberg,** and **Mrs. Shany Stiefel** all stand out for their love of their jobs and their professional work ethic. **Yisrael Killian** also played an indispensable role in many areas.

Thank you to **Rabbi Eliyahu Shusterman and family** of **Chabad of Georgia** for their impact on me during the beginning of my journey.

Thank you to **Rabbi Baruch Chazanow and family** of **Chabad of Manalapan** for giving me a wonderful synagogue in which to daven while visiting my parents in New Jersey, and for providing a *makom tefillah* for them.

Following college, I attended **Yeshivas Darchei Noam/Shapell's** in Yerushalayim and I am grateful to the *rabbeim* there for giving me an initial direction and grounding in learning. This was further developed by the *rabbeim* at **Yeshivas Madreigas HaAdam** in Queens, NY, and **Yeshivas Marbeh Torah** in Bnei Brak, Israel.

Thank you to **Rabbi Asher Schechter and his family** of the Ohr Moshe Synagogue of Hillcrest, Queens, who provided critical advice and focus to me and my wife and during our years in New York.

During this time I benefited greatly from the *shiurim* of **Rabbi Eliyahu Hartman.** His clarity and the scope of his knowledge left a strong impression on me as a model for my own learning. **Dr. Chaim Presby** also left a tremendous mark on me through his in-depth classes and his obvious love for learning and teaching.

My wife and I are grateful to **Bob and Carol Weissman** for being our adoptive *frum* family while we lived in New York, and to **Avraham and Ditza Verter** and **Chaim and Gila Mayerson** for playing a similar role while we lived in Eretz Yisrael. All three families introduced us to many of the practical ins and outs of the holidays and how to run an Orthodox home.

While we lived in Atlanta we were guided by **Rabbi Ilan Feldman** and we have gratitude to him for his assistance in numerous areas.

Thank you to our current Rav, **Rabbi Elimelech Kornfeld** of Kehillas HaGra in Ramat Beit Shemesh Aleph. He is the source of direction, knowledge, and guidance in our lives and those of our children in so many areas.

Since making *aliyah*, I have been most fortunate to be able to sit and learn full-time in Rabbi Kornfeld's *beis midrash* of Kehillas HaGra, amidst *talmidei chachamim* and writers of *sefarim*. It has been a special privilege. I also appreciate the letters of *haskamah* he wrote for this and my previous book, and for the encouragement he has shown for these projects.

I have attended the daily *shiur* of **Rabbi Yehudah Berinstein** for several years and have had the valuable opportunity to learn one-on-one with him and to help him develop written summaries of his *shiurim*. I am continuously impressed by his humility, serene nature, and sharp thinking, all of which have helped to shape my own learning.

My family and I also have tremendous gratitude to **Rabbi Kalman Rosenbaum** for helping to direct our children's education and our *aliyah* plans while we lived in Atlanta, for continuing to be a source of guidance and inspiration since then, and for making time to learn with me every week.

Thank you to **Rabbi Yehudah Silver** for his warmth and availability to us to help us navigate numerous critical questions in our daily life in Israel.

Much of the material in this book originated in a monthly column that I have written since 2007 in **The Jewish Press** entitled "The Teshuva Journey." I am grateful to the staff, especially **Mrs. Naomi Klass Mauer and Mrs. Chumi Freedman,** for their enthusiasm and encouragement for the column and for allowing me to use the articles in this format.

Several other stories appeared in **Hamodia**. Thank you to **Mrs. Ruth Lichtenstein, Mrs. Rivky Goldberger, Mrs. Sarah Birnhack, and Mrs. Esther Ehrlich.** My articles have also appeared on **aish.com**. I am grateful to the editor **Rabbi Nechemia Coopersmith,** for his editorial input and keen eye.

Thank you to all of the subjects profiled in this book and in my column for taking the time to share details of their journeys with me, and for inspiring me with their words.

Thank you to all our family members and friends who helped by sponsoring portions of the book which enabled me to bring it to publication.

Thank you to the **Feldheim** staff for their talent and experience to guide this project from mere words on a computer screen to a beautiful finished product. Thank you to **Rabbi Eli Meir Hollander, Rabbi David Kahn, Rabbi Yehudah Dombey, Mrs. Dena Belsky, Mrs. Eden Chachamtzedek, Mrs. Brocha Schreiber, Mrs. Chana Devorah Sklar, Mrs. Judy Mernick,** and **Mr. Menachem Deutsch.** Special thanks to **Mr. Michael Silverstein** for the stunning cover design.

Thank you to the Roshei HaYeshivah **Rabbi Ruvein Feinstein** *shlita* and **Rabbi Shmuel Kamenetsky** *shlita* who took from their valuable time to look at the text of this book and to write letters of *haskamah* for it. Thank you to **Rabbi Shalom Kamenetsky** *shlita* and **Rabbi Mordechai Eisenberg** for their help in attaining these letters; and to **Matty Rubenstein**, who was instrumental in this process as well.

An additional rabbi played an important role in the development of this book by providing timely encouragement for it. Among his many roles, the **Kaliver Rebbe** of America, **Rabbi Moshe Taub**, travels to the ends of the world to seek out Jews and give them encouragement. I had met the Rebbe in the winter of 2001/2002 when he visited Yeshivas Madreigas HaAdam while I was learning there. During his visit, he met privately with each student.

One evening, five years later, I received an unexpected phone call from his *gabbai*. At the time I was contemplating writing this book. The Rebbe instructed the *gabbai* to call me, to give me encouragement for my life and to wish me *hatzlachah* on any projects I was working on. I do not know how the Rebbe knew to call at just that moment, but the message was clear — full steam ahead!

I am grateful to several authors who live in Ramat Beit Shemesh who gave me valuable advice while I was working on this book: **Rabbis Nachman Seltzer, Michoel Fletcher** and **Reuvain Mendlowitz**.

Thank you to **Rabbi Dovid Greenwald** for his assistance during the final stages of this book. Thank you to **Ms. Yael Seruya** for her essential insights into the outreach world and **Rabbi Eli Gewirtz** for his invaluable suggestions on the text of the book.

With blessings,
Michoel Gros
Ramat Beit Shemesh Aleph, Israel
December 2017 / Kislev 5777

Introduction

AS I SIT AROUND our Shabbos table watching our eight lively children discuss the weekly Torah portion, it's hard not to reflect on where I have come from. Twenty years ago, when I began my journey of returning to my Jewish roots, I barely knew what the weekly Torah portion was. Today even our younger children know many of the ins and outs of each *parashah* and are eager to show off their *parashah* pictures colored in with every shade of crayon imaginable.

One of my own earliest childhood memories is going to my grandparents' house and watching my grandfather put on his tefillin each morning. He was not Orthodox, but in his parents' home in France, they had observed many of the mitzvos. When he arrived in America as a teenager, he brought with him a commitment to attend synagogue each Shabbos and to put on his tefillin every day. Even at such a young age, I remember being enthralled by the sight of him wrapping the black leather straps tightly around his arms and head and reciting a few short prayers to Hashem. The experience planted a seed in me that would one day sprout into a burning desire to do the same. Indeed, the mitzvah of tefillin was one of the first that I took on when I started my journey at age nineteen.

There were several other events and people throughout my life that pushed me onto the path toward Orthodox Judaism. When I was finally fully exposed to it in college, I jumped at the chance. I always knew there had to be more to Judaism than bagels on Sunday morning and occasional synagogue attendance. For Judaism to last for thousands of years through so many challenges and hardships, there had to be more substance than what I had been exposed to growing up.

Over my first nineteen years of life I accumulated plenty of questions about Judaism, the world, and my reasons for being here. I finally got the chance to start getting answers during my sophomore year at Emory University in Atlanta, Georgia.

Atlanta is home to a warm and welcoming religious community situated only two miles from the Emory campus. Anyone involved in Jewish outreach knows that free food is the key to getting participants to come to an event, and this rule holds true nowhere better than for reaching out to cash-starved college students. During my sophomore year in 1996, I began attending weekly (and free) pizza Lunch-N-Learns run on campus by rabbis from the local Atlanta Scholars Kollel.

Each week I heard fascinating ideas on upcoming holidays or the week's Torah portions and was able to ask some of the questions I had accumulated. No topic was left uncovered — I was able to explore and debate topics as diverse as the creation of the world and evolution, the after-life, feminism, and morality.

Every *ba'al teshuvah* has a different path back to Judaism and a different element which attracts them. The draw for me was Judaism's infinitely deep intellectual traditions. But I soon learned that the Torah is more than just a stimulating intellectual exercise. It is the ultimate guidebook to every detail and every moment of our lives. As the Rabbis explain, "Turn it [Torah] over and turn it over, because everything is in it" (*Pirkei Avos* 5:26).

For starters, the Torah is the decisive self-help book. The Torah and its commentaries teach people how to avoid anger, to overcome poor self-esteem, to become more generous, and to beat addictions. It teaches people how to become better parents, more effective bosses, and more loving spouses. But it is more than just a self-help book. It is the very foundation of our lives.

The Lunch-N-Learns and classes, combined with Shabbos meals in the local community and an assortment of additional programs from a Chabad family on campus, made for the ideal environment for myself and several other students to decide to return together to Torah-true Judaism.

For the summer after my sophomore year, I planned to return to my parents' home in New Jersey with the hopes of interning in New York City. A well-worn Yiddish expression teaches, "Man plans and G-d laughs." Not one of the dozens of companies I sent my resume to, or even the handful of interviews that I had, led to a job. Where did I end up for the summer? Back in Atlanta. I received an amazing internship at IBM, even though I do not recall ever submitting my resume to the company. When I was not working, I spent my time immersed in spiritual growth and Torah study. The summer culminated in a trip up north to Moodus, Connecticut, where I attended a week-and-a-half boot-camp for Jews returning to their roots. Being able to spend the summer in these environments helped to further cement my desire to become *frum*.

Over the next two years of college I grew steadily in my religious commitments. My dream was to attend yeshivah in Eretz Yisrael after graduation.

I met my wife Shoshana in June, 1998. She had just graduated from the University of Michigan and had become observant there. I still had one more year of college. When we first met, she told me that she was heading off to Israel for the next four years to attend medical school. I said, "Great, I'm going to yeshivah next year!"

Shoshana went off to Israel, I finished college and we married soon after. We spent our first year and a half together in Israel. Following medical school, we moved back to the U.S., first to Queens, New York and then to Atlanta, Georgia to follow our dream to get involved in outreach. There I joined the Atlanta

Scholars Kollel and became its Chief Operating Officer. I was able to work alongside the same Rabbis who had been my mentors at the beginning of my journey. It gave me a chance to give something small back to the people who had given me so much.

In 2009 we made *aliyah* and have lived in Ramat Beit Shemesh Aleph ever since.

It was my own journey home toward Torah observance that gave me the idea to write this book. I was repeatedly inspired by the stories I heard of other people's travels. I realized the value of collecting and sharing these stories to encourage others.

Homeward Bound profiles journeys of Jews returning to their roots. Jews who become observant are not blazing a new path for themselves; rather, they are returning to millennia-old traditions and customs that have withstood the test of time and ever-changing social norms. One young man identified to me the biggest hurdle when he began to learn more about his religion: he felt that becoming observant meant breaking from the mold of his non-religious family. But when he had an encounter with a memento from his great-grandparents and learned that they had been Orthodox, he realized that he was not running from the path of his family, but returning to it.

This book is not only a compilation of stories; it shows each of us the potential we have to grow and to connect to Hashem.

Throughout the book we travel alongside Jews on journeys of growth and we witness the Hand of Hashem gently guiding them with small everyday experiences disguised as "coincidences," and sometimes through outright miracles. We see them discover new strengths in themselves and muster their courage to pass the trials in their lives. In doing so, we discover their greatness and reveal the potential for greatness that lies within all of us.

Numerous Torah sources are quoted through this work. Any errors or omissions are the fault of my own research and translations as well as the limits of my knowledge and experience. As the Gemara says (*Megillah* 7b): "A poor person does not know he is hungry." This refers to a person being sadly unaware of how much Torah he is missing because of his own limited knowledge.

My deepest hope is that these stories will encourage all of us, regardless of our current level of observance, on our own journeys home.

Homeward Bound

1 Just One Shabbos

SHABBOS. IT'S A TASTE OF THE WORLD TO COME, AND A day of palpable holiness.

When a Jew experiences a truly beautiful Shabbos table, where family members sit together, singing, eating delicious food and sharing Torah thoughts, his soul soars. It is the doorway that often inspires a person to return to his roots. In the flicker of the Shabbos candles, he gets a glimpse of the beautiful, observant lifestyles of his great-grandparents. Their Shabbos tables were not much different than ours today. During their meals they gave blessings to their children, shared words of Torah and basked in the glory of Hashem.

The Shabbos experience enters a person's *neshamah* and makes a greater impression on him than any intellectual argument ever could. He is given the chance to step out of his everyday existence and contemplate his life — where he is headed and from where he has come. The day grants us spiritual clarity about where we are now, and where we want to be.

In the Friday-night prayer *Lecha Dodi*, we refer to Shabbos as "*Mekor HaBerachah* — the source of all blessing." Shabbos is a day of open miracles, and the single experience that best encapsulates the beauty of Judaism.

THE FIRE

SOMETIMES, IT TAKES patience to see the miracles and beauty hidden even inside tragedy.

In 1975, Mitch Rakover* decided to become observant, again. He had attended a yeshivah in his youth but had strayed in his observance. But when his second child — a son — was born, he had tremendous feelings of thanksgiving to Hashem, so he decided to return to his roots.

For him it was a real return. But for his wife Eve, the experience was brand-new. She had grown up in a nonobservant Jewish home and had never considered the religious path until Mitch suggested it. But she happily went along.

The Rakovers were living in Cleveland when they began rebuilding their life from scratch. From miles away in Philadelphia, Eve's parents, the Wolfs*, observed their changes. Though they did not become observant themselves, they said repeatedly how inspired they were by the changes they saw in their children's lives and the positive life-choices they were making.

One day, Eve's mother Anne called. She announced that she wanted to start lighting Shabbos candles each week. She was not yet ready to commit to observing Shabbos, but she wanted to take on this single mitzvah.

The Rakovers were thrilled at the news and told her how to light the candles and taught her the wording of the blessing. They waited expectantly throughout the whole Shabbos, looking forward to speaking to her afterward to hear about the experience.

Anne Wolf called after Shabbos, but it was not the news they expected. She had indeed lit candles on Friday night in her kitchen and then had left the room for another part of the house. She came back hours later to find her kitchen on fire! One of the candles had toppled over and caused a blaze that had quickly consumed most of the room. Miraculously the fire had not spread to the rest of the house and no one was injured.

The Rakovers expressed their shock and concern, and tried to calm her nerves. They said that they would help arrange for the insurance company to replace the kitchen.

Despite his attempts to maintain a calm demeanor, the news threw Mitch for a loop.

"I was confused. I had a talk with G-d in my mind: 'She decided to light Shabbos candles, and You burnt down her kitchen!' It was so hard to understand," Mitch said. "I tried to resolve it in my mind and said *gam zu letovah*. There must be a silver lining somewhere, but it was hard to understand. I left it at that."

The insurance company said it would take at least a week to send over a contractor to look at the kitchen. The week passed, and amazingly, Anne lit Shabbos candles again the following Friday night, this time placing them in her aluminum sink, one of the few items that remained untouched from the fire.

A few days later a contractor arrived from the insurance company. While he was there, Anne asked him to give her a quote for an additional job to repair and paint a crack in the middle of her bedroom ceiling. Years earlier the Wolfs had their master suite combined with an adjacent bedroom, which required knocking down one of the walls. The crack had developed sometime in the interim. It had never bothered them enough to fix it, but now that they had a contractor in the house, they decided to get it repaired.

The contractor climbed into the attic above the bedroom and returned a few minutes later, his face drained of color.

"I don't know who did your work, but they didn't reinforce it and your ceiling is about to come down. If it would have caved in while you were in bed, you could have been killed."

The news left her shaking. She had unknowingly been at death's door, only to be saved by the fire caused by her Shabbos candles.

Anne immediately called her daughter's house. Upon hearing the story, Mitch said he had gained greater clarity of the events that had trasnspired and he thanked Hashem for them.

"Usually we can't see the end of the story. I saw that she did good — she did the mitzvah — so Hashem made her kitchen go up in flames to save her from a possible bigger danger," Mitch said. "It was a great source of strength for me. G-d opened my eyes. I've learned that even if I don't see the end, I know there's something good."

In the kitchen fire, Mitch and Eve did not see a disaster, but a clear sign that Hashem had been manipulating events to bring about a salvation. The fire lit a bright spark of faith which continues to inspire and uplift them.

A TURBULENT FRIDAY NIGHT

SHABBOS IS A day of transformation. It's the key to the door of Judaism. It opens a person's eyes to a whole new world of meaning and substance.

The Torah contains a simple teaching about the profound impact of Shabbos. At the end of the Torah, Moshe foretold of a mass wave of *teshuvah* that will occur in the future as Jews return en masse to Hashem: "And you will return unto Hashem, your G-d, and listen to His voice, according to everything that I command you today, you and your children, with all your heart and all your soul" (*Devarim* 30:2).

What is that wave of *teshuvah*? The Chida points out that the letters of the first word of the verse, "ושבת (*V'shavta*) — And you will return," also spells "and Shabbos."

Returning to Hashem starts with Shabbos. The Shabbos table

offers a one-of-a-kind peek into the beauty and holiness of Judaism. Sitting at it opens the hearts of Jews to inspire them to return to their roots.

⇨ ⇦

Rabbi David Silverman of the Atlanta Scholars Kollel is a seasoned pioneer of Jewish outreach and education. He has taught thousands of people throughout Georgia, from students to seniors, inspiring them to gain a greater appreciation of their religion. He himself learned an important lesson early on in his career: never underestimate the profound impact of the Shabbos table.

One week Rabbi Silverman had invited a new family to come to his house for Friday-night dinner. It was their first taste of Shabbos. Rabbi Silverman and his wife tried to do everything to make it a perfect dinner. Before the meal he sat down with his young children and tried to encourage them to behave like little angels at the Shabbos table, saying *divrei Torah* and acting respectably. He told them this would make a great impression on their guests. (Today the Silverman children are pros at hosting newcomers and introducing them to Judaism. The oldest children have already grown up, married and have begun their own involvement in *kiruv*. But when they were still young, they needed a little pre-Shabbos pep talk).

"I wanted to make a good impression. I was concerned about how the food would taste, that my *d'var Torah* would be meaningful, and that it would be a beautiful, enriching, uplifting experience."

Things didn't go quite as he had hoped.

"Every possible thing went wrong. At one point we had one kid in the bathroom yelling, 'I'm done!' Other kids were fighting. One kid got on the table, crawled across it and spilled grape juice everywhere. Anything and everything that could have gone wrong, did.

"I was standing in the bathroom changing a kid's diaper and trying to get another kid to say a *d'var Torah* when there was a knock on the bathroom door.

"'I'm sorry, we have to go,' the wife said.

("'Oh no,' I thought to myself. 'We blew it!')

"'I'm sorry — we tried so hard to make it beautiful but everything went wrong,' I said.

"'No, I've never seen or experienced anything like this before,' she said.

"'Yeah, usually they don't spill as much,' I replied.

"'No, no, no — I just can't get over how your family gets along, how the kids play together and work things out. It was so uplifting and the singing was so beautiful.'"

Rabbi Silverman notes that he and his family were trying so hard to make things work that they forgot about the most crucial component — the intrinsic beauty and power of Shabbos!

"I was trying so hard to make it perfect. But what mattered most was that it was Shabbos. The environment of the Shabbos table is such a crucial key to opening up people to help them experience the beauty of Judaism."

The word Shabbos is an acronym for the words "*Shabbos Bo Tashuv*" — through Shabbos one returns. The essence of the day is returning to Hashem.

This power emanated from the first Shabbos in history. After killing his brother on the first Friday afternoon of creation, Kayin was seized by a wave of remorse. He did *teshuvah*, and Hashem placed on him a sign.

What was that sign? One explanation is that Hashem gave him the day of Shabbos to show him that his *teshuvah* had been accepted (*Midrash Tanchuma, Bereishis* 10).

That event gave Shabbos the unique role as being the channel for Jews to return to their heritage.

A Shabbos in the Middle of Nowhere

With the tremendous power of Shabbos to inspire our souls and even protect our bodies, it's no surprise that Hashem sometimes sends messengers to help people observe His holy day.

Gary Feldman* grew up as a Reform Jew in Manalapan, New Jersey. During high school he became close to four other young men from similar backgrounds. They called themselves the Roundtable and remained buddies for many years after.

Gary became observant during college. When the first member of the Roundtable announced he was getting married (albeit to a non-Jewish Filipino girl, and on Shabbos), Gary and the other members of the Roundtable decided to travel together to the wedding. They booked flight tickets together to San Francisco, after which they planned a ten day, 500–mile road trip to Newport Beach for the wedding. Gary thought it would be the perfect opportunity to share his newfound beliefs with his friends. Boy was he wrong.

"I was the quintessential flaming *ba'al teshuvah*. I was unshaven and righteous, wearing a khaki paperboy cap like that of a European immigrant, tzitzis hanging over my Levi's jeans and a gold "chai" necklace hanging around my neck."

Throughout the trip Gary's friends gave him the harshest of abuses. They mocked his praying, yelled at him for *bentching* after eating because it delayed the trip, made fun of him for trying to say *Tefillas HaDerech* in the car, and even tricked him into eating shrimp.

"Judaism was so fresh and new to me and I wanted to share it with every Jew. I felt like I'd discovered the secrets to understanding life and nobody cared. The bitter frustration left me seething."

His pain was magnified by his expectation that the members of the Roundtable, all Jewish and his friends for years, would share his excitement for their own religion.

"The irony was that we'd only been such close friends in the first place because we were Jews. There were deep, unsaid inexplicable bonds between us simply because we had Jewish souls, regardless of any affinity whatsoever to Judaism itself," Gary said. "Now that I brought Torah to the Roundtable, rifts of resentment began to form and the facade of our friendship began to crack. I honestly felt like a stranger in their presence."

Before leaving for the trip, Gary searched on the internet for a Jewish community close to the hotel where they would be staying during the wedding. The nearest synagogue was seven miles away, too far to walk. He decided to attend the wedding on Friday night, and spend the rest of the Shabbos by himself in the hotel.

After a week of abuse from his friends, all he longed for was a beautiful Shabbos experience. On Friday he planned to buy Shabbos candles, wine, and food. However, as they arrived in Newport Beach on Friday, he realized it was in the middle of nowhere. There was no place to buy the items he needed. His plans for Shabbos were doomed!

The group pulled up to the hotel on Friday afternoon and two members of the group went inside the hotel to check in. Gary stayed in the truck with the luggage and the fourth member of the group, Matt*.

Suddenly, Matt pointed out the window.

"Hey, here comes one of your friends."

Gary's jaw dropped. A boy with a *kippah* and tzitzis walked past, followed by another and another and another.

Gary raced out of the truck. Inside the hotel lobby were dozens of observant Jewish teenage boys and girls. He ran back outside to the parking lot, where tour buses were unloading even more *frum* teenagers. What were they all doing here, in the middle of nowhere?

Gary approached a man who was holding a clipboard.

"What's going on at the hotel this weekend?" Gary asked.

"NCSY is having their annual West Coast conference."

Gary said it was impossible to describe what he felt at that moment. NCSY, the largest Jewish youth outreach organization, just happened to be making their Shabbaton in the same hotel. Over five hundred Jews from all across the United States and Canada had flocked to Newport Beach.

After roaming around taking in the scene, Gary ran into the groom and his parents at the hotel's entrance. They looked completely bewildered.

"Did you have to invite your whole congregation?" the groom's father asked.

A few minutes later Gary met Rabbi Steven Burg, one of the organizers of the weekend who later became the national director of NCSY. Gary explained his predicament. Rabbi Burg invited him to spend the entire Shabbos with NCSY, and to attend all of the meals, classes, and festivities for free.

Shabbos was saved!

The Shabbaton was absolutely beautiful. The meals were delicious, the spirit was uplifting, and the classes were inspiring. The Shabbos morning Shacharis literally brought tears to his eyes, tears of gratitude to Hashem for having saved Shabbos.

"It was one of the most powerful *tefillah* experiences I've ever had. In a huge white tent, I was surrounded by hundreds of young Jews who all believed in Hashem. The setting, the circumstances, the *kavanah* I was having — all felt right on. This was the first minyan I had davened with in a week and the biggest minyan I'd ever davened with in my life. I thanked Hashem with all my heart for everything He was doing and had ever done for me."

From the sudden turnabout of events, Gary gained a newfound appreciation of G-d's involvement in the world. He committed himself to growing further in his observance and knowledge of his religion.

Before the trip Gary, had received calls from Rabbi Elazar Meisels. The rabbi invited him to attend the Sinai Retreats, a ten-day program in upstate New York that teaches Jews about their heritage. Each time he called, Gary declined, saying he was too busy looking for a job. But when Rabbi Meisels called him during the week after the road trip, he jumped at the chance.

The program picked up where the NCSY Shabbaton left off, and Gary grew in his excitement for Torah study. When a rabbi at the Sinai Retreats approached him to ask if he would like a chance to learn in yeshivah in Israel, he immediately agreed.

Gary packed up his few possessions in America and moved to Israel to learn. He dove into his studies. After learning for awhile in Israel, Gary typed up the story of his return, the road trip and the Shabbaton. He showed it to one of his teachers, Rabbi Dovid Orlofsky. As he read the story, Rabbi Orlofsky said it made him think of a young woman in a class of his at the Neve Yerushalayim seminary. He showed the story to her; she asked to meet Gary, and they were married thereafter.

After spending three years immersed in total learning in yeshivah in Yerushalayim, Gary and his bride returned to America. On the desk in his childhood room, he found the invitation to his friend's wedding, just where he had left it three years earlier. He smiled as he looked at the invitation and reflected on the incredible turn of events that had come from it. One item caught his eye which he had never noticed before:

The name of the yacht where the wedding had been held was "Destiny."

Hashem performs miracles for Jews who extend themselves to defend His name (*Berachos* 20a). Gary spent his week with the Roundtable trying to do just that — to maintain his observance and to spread the light of the Torah. All he wanted was to end the week with a beautiful Shabbos, and Hashem meticulously arranged all of the details to give him just that.

What Not to Do at the Shabbos Table

Kenny and Beth Broodo of Dallas, Texas were both raised in non-Orthodox Jewish homes. Kenny is a lawyer by trade, and years ago he and Beth ran a small multi-level marketing business.

The business recruited people in local communities to sell its products and provided them with ongoing training, sales seminars, and classes. Salespeople were strongly encouraged to attend the seminars, which were always held on Saturdays. The Broodos were not observant at the time, so they attended the events without any qualms.

At one of the regional sales conferences, the Broodos attended a sales seminar given by the motivational speaker Les Brown. One pithy comment hit home with them:

"If you put G-d first, you'll never come in second."

The Broodos had not thought much about G-d outside of the Seder table, Chanukah, and the High Holidays, and especially never thought about bringing Him into their business. But this one comment made them realize that they were missing the spiritual element to business success.

At a later business event in Conroe, Texas, the Broodos had another epiphany, also from an unexpected source.

They had arranged a meeting with one of the top-selling marketing representatives at the time, a non-Jew from the Deep South. People flocked to meet him for his advice and guidance. He was in such high demand that the Broodos had to wait for hours to meet with him, and finally got a chance to sit down with him at 3:00 A.M. in a local donut store.

The Broodos spoke with him about his successes, their business, and life in general. One of his comments made a profound impression on them. Kenny recounts the conversation:

"We were sitting there talking about G-d and G-d-type topics. Not Christianity, not Judaism, but just G-d. I said to him jokingly, 'It's like you're becoming my Rabbi.' His eyes suddenly got very big. He said, 'No, I'm not, and you need to go find one.'"

These two comments led the Broodos to start thinking introspectively about their life, their values and their religion. They began thinking that maybe they were missing something spiritual.

After returning home, Beth and Kenny began checking out different non-Orthodox synagogues in their area.

"Nothing rang true. They all seemed somehow spiritually superficial," Kenny said.

Shortly after, the Dallas Area Torah Association (DATA) outreach organization sponsored a onetime lunch-n-learn at Kenny's law firm. It was delivered by a big-name visiting rabbi. Kenny attended the event ("Judaism and the Art of Motorcycle Maintenance") and enjoyed it, but didn't feel particularly changed by it.

The event put the Broodos on DATA's mailing list, and six months later they received an invitation to a DATA seminar on the upcoming holiday of Purim. At this point they were still synagogue shopping and were curious to learn more about Judaism, so they decided to attend.

One class at the event, entitled "The Hidden Mask of Nature," particularly piqued their curiosity. The speaker, Rabbi Aryeh Feigenbaum, showed how Hashem's name is never mentioned in *Megillas Esther*, but His hand is apparent throughout the whole nine-year story.

"Only when you look back do you see Hashem's Hand in it. Even when I say it now I get chills. I had never heard something of that depth about the Torah. It was more than interesting to me," Kenny said. Kenny was fascinated by the presentation and even more, was impressed by Rabbi Feigenbaum. Kenny stayed afterward to drill him with a slew of other questions.

Following the seminar, the Broodos began attending other

classes sponsored by DATA. Kenny began studying one-on-one with Rabbi Feigenbaum each week. They began hearing the truth about Orthodox Judaism and the Jewish outlook, and saw that it held the spiritual content that they were looking for. The advice they had heard from the marketing people were right — they needed to bring G-d into their life, and they had finally realized that their Judaism was the way to do it. Still, they were somewhat intimidated by the observances and cautious about jumping into anything too religious.

Rabbi Feigenbaum had given them an open invitation to come to synagogue on a Friday night and to his home for Shabbos dinner. One Friday night they decided to take him up on it. While they were excited about the opportunity, they were uncertain about what the experience would be like.

However, as soon as they entered the Feigenbaum's house, the family's warm welcome immediately melted their discomfort. This feeling was only reinforced by the beauty of their Shabbos table and the obvious familial love and holiness that filled the home.

"It was my first Shabbos dinner. I was very taken by the whole scene — the white tablecloth, the silver Kiddush cup, the candles, the singing and the *divrei Torah*," Kenny said.

Kenny especially loved Mrs. Feigenbaum's homemade challah. He had never tasted homemade challah before, and he found it to be absolutely delicious.

After finishing his first piece, Kenny wanted a second. The challah was sitting in a napkin-lined metal wire basket in the middle of the table, just on the other side of Mrs. Feigenbaum's silver Shabbos candlesticks. Kenny tried asking other people to pass him the bowl, but he couldn't get anyone's attention. So he leaned across the table and picked up the bowl himself.

He lifted it over the Shabbos candles, just above the flickering flames. Within a second the napkin burst into flames and the basket turned into a giant bowl of flaming challah!

Kenny dropped the burning basket onto the table and picked up his glass of water. He was about to douse the flames when Rabbi Feigenbaum said, "Stop!" The rabbi picked up the basket, calmly carried it to the front porch and let it burn out.

There are no words to explain the embarrassment that Kenny felt. He wanted to leave the meal immediately and never come back. He apologized repeatedly. The remainder of the meal slid by, but not fast enough for Kenny. He felt like he had committed some kind of crime.

The meal finally ended, and Kenny was eager to run out of the house. Realizing his discomfort, Mrs. Feigenbaum made a comment as they were leaving that put an immediate smile back onto Kenny's face. It also helped the Broodos stay on their path of growth toward Jewish observance.

"Will you stop worrying about it?" she said. "The next time you want toast for Shabbos, just let me know in advance!"

That episode, and the Rebbetzin's response, was a critical point in the Broodos' life. If their hosts had handled it in any other way, they might have never come back. Instead they returned for many more meals in the Feigenbaum home and grew extremely close to the family. They began attending additional classes and started coming to the community frequently for Shabbos.

"When Mrs. Feigenbaum said that, we all laughed. I realized that no one judged me for making such a ridiculous mistake. Then I felt accepted," Kenny explained. "When you're not *frum* and you're around people that are, the one thing you feel sure of is that you are being judged and not accepted."

Sefer Pele Yo'etz teaches: "All Jews are one body and one person. It is proper to rejoice over the good fortune of your fellow Jew and to feel pain at his suffering, as if it were your own. ... When a person is in distress and pain, he is not able to serve his Creator" (*Perek Kinah*).

Rebbetzin Feigenbaum sensed Kenny's embarrassment and

pain. With her caring response, she picked him up and changed the future of his family and that of countless other Jews whose lives the Broodos have touched.

Following that burning challah episode, the Broodos began spending Shabbos at the home of the Feigenbaums and other families in the community. They were attracted by the lifestyle and the values they were seeing. They wanted so much to become part of the community and knew that committing to observing Shabbos was an important step. However, they felt unable to commit to becoming *shomer Shabbos*. It seemed like too significant of a commitment to make. They thought that Shabbos was an all-or-nothing thing, that they had to commit to keeping it in its complete entirety or to keeping none of it. Rabbi Feigenbaum showed them instead how they could take it on gradually via small, progressive steps.

"He taught us to make Kiddush before going out on Friday night, and to make havdalah when we came back from our outings on Saturday," Kenny said. "He showed us that doing these things was a separate mitzvah of *zachor*, of remembering Shabbos and marking the day."

Rabbi Feigenbaum gave them other practical suggestions. The Broodos followed his advice and began slowly taking on some of the observances of Shabbos. But it took them some time to grow into full observance.

The Broodos eventually moved close to an Orthodox synagogue. Later still, a new Orthodox synagogue called Ohr HaTorah was founded in their living room, and held its first services on Sunday morning, 14 Shevat, 1999. The day before, the Broodos had attended the annual DATA Shabbos retreat. Rabbi Dovid Goldwasser was the guest speaker of the weekend, and the Broodos made sure to speak with him.

In particular, they asked him for advice about a major source of sadness in their lives — after many years of marriage, they were unable to have children. Even repeated medical treatments and experimental procedures were unable to help. Kenny and Beth almost literally cried on his shoulders asking for guidance.

When Rabbi Goldwasser heard that Ohr HaTorah was planning to start in their home on the following morning, he gave them a blessing that in the merit of that event, Hashem should fill the same home with children.

And exactly one year later on 14 Shevat, 2000, the Broodos were blessed with twin girls, whom they named Rachel and Leah Esther.

The Broodos have been growing spiritually ever since, and are now committed members of the Dallas community. They frequently host Jews who are new to Orthodoxy. And if Kenny senses that a visitor feels uncomfortable by being in an Orthodox home for Shabbos, he calms his guest's nerves by telling him about the Friday night when he set the rabbi's challah on fire.

JUST ONE MARBLE

MIRA BERGEN OF Atlanta, Georgia, also experienced an unease related to Shabbos. She loved spending Shabbos in the local *frum* community, but found herself intimidated by the label of calling herself *shomer Shabbos*. It just seemed like too drastic a change to commit to observing Shabbos for the rest of her life. But then she found a creative solution.

Both of Mira's parents were Jewish and her home had "a Jewish feeling." Her father was a career soldier in the U.S. Army and so the family was always on the move. They never lived in a Jewish community, and the only Jewish education she received was the little that her parents were able to give her.

She was named after her father's grandmother Miriam who

had been observant. When Mira eventually returned to her roots and became religious herself, she felt like she had come full circle, continuing the life of her great-grandmother.

Mira married a Jewish man, but they divorced after five years. She received a civil divorce.

In 1978 Mira went to Israel for the first time. It was on that trip that she initially discovered the beauty of Shabbos.

"I had a feeling. I didn't know what it was, but I felt so good about it. I felt like I had been transported back five hundred years," Mira recalled.

Several years later, an acquaintance (who happened to be Reform), told Mira that her civil divorce was insufficient in the Jewish world. He told her that if she wanted to be considered properly divorced, she would need to receive a *get*.

The information stopped Mira in her tracks. She had never heard of a *get* before. Plus, she had always felt "connected" to Hashem. However, once she learned that she was lacking a complete Jewish divorce, she felt like this was disrespectful to Hashem.

"I had always had a personal relationship with the Creator of the universe. I remember talking to G-d from the moment I knew in my heart and soul there was a G-d," Mira said. "When someone told me that I wasn't divorced in the eyes of G-d, I thought how can I have a relationship or get remarried if I'm not properly divorced?"

Mira decided that she wanted to receive a get it in the most proper way possible. Someone gave her the name of Rabbi Emanuel Feldman from Congregation Beth Jacob. She set up a meeting with him. He completely shattered her stereotype of the old-fashioned, out-of-touch rabbis she had always imagined.

"I saw the joy, humor, and loveliness of dealing with someone who was close to G-d. I never knew that. To me, rabbis were always off in their own aura, never talking to you, just around you. They never made eye contact with you, never gave you answers.

Here was a rabbi who was relating to life and reality."

Rabbi Feldman once called Mira's office to speak to her. Her secretary answered, and asked him which company he was with. He told her: "G-d."

"I thought that was so funny!"

Rabbi Feldman spoke to Mira's ex-husband and prepared the get. Finally, in 1986, eleven-and-a-half years after her civil divorce, she received her "kosher" divorce.

"I felt like in order to move on with my life and in a relationship I needed to be divorced in the eyes of G-d. G-d was the ultimate."

The process of receiving the *get* inspired Mira in another way as well.

"I was so moved by the ceremony. When Rabbi Emanuel told me they've been doing this for thousands of years without changing it, I felt very moved. I felt part of the fabric of Jewish life.

"He could tell I was very touched. He told me he was always available for any other questions, and would love to meet with me again."

Mira graciously appreciated his offer, but did not take him up on it — at least not initially.

However, this initial experience with Rabbi Feldman left Mira with a stronger connection to Hashem. Over the next two years she felt herself growing closer to Hashem, but she did not know how to demonstrate it or act on the feeling. She recalls once specifically asking Hashem to show her how she could become closer to Him.

Shortly afterward in 1988, Mira was on a flight to Maryland. Sitting in the seat next to her was none other than Rabbi Emanuel Feldman.

"He was looking at the Wayfarer's Prayer. He asked if I would want him to say it for me."

During that flight, Mira felt the same feeling of warmth and acceptance from the rabbi. He again repeated his invitation to meet with her whenever she wanted. She felt like her request to Hashem had been answered — Hashem was giving her a sign that she should try to find ways to get closer to Him.

Sometime later she decided to attend a class at a local Chabad House about the Jewish lifecycle, from birth to death and the afterlife. When the rabbi spoke about death and that a person's *neshamah* can sometimes be resurrected in a different body, the idea sounded very familiar to her from other religions she had studied.

"I said, 'Oh my gosh, this is what I believe. This is New Age!' I raised my hand and said, 'You're talking about New Age!' He said, 'What's New Age?'

"At that moment I realized that one-hundred percent of what I believed in, one-hundred percent, was rooted in Judaism and nowhere else."

Eager to learn more, Mira called Rabbi Feldman soon after. He met with her for an hour and a half, during which she opened up to him about her deep spiritual feelings and her hesitancy about becoming observant.

"I just sat there and said, 'I'm totally intimidated by my Judaism. I don't know the practices, the prayers. I talk to G-d but I don't know what to do.'"

Rabbi Feldman gave her two recommendations: he told her about the Beginner's Service held each Shabbos morning in his synagogue, and about an upcoming Discovery Seminar weekend.

Mira followed both suggestions. In the Beginner's Service she felt accepted and welcomed. Local families invited her for Shabbos and Yom Tov meals.

"Shabbos is like an introduction to the *frum* lifestyle, to see a family having lunch together in the middle of the day on Saturday when you're supposed to be having your nails done," Mira said. "It's so nourishing spending time together."

Mira loved the environment and the experience of Shabbos,

but she was in no rush to become observant.

"I was quick to tell people that I drive on Shabbos and eat shrimp, and they didn't bat an eyelash. One of the things I loved — nobody was trying to change me, they were just being," Mira said. "I didn't want to be Sabbath observant or keep kosher. I just wanted to be around these people whom I saw, watch how they were leading their lives, how they were with their children. It was so amazing."

During this time the Beth Jacob community was going through its own transition, as Rabbi Emanuel Feldman was gradually turning over the reins of the synagogue to his son Rabbi Ilan. Mira soon grew as close to him as she was to his father. That closeness helped to encourage her journey further.

The younger Rabbi Feldman's wife once invited Mira to spend Rosh Hashanah with their family. She invited Mira to stay for the whole Yom Tov at their house, but she demurred, saying she had a cat at home to take care of.

"Why don't you bring him along?"

Mira graciously accepted her offer.

"Traveling with a cat is like traveling with a toddler — you have to bring his bowl, scratching post and litter basket. That afternoon, after I arrived, the Rabbi saw me and asked where my cat was. I said he was in the in living room. After the Rabbi saw my white cat, named Mazel Tov, he said, 'He's perfect. He is already dressed for Yom Tov.'"

"What do you mean?" Mira asked.

"He's already wearing white!"

Mira discovered that the same humor she had been drawn to in his father was present in Rabbi Ilan as well.

In 1991, Mira became a member of Congregation Beth Jacob. It was the first synagogue she had ever joined. Even though she was still not observant, she felt welcomed and at home in the shul. Joining the synagogue represented a major step in her life.

Over the next decade, Mira spent nearly every Shabbos in the community. She absolutely loved everything she was experiencing. However, she still felt like it was too much of a commitment to say she would observe Shabbos for the rest of her life.

Finally, in 1999, Mira felt like it was time to make the jump. In December of that year as everyone was talking about the New Millennium and Y2K, Mira saw something else. When New Year's Eve fell on a Friday night, Mira saw the intersection of Shabbos and the new Millennium as a sign from G-d that it was time to commit to becoming *shomer Shabbos*.

"I decided it was time, but I couldn't give myself the label of being *shomer Shabbos*," Mira said. So she decided to keep just that one Shabbos. "I said, 'I'm making a commitment one Shabbos at a time.'"

Mira learned the lesson from her mother, who had taught her that if you're trying to cut a roll of salami it can be overwhelming to do it all at once. But if you slice it one bit at a time, it's much easier. So Mira resolved to observe just that first Shabbos of the year.

"Many people think that observing Judaism is an all-or-nothing action, that you must take on all the obligations at once. But growth in Judaism is really about constant baby steps, about taking on small commitments," Mira said. "G-d appreciates anything we do to get closer to Him."

For Mira this meant making one commitment at a time. In every area of her Jewish growth she heeded her mother's advice and cut off only a small bit at a time.

"If someone is not ready to keep Shabbos each week, why not try to keep it only for an hour? If someone is not ready to keep kosher full time, then try to give up only one particular food," Mira said. "People think they have to do everything at once. They don't know that G-d looks highly at everything we do. You're making a distinction; you're trying to have a relationship with Hashem."

So on Friday night, December 31, 1999, she was sitting with a local family watching the clock as it struck midnight. It was the first time she had ever spent New Year's Eve not watching the ball drop in Times Square on television. But instead of lamenting that she was missing the televised celebrations, Mira felt wonderful as she reflected on the start of the new millennium quietly and in G-d's way. The frenzied revelry of the secular New Year had been replaced by the spiritual bliss of Shabbos.

The next week, Mira again decided to observe "just that one Shabbos." Within a short time, she had kept Shabbos for a month. She began to keep track of each Shabbos by placing a marble into a wine decanter. Now, hundreds of marbles later, she had to buy several other jars and decanters to hold her collection.

With each marble she added, the number of that marble also took on a deeper meaning. Each Shabbos she looked for a connection between the week's number and an idea in the Torah portion of the week or other current event. Members of the community heard about her collection and began pointing out some of the deeper connections of the number of her marbles.

For example, on Shabbos number thirteen, a rabbi in the community taught her about the Thirteen Attributes of Hashem. Mira's fortieth Shabbos was Rosh Hashanah. The number forty is deeply related to birth and new beginnings, so the timing was perfect.

On Mira's fiftieth Shabbos, the family with whom she was staying baked a special challah in the shape of the Hebrew letter *nun*, which has the numerical value of fifty. When she traveled to Israel and spent three Shabbosos there, she added three unique items to her collection: a small blue *chamsah* "hand," a blue glass circle, and a blue fish. For her one-hundredth Shabbos she put a battery into the jar because: "Shabbos keeps me going!" People in the community have bought other special marbles for various Shabbosos, such as the handmade marbles a friend brought her from China.

Even once she committed to observing Shabbos, Mira still lived outside the community and therefore needed to drive in each Friday afternoon to stay with a local family. Oh how she longed to be able to purchase a home in the community!

One day she circled Shabbos 120 in her Day Planner. By that number Shabbos she hoped to be living in the community.

In the fall of 2001, she put her condo on the market. She received a contract from a buyer on January 25, 2002, and moved into the community on February 28, Shabbos number 114.

"As I lit my candles that Friday night, I was crying. I could not thank Hashem enough for letting me move into the community."

When Mira first began collecting the marbles, she did it to make herself accountable and maintain her Shabbos observance. Soon the collection took on a mission of its own, and she now looks forward to each Shabbos and especially to putting another marble into the decanter. With each new marble, Mira has gained a deeper level of appreciation for Shabbos.

"A lot of people don't understand. They think that I live the most rigid life, full of shoulds and have to's, that I have to do this and that. However my life is filled with such pleasure and joy and laughter," Mira said. "G-d loves me so much because He gave me Shabbos."

When Hashem decided to give the gift of Shabbos to the Jewish people, He told Moshe to bring it to the Jewish people:

"I have a precious gift called Shabbos in My storehouse that I want to give to the Jews. Go and tell them."

What was the purpose of this special gift? Rashi says that Hashem gave us the gift of Shabbos to make us holy. And about what specific element was Moshe to tell the Jews? About the incalculable reward for people who observe Shabbos (*Shabbos* 10b).

It took more than a decade for Mira to commit to observing Shabbos. But since making the decision to do so, she has constantly grown in her excitement and sheer thrill of keeping it, repeatedly seeing the beautiful rewards of its observance.

DISCOVERING WHAT TRULY MATTERS

RABBI ARYEH GIBBER also learned important lessons about the power of Shabbos and personal commitment during the few years he spent as part of the Norfolk Area Community Kollel in Virginia.

Rabbi Gibber moved to Norfolk in 2001. Over the next few years he became close with Sam Perkal*, a prominent member of the local Jewish community. Sam was a real-estate mogul and owned several buildings in the area. He attended classes at the local Orthodox synagogue, B'nai Israel Congregation. He had begun taking his first tremulous steps toward becoming *shomer Shabbos*.

Sam was home one Shabbos afternoon, trying to keep Shabbos, when someone ran over to his house in a frenzy. The man had just heard on the radio that a major fire was sweeping through the area of Portsmouth, across the river. He knew that Sam owned several buildings there and would be concerned.

Sam instinctively jumped up, ran to the other room and picked up the phone. Then he froze.

As he held the phone to his ear, Sam said to himself: "If I'm going to pick up the phone on Shabbos to see if my buildings burned down, why I am spending time in shul, not driving?

"And if I'm keeping Shabbos, what does it matter if my buildings are burning?"

Sam held the phone to his ear for a long time, wavering between placing it down and making the call. Finally, after what felt like an eternity, he placed it down and walked away.

Sam was able to push through the tumult of emotions inside of him, and make a concrete decision to not break Shabbos.

That event happened years ago. It took tremendous effort and willpower, and even though the entire episode took only a few minutes, it was the spark that Sam and his family needed to concretize their steps toward becoming observant Jews. They have lived lives of firm Jewish commitment ever since.

Another member of the community faced his own challenging life decision, made easier by a jovial retort. Benjamin Korniver* and his family lived in Norfolk, but not close enough to the synagogue to walk on Shabbos. He and his family were interested in becoming more religious, but their physical distance from the community was an obstacle.

The family knew intellectually that they needed to move into the *eruv*, but refused to move away from their scenic lakeside house to do so.

One day he was explaining his dilemma to Rabbi Yosef Friedman, then the synagogue rabbi.

"Rabbi, every Saturday morning I wake up and go outside. I see ducks coming out of the water onto our lawn. It's touching."

The rabbi replied, "Ben, you just have to make a choice. On Shabbos morning, do you want to wake up and see ducks or see Jews?"

That comment was the turning point in the family's growth. Benjamin is a psychologist by trade, and that comment pierced through his thoughtful, analytical mind to leave a mark.

"It's amazing — you just don't know how an off-hand remark about ducks or someone standing there holding the telephone will do it," Rabbi Gibber said. "You never know what will make an impact."

In Hebrew, the word "Shabbos" is related to the word "*shuv*," "return." Everything returns to its source on Shabbos. When Benjamin and Sam became aware of the power and greatness of Shabbos, it penetrated to their deep insides to bring them home.

THE SHABBOS OF THE MISTAKEN IDENTITY

MEETING AN UNKNOWN holy woman on Shabbos taught Susan Rosen* a vital message that has stayed with her forever since.

Susan grew up in Philadelphia, Pennsylvania, in a neighborhood that was primarily Jewish, but barely religious. Everyone she knew was Jewish, and they all went to afternoon Hebrew school and had lavish bar and bas mitzvahs. Surrounded by so many other Jews, people in her area took their Jewish identity for granted and felt no need for religious activities.

However, even as a young girl, something gnawed at Susan's insides. She felt that she was missing something. Susan had a deep desire for purity, truth, and a meaningful life. When her nursery school teachers in the Conservative synagogue sang about Shabbos and talked about kosher food, Susan decided this was for her.

"I really wanted to live a life that had more to it," Susan said. "I wanted to keep kosher to be close to G-d."

Growing up in Philadelphia meant frequent school trips to the nearby Amish Country. Susan loved seeing the simple, basic lives led by the Amish. Having never come into contact with religious Jews, she assumed that the Amish were the only people living a pure, clean lifestyle.

"I thought I belonged there," Susan said. "I told my mother I was born in the wrong generation. I should have been born in the time of *Little House on the Prairie*. I wanted to move to Amish Country."

After college Susan went not to the Amish Country, but to Atlanta to attend chiropractic school. Soon after arriving, she was invited to attend a Revival Meeting by a local born-again

Christian group. Susan accepted the invitation out of curiosity as to what it was.

At the Revival Meeting there were hundreds of people singing, clapping, and standing on chairs. Energy filled the room but Susan felt completely out of place.

"I thought to myself, 'What is a nice Jewish girl doing here?'"

The event made Susan realize that she could no longer take her Jewish identity for granted. In Philadelphia it was easy to feel Jewish, but now in the Bible Belt, under the threat of missionaries, she realized she needed to be proactive to protect and maintain her Jewish beliefs.

Not sure where to turn, Susan called the Jewish Federation and asked them to send her materials on local Jewish life. One of the items they sent was a copy of the city's Jewish paper, the Atlanta Jewish Times. Flipping through it, she saw an ad for the Atlanta Scholars Kollel, a local Jewish outreach and education organization that had just opened. For some reason she was drawn to the ad and called the number.

Susan was invited for a Shabbos meal and loved it!

Shortly thereafter, Susan was working in a gym in Atlanta when she noticed a man passing by who looked like he had stepped straight out of Amish Country: he had a black beard and was wearing a black hat and suit.

"I saw this man. He looked Amish, but I knew he wasn't. I thought he was the Jewish version of the Amish," Susan said. "I ran over to him and said, 'I think I need to talk to you.'"

The man and his wife lived in the local Orthodox community, and in time they became close friends of hers. Susan began meeting more people in the community, and saw that they were the models of the purity and truth she craved. By this point, Susan had decided that she no longer wanted to be Amish; she realized that her own religion held the answers for her.

She began attending events in the local Orthodox community

and returned for more Shabbosos. She was touched by the pure attributes and sincere morals of the people in the community.

"I just wanted truth and wanted to be around people living a life of truth," Susan said. "I just wanted to be close to G-d."

One other event at this time convinced her of the existence of G-d and the truth of Judaism. During the first semester of chiropractic school, Susan was in the anatomy lab and saw a cadaver for the first time. She stared at its face and had an epiphany.

"I looked at the face and nothing looked back at me. It was just flesh and muscles and fat and organs. At that moment, I almost felt that Hashem is palpable. When I look at you and you look at me, who is looking at me? It's not your eyeball in you, it's the Hashem in you looking at the Hashem in me," Susan said. "My ears started ringing. I said, "That's it; it's Hashem! That was a major realization for me."

Soon after, Susan met Miriam Feldman, the Rebbetzin of the Atlanta community. She saw in the Rebbetzin a holy woman — a role model of whom she wanted to become.

"When I went to Miriam's house, I felt as if I was in Yerushalayim. When I [had attended a year of] Hebrew University, I felt like there was more oxygen. I felt I could live better there. After I got back from Israel, I never felt it until I went to Miriam's house.

"Some people are into family, food, music. Everyone gets excited by something. For me it was *emes*. My whole drive to be *frum* was all about *emes*. I can't breathe around people who are not straight. Miriam is very straight, honest, full of *emes*. She gave me the tools to live a life of *emes*."

After becoming observant in Atlanta, Susan spent several months learning at the Neve Yerushalayim seminary in Israel.

After seminary, Susan was planning on returning home to Philadelphia to visit her parents. Because she had not spent time in Philadelphia since becoming *frum*, one of her teachers from seminary thought it would be helpful for her to get to know a local religious family. Therefore she gave Susan the name and phone number of one of her own teachers, Rebbetzin Temi Kamenetsky, the wife of Rabbi Shmuel Kamenetsky, the Rosh Yeshivah of the Talmudical Yeshivah of Philadelphia.

Susan was still newly religious and had heard the Kamenetsky name, but was not very familiar with it. She called them soon after returning to Philadelphia. The Rebbetzin invited Susan to spend a Shabbos with them.

Susan did not realize the special privilege she had just received, to spend Shabbos with one of the leading rabbis of America.

The Kamenetskys lived in a different part of town than Susan's parents, so Susan's mother offered to drive her before Shabbos and pick her up afteward. Unfortunately, Friday's pre-Shabbos rush delayed their departure from home. They got lost on the way and arrived late, in the few minutes after candle lighting and before the actual start of Shabbos.

Susan jumped out of the car, waved goodbye to her mother and frantically ran to the front door of the house. She did not see a name on the door, but knocked anyway. After a few minutes, a short, older woman opened the door.

The woman had already lit candles and was praying. She didn't introduce herself but motioned to Susan to join her. She pointed to a place where Susan could put her bag, handed her a siddur, and returned to her own prayers.

"As she was praying, she was putting her finger next to every word like it was her first time saying it. '*Baruch ... Atah ... Hashem.*' I looked at her, and I thought, 'I'm in the wrong house! This lady doesn't even know how to daven!'"

Susan began to have an anxiety attack. In her stress to find the right home before Shabbos, she must have knocked on the wrong door!

The older woman continued davening, calmly and methodically sounding out each word. Next to her, Susan was in the exact opposite state. She was panicking. What could she do? Shabbos had just begun so she couldn't leave, but she didn't know the woman's religious level so she wasn't sure if she could even eat her food! Plus she knew no one else in the area and so had nowhere to go.

Susan decided that she would stay in the house for Shabbos, but would fast until the end of Shabbos. Yes, that sounded like the most reasonable option.

The woman's prayers seemed to stretch out forever. She finally finished praying just as the voices of men returning from synagogue were heard from outside. There was a knock on the door and an older man entered, presumably the husband of the house. Following him was a group of younger men.

Once inside the young men crowded around him, asking him questions and inquiring if they could bring him anything. Susan strained to try to get a glimpse of him and to hear bits of the conversation.

She could neither make out nor understand the topic of the discussions, but heard repeatedly the young men referring to the older gentleman as "the Rosh Yeshivah."

After all her tension and panicking, she finally realized that she had been in the correct house the whole time!

But now Susan was even more puzzled — if he was a great Rosh Yeshivah, why did his wife pray in the way she did? Later that evening Susan approached Rebbetzin Kamenetsky and asked. Her response taught Susan an essential lesson about prayer that has remained with her ever since.

"She told me that these words are the only weapons we have to fight our war. We can't just look at them. They can't be just words that we say out of our mouths. We have to be aware of them, know them, and internalize them."

Rebbetzin Kamenetsky's attention to her prayers was not the result of being unfamiliar with them, as Susan had thought. On the contrary — it was because she knew their significance and how careful we must be with them.

Those words from Rebbetzin Temi Kamenetsky more than twenty years ago have stayed with Susan and guided her perspective on prayer every since. She has faced formidable challenges throughout the years, and has responded to them primarily through prayer and by working on her faith in Hashem.

"I grew up not knowing there was a G-d in the world. Now I know Him. I have a relationship with Him. *Dayeinu*. I would feel complete even if I died today. Every day in my prayers I say I return to Him. I will keep on returning to Him.

"I have had tremendous disappointments in my life but I still love Him. I keep reminding myself that I'm alive for only one reason: to relate to Him."

That first Shabbos in Philadelphia created a strong bond between Susan and the Kamenetskys and she has remained in touch with them ever since. But even more importantly, the lessons of *tefillah* that she learned from Rebbetzin Kamenetsky taught her how to have the ultimate bond with her Creator.

---

2 Shabbos: The Greatest Test

AS PEOPLE GROW IN THEIR OBSERVANCE OF JUDAISM AND accept upon themselves particular religious commitments: Hashem sometimes tests them to measure their level of dedication. The tests are very personal and are designed to prove their level of commitment to themselves, those around them and G-d.

One of the biggest steps a person takes while becoming religious is committing to the observance of Shabbos. The Chafetz Chaim said that just as a king may own many castles and other residences, he will mark the particular home in which he is residing by flying his royal flag outside.

Shabbos is the flag showing a Jew's commitment to his religion. It's an open statement of his growth and beliefs, and its observance has a significant impact on his overall religious life. So it's not surprising that many people receive direct Divine tests measuring their level of commitment to Shabbos. And if they pass the tests, the rewards are awe-inspiring.

Face-to-Face with the Boss

FOR THIRTEEN YEARS, Jimmy Baron worked as a radio announcer in Atlanta as the Morning Drive Radio host on 99X

Radio. On his daily radio program, he often recounted experiences from his religious journey, such as the many days he came to work with "hat hair" from the *kippah* he had worn in synagogue that morning.

Committing to Shabbos observance was a gigantic step for him, because much of his job revolved around concerts and other events on Friday nights. But he loved Shabbos and found ways to hold onto his job without having to attend Friday night music fests.

Outside of his developing religious observance, Jimmy had one other passion in life: the musician Bruce Springsteen, a.k.a. The Boss. Jimmy describes himself as "an absolute obsessed Bruce Springsteen fan." He has traveled around the country to attend Springsteen concerts, spending thousands of dollars and burning up vacation days to see him perform.

Several years ago, Springsteen announced that his tour schedule would include a major concert in Atlanta on a Friday night. Jimmy had been keeping Shabbos for only six months and was still growing in his observance, and he was very tempted to go. However, for the first time in his life, he did not purchase tickets to the concert.

A few days before the show, a friend of Jimmy who worked in the record industry called him to invite him to go backstage after the concert and hang out with Springsteen in his dressing room.

This was a dream come true! He had never met Springsteen in person and he knew this was a once-in-a-lifetime opportunity. But how could he turn his back on his religion and his commitment to keep Shabbos? He was torn, but he gathered up his strength and replied that he would be unable to go to the concert because it was on Shabbos. His friend was shocked.

"You did hear what I said, right?" his friend asked.

"Yes, I heard you, but this is my life now. I've made this commitment," Jimmy replied.

"Jimmy, G-d will forgive you," his friend said.

"Boy, you must have some inside knowledge."

It was a powerful moment for Jimmy. He had taken a critical step in proving his dedication to Shabbos by refusing his friend's offer. Passing that test also made him realize the depth of his devotion, because he was able to respond immediately.

"It was a real landmark in my Jewish growth, choosing between my commitment to Judaism and what I just wanted to do," Jimmy said. "The satisfying thing was not only being able to make the right decision, but being able to make that decision without even thinking about it. Six months earlier I would have been at that concert."

Jimmy attributes his strength in overcoming the challenge to have come directly from Hashem. For others faced with similar tests, he said it is important to look beyond the moment and measure how you will feel about the choice in the future.

"If on that one night I would have made an exception because it was Bruce and I would have gone to the concert, I know I would have regretted it for the rest of my life," he said. "You have to look within yourself and think: Is this something that tomorrow, or next week, I will be happy about or will I beat myself up about it?"

The Friday night came and Jimmy and his wife were at a friend's house for Shabbos. The holiness of Shabbos, the camaraderie of his close friends, and the spiritual high he received each week from Shabbos reminded him just how correct his decision had been. Jimmy's friends knew about the concert and how difficult his test was. So after dinner they brought out a custom-made cake decorated with the words "I missed Bruce Springsteen for Shabbos."

Jimmy was deeply touched. To this day he still has the top of the cake in his freezer.

A few years after that Friday night concert, Jimmy received even more clarity that he had made the correct choice. He was in a bar in a fancy Atlanta hotel one night when he noticed a familiar face walk in. There, by himself, was none other than Bruce Springsteen.

Jimmy walked over to him and offered to buy him a drink. It turned out that Springsteen was in Atlanta recording a new album. The two men sat down and spoke uninterrupted for thirty minutes, which was much longer than he would have gotten in the dressing room after the concert.

"Favor and glory does Hashem bestow, He withholds no goodness from those who walk uprightly" (*Tehillim* 84:12). For Jimmy, making the correct choice earned him tremendous rewards in the eyes of Hashem, and in his own. It also helped him realize who The Boss really is.

Knowing What to Answer

RABBI YEHOSHUA (JOSHUA) LOOKS now works in Jewish community work, but was previously the president of the international division of Edison Brothers Stores, a $1.5 billion retail firm.

Yehoshua's religious growth came with some challenges at work. One of his superiors in the company was particularly unsettled with Yehoshua's need to leave early on Friday afternoons in the winter. The boss began keeping track to the minute the time that Yehoshua left each Friday, and became increasingly cold to him.

One Friday the executive called Yehoshua into his office. He angrily berated Yehoshua, accusing him of slacking on the job by leaving early. After several minutes of harsh attacks, he roared at Yehoshua, "What am I going to do if the business falls apart on Shabbos and you're not there to take care of it?!"

"You would fire me. If the business can fall apart in one day, I'm obviously not doing my job."

Yehoshua's boss had no rebuttal. Yehoshua calmly turned and walked out of the office and his boss never said another word to him about Shabbos.

THE BIG GAME

HASHEM OFTEN TESTS people to help them grow into new roles in life. For Rebecca Kalmanovitz*, a dramatic test of her Shabbos observance sent her skyrocketing into an entirely new dimension.

Rebecca grew up in a "very committed Reform household" in Cleveland, Ohio. She was president of her temple's youth group. To her, being Jewish meant belonging to a big, fun club with plenty of social events but few official observances.

Rebecca headed east for college where she attended an Ivy League school. During her freshman year, she joined a semester-long class sponsored by a Jewish outreach program on campus. She dutifully attended all of the classes, but her mind was elsewhere.

"I was not the most interested student. I was pledging a sorority at the time. I spent the entire time texting in the back of the classroom. I was really not present, and missed both Shabbatons."

The semester ended and Rebecca moved on with her life, expecting to quickly forget about the program. However she then heard about a trip to Israel that the group was offering. It happened to be timed perfectly to fill the week and a half between the end of her spring break trip and the beginning of classes. She had always been Zionistic; how could she turn down a free ticket to Israel?

She signed up for the trip, packed her bags, and was soon

seeing the sights of Israel. The trip progressed much like her time in the program — even though the trip combined classes with excursions, she did not pay much attention to the lessons, but loved the activities.

"It was an absolutely amazing time. The staff was great; the traveling was fun. I still didn't see myself making any changes or doing anything differently."

Rebecca had to leave the trip a few days early to return to America for a cousin's bas mitzvah. This very fact would soon change her life.

"The last night of the trip, we had done the Kosel tunnel tours. I had a huge epiphany while standing at the Kosel. I said if the Beis HaMikdash really existed, I would have to make significant changes in my life.

"I was the student on the trip who had the most fun. I was always hanging out, and I never really spoke to the staff members. But that night I said to myself, 'I'm leaving tomorrow. I should ask every question I wrote in the back of my journal now.'"

The time was seven P.M. Rebecca's ride to the airport was due to come the following morning at five A.M., and she spent those ten hours speaking with Ariella Cohen*, one of the staff members, bombarding her with every question she had thought of during the previous week and a half.

"The poor woman. I kept her up all night."

During those ten hours, Rebecca saw her entire understanding of Judaism, and of her life, crumble. Her conversation with Ariella helped her to realize that she had spent the previous nineteen years pursuing shallow goals and momentary thrills.

"I spent all night asking my questions, laughing with her, and crying on her shoulder. At one point, I even yelled at her."

That night Rebecca experienced a rollercoaster of emotions. They came from a nineteen-year build up of numerous unanswered questions and issues that she had always ignored. Even during her moments of frustration and seeming hostility to Ariella that night, she was never upset at her, but was frustrated by her realization of the many opportunities she had missed in life.

Finally, as morning broke, Rebecca arrived at a new and beautiful understanding of what her true path in life needed to be. She had always been stuck in her view of what Judaism should be. She had always wanted Judaism to fit into her view of life and her priorities, without realizing that she needed to bend her life to Hashem's rules.

For her bas mitzvah seven years earlier, Rebecca had learned to read from the Torah and lead the prayer services. She continued to do so in college. She thought this was her role in life. She never realized that her true position as a woman encompassed other far more beautiful and fulfilling roles.

"I realized that night that most of my relationship to Judaism had been misguided. At college, I *leined* every other week. I was the go-to *chazanit*. That's how I connected. I was one of the leaders in the community. This had been a big issue — my relationship with Judaism and how I wanted to connect.

"Once I was able to sit down and talk to someone about it, my understanding ceased to be a problem. Once I accepted that the Torah was from Hashem, I realized that the goal of mitzvos is to connect to Hashem. I'm only commanded to do specific mitzvos, and I need only those to connect to Him. I have learned since then that it is only through those ways that I can connect best with Hashem.

"We are so blessed that we were given a guide book on how to connect to Hashem," Rebecca said. "I have the ultimate how-to book on life. My job is to follow that — to learn how to connect to G-d."

Looking back, Rebecca also marvels at the turn of events that led to her epiphany that night at the Kosel and the uninterrupted time she was able to spend with Ariella.

"It was *hashgachah pratis* — if I had not left early, there would have been a million people asking questions the last night of the trip and I wouldn't have been able to."

Rebecca returned to college after her trip with a newfound enthusiasm for her religion. She was eager to learn more and grow in her observance. She began attending Jewish classes on campus, and started to study one-on-one with Ariella.

Rebecca's growth continued through the beginning of her sophomore year. That fall she decided to become *shomer Shabbos*.

Then came the Big Game, and with it, the Big Test.

"I was going home three weeks later for Thanksgiving. I had a huge debate — should I tell my parents? I didn't want to drive with them on Shabbos to visit our family. Would I actually keep Shabbos at home? I finally called them and told them I wanted to keep Shabbos. *Baruch Hashem* they accepted it, and they have been supportive of my whole journey since then."

Ten minutes after telling her parents, Rebecca received a phone call from Annie, her best friend since childhood. They had grown up in the Reform temple together. Annie had just bought tickets for them to the Ohio State–Michigan University football game to be held in Cleveland on the Saturday of Thanksgiving weekend. The tickets were only $100 each, a bargain for such a major game.

The annual Ohio State–Michigan game is not just a tranquil, friendly competition. It's a culmination of a bitter rivalry which dominates not only the two universities but also the cultures of the cities that surround them. Getting tickets to the game was a big deal. "I told her, 'I'm freaking out. I want to go, but it's not so appropriate for Shabbos!' For a solid day and a half, I didn't know what to do. I was freaking out."

Rebecca decided to call Ariella for advice.

"Ariella talked me through it. There was no pressure."

Having heard similar questions from other students over the years, Ariella gave Rebecca guidance, but stressed to her that the decision was ultimately hers.

"Any decision a student makes must come from within herself," Ariella explained. "Otherwise she will come to resent the whole process."

Even though her commitment to observing Shabbos was only a few weeks old, Rebecca knew it was the right choice. She finally picked up the phone and dialed Annie. However, she still did not know how to break the news to her.

"As soon as she picked up the phone, Annie said, 'I was about to call you. Someone just offered me $1600 for our two tickets, so I sold them.'"

"I said 'Perfect!'" *(I didn't tell her that I was going to cancel.)*

"Hashem knew it was such a big *nisayon* and I was having trouble backing out, so He took the *nisayon* away from me."

She immediately called Ariella to tell her the great news.

"You just made $700 for keeping Shabbos!"

"When I hung up the phone from Ariella, I said to myself, 'Wow, I really made the correct decision. Hashem took care of me and gave me such a perfect reward.'"

In addition to being a confirmation about her choice to observe Shabbos, the money enabled her to grow in another area as well. She had longed to return to Israel to study in seminary to further broaden her Jewish knowledge, but she hadn't had the means to pay for a plane ticket. So Rebecca took her newfound $700 and put it toward a ticket to Israel for the upcoming summer, where she learned at Neve Yerushalayim seminary. Following graduation, she returned again to learn for the year at Midreshes Rachel V'Chaya.

"Hashem presented me with opportunities, and brought people into my life who showed me the Torah. I grabbed onto those. Ultimately that's what every Jew's *neshamah* wants.

"I was blessed. I was given the right people during my journey and was able to connect to what they were saying."

Rebecca had originally chosen her university because of the professional opportunities it would grant her, but she did not expect just how important the choice of college would be for her Jewish growth.

"I chose it because it was an Ivy League school and because it promised a great social life. After becoming *frum*, I discovered its active Jewish life, the ability to keep Shabbos and kosher. It was an easy place to be *frum*.

"My whole journey was challenging, but Hashem put me in places that aided me, and gave me a *nisayon* I was able to handle."

Rebecca says she sees that Hashem had hand-picked her particular test of Shabbos observance, and He sent it at the perfect time to solidify her growth.

"I went through a stage — intellectually I was on board, and I knew it was true, I knew the Torah was *emes*. However, I had a very happy childhood, so it was very hard for me to say that I was emotionally ready to commit to changing my life to become *frum*."

It was that very test of Shabbos observance and the Ohio–Michigan Game which pushed her to grow, helping her to truly commit to her new direction in life.

Singing a Brilliant New Song

THROUGHOUT HIS THIRTY years working in *kiruv* on college campuses and in other locations in Michigan, Rabbi Avraham Jacobovitz said he was repeatedly inspired by the *mesiras nefesh* of his students. He watched as many of them overcame tremendous obstacles on their paths toward religious observance and displayed levels of strength that even he envied.

Take, for example Noah Lindenberg*. He attended Wayne State University with a lifelong dream to pursue a career in musical theater. A talented singer, he was a member of the university's choir and sang at every concert they performed. Soon after

Commencement, Noah met Rabbi Jacobovitz and began attending his classes on Judaism. He was a frequent guest at his home for Shabbos meals and soaked up everything he learned from him.

One Thursday night in the early part of the winter, Rabbi Jacobovitz received a phone call from Noah. He was struggling with a difficult dilemma. Over the previous few weeks the choir had been practicing for their major event of the year, their upcoming Xmas concert, which was to be held in a large Detroit church. Not only that, but to get ready for the concert, the choir had been holding their practice sessions in church! As the date of the concert neared, practices were scheduled for each coming Friday night and he was required to attend. With his newfound love of Judaism, singing Xmas music had begun to bother him. But more importantly, he was dismayed at the thought of missing Shabbos dinner at the rabbi's table.

However, Noah felt like there was nothing he could do. He was torn between his lifelong dream of the theater and his newfound love of Judaism.

Rabbi Jacobovitz struggled to find the right words to tell him, and he suggested that Noah speak with his music professor and explain the predicament. Perhaps the professor would come up with a solution.

The next day, Friday, passed uneventfully with no news from Noah. He did not attend synagogue Friday night. Rabbi Jacobovitz's heart sank as he looked around his table at the many assembled students, with no sign of Noah.

In the middle of the meal, there was a knock at the door. Noah came running in, full of excitement.

"Rabbi, I need to talk to you right now! I got up the courage to speak to my professor this morning in his office before class."

Noah described how he had unburdened his personal turmoil and inner struggles to the professor. He told the professor that he had decided he would not sing in the concert, regardless of the consequences.

The professor asked him, "Are you serious?" Noah froze in fear.

"This is so beautiful," the professor continued. "I can't believe that nowadays a young man can be so connected to his religion to stand up for his beliefs. I will stand behind you one hundred percent. Don't worry, nothing will happen to you. I'll protect you."

At the beginning of class that morning, the professor called Noah to the front of the room and told everyone what had happened.

"Do you see this young man? Everyone should be proud of him."

The event was a decisive moment for Noah. From there he followed a meteoric path to becoming fully observant, and subsequently learned in yeshivah. He eventually married, and is raising a family of ten children in a home saturated with Torah values.

Looking back, Noah said he is still amazed at the multitude of blessings that have come from that single event of committing to observing Shabbos. In giving up his dreams of the theater, he paved a bold new path for himself and his whole family.

"The repercussions of that choice, thirty-three years later, changed not only my life but led to my siblings and parents joining me on this journey. I've been able to see my own children and many nephews and nieces raising *frum* families. Many are learning in kollel today — it's a *berachah* with ripple effects that I have been fortunate to witness in my lifetime. It is a dream come true."

Rabbi Jacobovitz himself was greatly inspired by the story.

"I've used the story many times to teach students," Rabbi Jacobovitz said. "People are given tests. Hashem pushes them to make a decision to prove in which direction they want to go. A person gets tremendous *siyatta d'Shemaya* once he shows Hashem his level of commitment."

Rav Moshe of Kobrin, the Kobriner Rav, teaches an important lesson from the words of Friday night Kiddush. There, Shabbos is called "*techilah l'mikra'ei kodesh*" — the beginning of the holy days. The Kobriner Rav explains: if a person wants to become holy, he must start with Shabbos. A person shows his desire to do *teshuvah* by committing to observe Shabbos.

He writes that it is impossible for a person to fully purify himself without allowing the light of Shabbos to penetrate into him (cited in *Nesivos Shalom*).

Those Friday-night choir sessions were the beginning of Noah's journey. He was filled with such a tremendous yearning, a great love for Judaism, that he was able to rise above the formidable challenge and dedicate himself to Hashem. And once Hashem saw his commitment to keeping Shabbos, He smoothed the way to make it possible.

Hashem took note of Noah's sincerity and his commitment to keep Shabbos and sent him exactly the help he needed.

Fred Sugarman* faced a similar challenge after he became observant during college. He worked as an investment analyst and had a boss named Julio. One year in the autumn he explained to Julio the details of Shabbos and why he would need to start leaving early on Friday afternoons. Julio was very supportive.

Julio was so supportive, in fact, that on one Friday afternoon he barged into Fred's office at 2:00 P.M. and yelled at him to go home to get ready for Shabbos.

"Julio, it's the middle of June!" Fred replied.

A Heartfelt Shabbos

WHEN A JEW is tested, he needs to remember that G-d is watching out for him and arranges every event with a purpose. I had such an experience early on in my own *teshuvah* journey in which I perceived G-d watching over me and my grandmother.

I started to become observant at the beginning of my sophomore year at Emory University in Atlanta. By the beginning of my junior year, I was already keeping Shabbos.

In March 1998, toward the end of my junior year, my seventy-five-year-old grandmother Isabel Gros flew down from New York to visit me for a week. She had always been the epitome of good health, the kind of grandmother that you have to run to keep up with. A few days before coming, she had a routine checkup with her cardiologist in New York. He found a very small amount of blockage in her arteries, but said it was nothing to worry about and gave her a clean bill of health to fly.

My grandmother arrived in Atlanta on a Friday. The following Wednesday afternoon, in the middle of her trip, she began to experience severe chest pains. She went to Emory University Hospital's ER. She knew very little about the hospital, and chose it mostly because it was close to her grandson.

Tests in the hospital found that her arteries were over ninety percent blocked. Her doctor back in New York had completely misdiagnosed her. Additional tests showed that she needed an immediate angioplasty procedure to clear the blockage and a coronary stent inserted to keep the arteries open. As it turns out, Emory Hospital is a leader in the procedures she needed. The first coronary stent procedure in America was performed at Emory in 1987, and the hospital has more experience than most — especially more than her doctors back home.

The procedures were scheduled for Friday morning, but were pushed backed several times during the day. She finally went into the surgery ward on Friday afternoon. That evening I attended the Friday night Shabbos services on campus as usual, had a quick meal in my dorm room, and then walked to the hospital to wait for her to be released from the recovery room. (In another sign of G-d's beneficent Hand, my dorm, Harris Hall, was located next door to the hospital.)

It was already after nightfall. All of the entrances to the hospital were closed except for one. Directly inside the door a burly African-American security guard was sitting at a desk with a sign that read, "After 6:00 P.M. All Visitors Must Sign In."

My mind began to race. How could I explain to the security guard that I couldn't sign my name on the pad?

I had been keeping Shabbos for less than a year, but I knew I could not bend for this. Giving in and signing my name would have been an easy way out, but I would not do it.

But what could I tell the guard? I figured he was from somewhere else in the Deep South. He had probably never met a Jew in his life, and almost certainly would never have heard of an Orthodox Jew. How could I say that because the sun had set I could no longer write? In my mind's eye he was going to either slam the door in my face or call the psychiatric department. I needed to find a solution, but had no idea what it would be.

After several minutes standing outside the door pondering what to do, I nervously entered and walked up to the guard.

"Hi, my name is Michael Gros and my grandmother Isabel Gros had surgery today and I'm here to visit her," I blurted out as fast as I could, hoping not to sound too anxious. "I'm an Orthodox Jew. On the Jewish Sabbath from Friday evening until nightfall on Saturday night we don't use electricity, write or drive. Therefore, unfortunately I can't sign in."

The guard paused for what seemed like an hour, though it was really only a fraction of a second. Then a huge smile erupted on his face. "Oh, the sunset thing. I'm from Brooklyn. I know all about it. Go right in."

The Hand of G-d was apparent to me throughout this story. At every step of the way He arranged the events to make sure my grandmother received the finest care possible. Then, when I faced my test measuring my commitment to Shabbos, He sent the perfect emissary to assist me. How else could this security guard just happen to have been from Brooklyn, just happen to know about Shabbos, and just happen to be at the hospital that night? The chain of events was too perfect to be coincidental.

But if G-d was going to arrange the events to help me get into the hospital that night, why did He need to test me at all? He could have orchestrated the events in some other fashion so I wouldn't have had to endure the pressure of the moment.

The Rabbis write, "If one comes to purify himself, he is helped" (*Shabbos* 104a). Rashi explains that if a person sincerely tries to change his behavior, he receives help from Heaven. A person must first put in genuine effort, and then G-d sends him support. On that Friday night, G-d waited to see my level of commitment to Shabbos, and then sent assistance to help me complete the mission.

Telephone Temptations

EVERY JEW HAS a different road back to Orthodoxy and unique events which inspire his journey. For Mark Schwartz*, his journey toward becoming observant was ironically marked by two events — a spiritually uplifting experience which he barely appreciated, and a religious test which he failed. Only when he later appreciated the significance of the two moments did he realize the impact they had on his life.

Mark grew up in a completely non-observant home. His father had been raised Orthodox, but turned away from it, and he and his wife raised Mark and his siblings with no religious practices. However, most of his extended family remained observant. When Mark was a young boy, he was very close to his first cousin Shloimie who was *frum*. The two spent a lot of time playing marbles in the streets or in each other's Lower East Side apartments. Shloimie descended from a long line of rabbis and his family was well-connected to the religious establishment of New York.

When Mark was five he was once at Shloimie's house on a Shabbos afternoon. After hours of playing together, night had already fallen and it was time for havdalah. Mark still clearly remembers being chosen to hold the havdalah candle, but recalls nothing else of the evening. Years later his cousin told him at havdalah that night in his apartment were two of the leading rabbis of America: Rabbi Moshe Feinstein and Rabbi Joseph B. Soloveitchik. (Rabbi Feinstein lived in the same building as Shloimie's family, and was related to Rabbi Soloveitchik. The latter had come to visit him that Shabbos afternoon and the two had joined Shloimie's family for havdalah.)

Righteous individuals such as Rabbi Feinstein and Rabbi Soloveitchik bring a feeling of holiness to their surroundings that leaves an impression on those around them, whether they realize it or not. For Mark, the experience lit a spark in him that would eventually burst into a flame to guide him back to Judaism.

For over twenty years that flame flickered silently inside Mark. He grew up, went to college and married a Jewish woman, Donna, in 1970. They settled in New York. But their lives felt empty and they soon realized they needed to find spiritual meaning. They started attending a local Conservative synagogue and began taking on some Shabbos practices.

Over the next few years, they slowly grew in their Jewish observance and considered becoming Orthodox. For Mark one of the hardest challenges in their growing religious practice was not being able to answer the telephone on Shabbos. Answering machines were not yet common and the Schwartz family did not own one. Mark felt that every phone call was urgent and needed to be answered. Donna tried to persuade him to stop answering the phone, but he was reluctant to give it up.

"Each individual phase of our growth took a little bit of self-control. But the phone was different. It rang all the time," Mark said. "You can put your lights on timers and then you don't have to worry about them. But the phone was a constant."

After several years, Donna and Mark decided to move to a community better suited to their changing needs. They were the only young couple in their synagogue, and they wanted a congregation with families their age and one that could provide more opportunities for spiritual growth. They were still straddling the fence between being Conservative and Orthodox, but they chose an Orthodox community in Long Island.

They eventually found a house near an Orthodox synagogue and applied for a mortgage. It was a stressful time period: they were at a crossroads in their lives religiously, were anxious about their move, and were unsure if they would be approved for a mortgage.

A Yom Tov came during this period and offered a much-needed respite from their worries. The Yom Tov fell in the middle of the week, and Mark and Donna were at home in the afternoon. The phone rang and Mark could not resist picking it up.

It was the bank. The mortgage application for their new house had been — rejected!

"I looked at Donna, Donna looked at me, and we said: 'Enough is enough.' It was a clear message from Hashem," Mark said. "That was the last time I answered the phone on Yom Tov or Shabbos."

After months of trying to wean himself from his dependency on answering the telephone, it took just one big slip to make him stop. A mistake can be compared to a trampoline: sometimes if a person slips and then recovers, the event can propel him much higher in his growth than he would have achieved without it.

"When people decide to go to therapy for help, they decide to go because they finally admit that something is wrong. That call told me, 'This is the message. You've been wanting to stop answering the phone, so just stop it.'"

Mark and Donna eventually applied for another mortgage and were approved. Several months later they moved into their new house in Long Island, and within a few years became fully Orthodox. And Mark never picked up the phone on Shabbos or Yom Tov again.

When G-d tests us, He only gives us tests that He knows we can pass. The same strength that helped Mark finally persevere in his test is planted in all of us.

Early in the Torah, G-d made a covenant with Avraham, promising him that his descendants would inherit the land of Israel. Hashem appeared to him and commanded him, "Walk before Me and be perfect" (*Bereishis* 17:1).

Rashi said that these words were a powerful blessing for Avraham. When G-d blessed Avraham that he should "be perfect," He was telling him: "You should be complete in all of My trials." G-d gave Abraham a blessing that he would be able to pass all of the tests he would face. So, too, G-d gave us all a blessing to help us overcome the hurdles in our religious observance.

A BUMPY ROAD

JOEL KESSLER'S PATH toward becoming Shabbos observant was filled with potholes and speed bumps, but he was guided by G-d's Hand. In the end, he received an unexpected and unbelievable salvation.

Joel's journey began in April of 2005. His father had just passed away and he made a commitment to go to synagogue every day to recite the Kaddish prayer in his father's memory. Joel began attending his Conservative synagogue's 6:30 A.M. daily prayer service, but Saturday mornings posed a challenge. He worked as the manager of a mobile electronics store near his home. He needed to open up the store at 8:00 A.M., well before the 9:00 A.M. start of the Shabbos morning service at his synagogue.

A friend who prayed in his Conservative synagogue told him that the local Orthodox synagogue, the Young Israel of Plainview, had an early Saturday morning service at 7:30. Joel decided to try it once. He knew that he would not be able to stay for the entire service, but at least would be able to say Kaddish a few times before he had to leave for work.

That Shabbos morning he drove to the Young Israel. Since he

was going directly to the store afterward, he came in his work clothes. He opened the door and immediately froze out of anxiety. Between knowing that he would have to leave early, not being properly dressed, and being unsure about the prayer book, he felt very uncomfortable.

Almost immediately a man walked over to him.

"Hi, my name is Harry Fruhman. Come in, we don't bite," he said with a warm smile.

"I'm a little embarrassed," Joel replied. "I don't know what to do."

"That's okay. Come in, sit down. I'll show you," Harry said.

Harry found Joel a seat and showed him the proper place in the prayer book. Joel stayed in synagogue long enough to catch Kaddish a few times and then excused himself and drove off to open the store.

Though he was only in the synagogue for a short time that morning, the warm welcome he received left an impression on him and he decided to return the following Shabbos.

Joel began attending the Young Israel every Saturday morning and started going to the morning service during the week as well. Over the next few months he became friendly with other members. They became an ad-hoc support group for him and helped him through his bereavement. He felt part of a huge, caring family.

"I was brought there; I was guided there for a reason. You have to believe in Hashem. Things like finding that synagogue don't just happen by accident," Joel said. "I never thought I would find myself in this position, but I love it. The people that I became involved with at the Young Israel are more content than any other people I've met."

After a few months, the Saturday morning service had become a staple of his life and he looked forward to it all week. But now he had a different challenge. He enjoyed the service and the people so much that he dreaded having to leave early.

Just at this point, a perfect opportunity arrived. For many years Joel and a friend had contemplated opening their own mobile electronics store. By the summer of 2005 they had finally saved up enough money and opened a store. For Joel, the excitement was not just having his own business, but he now had a partner who could watch the store while he was in synagogue!

Joel was now able to attend the entire Shabbos morning service each week and stay for Kiddush afterward. He still drove to his store after services, but often returned to synagogue for the Minchah and Maariv services at the end of Shabbos.

However now he had a new problem: he longed to quit his job altogether and commit to keeping Shabbos! But he saw no way out. He was the co-owner and therefore felt he had to be there to run the store.

Joel eventually got his wish, though not in quite the way he had hoped. From almost the beginning, the store had financial problems and through much of 2006 business was on a downward spiral until the store finally went bankrupt. He and his partner officially closed the doors on October 31, 2006.

Joel was absolutely frightened. The store was his livelihood and he wasn't sure how he would be able to make ends meet. It was a time of significant introspection and he frequently beseeched G-d for help.

"In shul sometimes I would just sit and look at the book, talking to Hashem. I would cry out to Him, 'Help me, where am I going, how will I make it?'" Joel said. "When you're in that position, you just look at the words and you're staring into space. So many things are on your mind."

Joel was nervous, but at the same time he was beginning to see G-d's Hand in his life. He realized that G-d had provided him with the opportunity he so much desired: to keep Shabbos.

"In one way it was the scariest thing in the world. I had put a lot of money into [the store]. But it was also a relief. I knew that part of my life was ending, but I knew that something new was beginning," Joel said. "It's such a calming feeling to have Shabbos."

Joel now began spending the entire Shabbos in synagogue and with families in the community. His family joined him from time to time, and his teenage son began walking to synagogue every week with him. For years he had felt a nagging feeling of not having sufficient time with his family, but now Shabbos became the day each week he could dedicate to his family and himself.

"That took me to another point in my life. It gave me the opportunity to have a half-hour talk with my son every Saturday, which is something I didn't have before," Joel said. "These became — and still are — beautiful walks with my son."

It was also the first time in Joel's life that he had found peace and quiet. During his sixteen years as a store manager, employees constantly called him at home or on his cell phone — even during vacations and Jewish holidays. For those sixteen years, every Rosh Hashanah was spent the same way: in the morning he went to synagogue with his family, and in the afternoon he had to return all of the work calls that had piled up while he was praying. Committing to keeping Shabbos gave him a feeling of freedom.

"It's such a calming feeling to have Shabbos and to know that nobody will call me or beep me," Joel said. "I was never at peace on Shabbos. Now I found peace... It took me fifty years to find it, but I finally did."

At the end of 2006, a year and a half after he first stepped foot in the Young Israel, Joel began keeping Shabbos. But he was now unemployed. People in the synagogue recommended job openings to him, and he went to many interviews but nothing came through. During each interview he explained that as an observant Jew, he would not be able to work on Saturdays or Jewish holidays. Since Saturday is the prime day in the retail world, no one hired him. But despite all the rejections, Joel remained optimistic and never compromised regarding Shabbos.

"It was really scary. Nothing was working, but everywhere I went I stuck to my guns about Shabbos," Joel said. "I made the decision that this was my life and I'm not going back."

A friend from synagogue had heard that the electronics store B&H Photo in Manhattan was expanding and suggested he apply there. Joel went on an interview. With his years of sales and electronics experience, he was immediately hired to work in the home entertainment division! He was overjoyed beyond belief.

B&H offered him not just a job, but the perfect environment in which to sustain his Jewish growth. The store is owned by Orthodox Jews and is closed on Shabbos and Jewish holidays. It closes early on Fridays. The store even has a Minchah service each afternoon. When Joel started the job he began wearing a *kippah* to work and felt completely comfortable doing so.

The B&H job was Joel's salvation. He still marvels at the incredible turn of events and the power of G-d's guiding Hand that brought him first to the Young Israel, then to a store which would go bankrupt, and finally to B&H.

That's the power of our commitment to Shabbos. Joel repeatedly demonstrated his passion and excitement for Shabbos amidst all obstacles, so G-d sent him a work situation that allowed him to observe it. If we exert ourselves to keep Shabbos, G-d will reciprocate and arrange events to help us do so.

David HaMelech refers to G-d as "your shadow" (*Tehillim* 121:5). Just as a shadow follows its master and copies his actions, so, too, G-d responds to our actions and reacts accordingly.

A second theme of the story is the tremendous impact that the members of the religious community have had on Joel, guiding him and inspiring him throughout his journey.

"I have faith in Hashem, and He's leading me somewhere. The whole time He's been taking me by the hand and leading me," Joel said. "I have to believe my father's passing led me to the Young Israel and the Young Israel led me to find Harry. During all our walks to synagogue I had so many questions. He was my mentor."

In June 2007, Harry moved to Florida with his family. However, he and Joel have still kept up their friendship despite the distance. Every Friday afternoon Harry calls Joel to wish him a Good Shabbos and the two men make a *l'chaim* together over the phone.

As a further sign of the close support of the community: Joel had been a Commissioner on the Board of Commissioners of the Plainview Water District for many years, and in 2007 was up for re-election for a fourth term. For the first time, he had competition and it proved to be a tight race. However, the entire membership of the Young Israel voted for him and he won in a landslide.

Addendum: in April 2010, Joel decided to leave B&H to take a full-time job in the local Nassau County government. However, his years at B&H, and especially seeing how Hashem arranged events for him to get the job, left a mark on him that he will never forget. The position gave him *parnasah* when it was sorely needed and it precisely fit his previous work experience. It also supported his new religious growth, allowing him to become fully observant, and gave him the confidence to proudly proclaim himself as a *kippah*-clad, Torah-abiding Jew.

He wears his *kippah* to work now in the county government. He has had only positive experience in his current position, with no challenges from his supervisors or co-workers when he requests to leave early for Shabbos or to order kosher food for department events.

Joel also has a new role in the Young Israel — he serves as the *gabbai* for the synagogue's early-morning minyan.

"Wow, who would have ever thought ten years ago that I'd be running a minyan there?"

3 Messengers Sent from Above

IF THE KING'S CHILD GOES MISSING, HE WILL MUSTER HIS entire army and all of his officers to track him down. How much more so does this hold true when Hashem calls one of his precious children to come home. He will arrange the most unpredicted circumstances and even use people who are the farthest away from Him to save one of His beloved souls.

The narratives of Jews returning to their roots are full of drama, twists, and turns. They show the strength of the Jewish soul to pursue truth even when it is difficult, and the rewards that come from above when they persevere. And they show the magnificence of the Hand of Hashem, which reveals itself in the most unexpected ways to guide Jews home.

His Whole Life Turned on a Sandwich

SOMETIMES HASHEM WILL send the most unlikely emissaries to inspire a Jew to grow. For Art Sherman, that messenger was a dreadlocked Rastafarian from the island of Jamaica, who made a single comment that turned Art's whole life upside down.

Art grew up in a loosely affiliated Jewish home in Margate, New Jersey, outside Atlantic City. In 1973 he married Karen, a Polish

Catholic woman. The young couple moved from place to place — first to Philadelphia and then to Brooklyn. There, he decided to open a small sandwich store. He made all types of sandwiches, from five different kinds of cheese steaks to Italian hoagies stacked high with ham, pork-salami, and provolone cheese. Customers loved the sandwiches and business was great.

Over time, he started noticing specific groups of people who would not eat particular sandwiches. He had a lot of Jamaican, Seventh Day Adventist and Muslim customers who said they didn't eat pork because it was prohibited in the Old Testament.

Art continued to devour his non-kosher sandwiches, but over time he began to sense the irony of his non-Jewish customers attempting to follow religious dietary laws which he ignored completely.

"The Muslims would make me wipe off the slicing machine before I cut roast beef or corned beef for their sandwiches. For myself, I couldn't care less," Art said. "I could eat so much pork it would make the Pope sick. I had all these non-Jewish people coming in who had more respect for where I came from than I did."

One of his employees, who was a Rastafarian, refused to eat meat altogether. He was a vegetarian, because as he told Art, "The Bible forbids the consumption of blood." Rastafarians take this Biblical statement to prohibit the consumption of any animal flesh.

Art continued to consume away. One day in his store, he had a craving for a huge hoagie, with everything on it.

"I wanted a 'Marciano' Italian Hot Ham and Provolone cheese sandwich. The sandwich had to have the perfect balance. It was my place. I could put on as much meat or cheese as I deemed appropriate. But too much meat, not enough cheese, and the balance would be thrown off. I had to have room for the lettuce, tomatoes, thinly sliced onions, hot peppers, oil, and oregano," Art said. "I was in Alpha concentration. I was totally focused on the task at hand."

As he was about to finish preparing the sandwich, he heard from behind him the deep voice of his Rastafarian employee:

"You know Art, you really shouldn't eat ham."

Something about the statement caused Art to stop and think about what he was doing.

"I felt like I had been slapped in the face! Shot in the heart! It woke me up," Art said. "I knew I really shouldn't eat ham. I went to Hebrew school. But the last person I expected to call me on it was this guy. What could I say? He was right."

Art made a commitment at that moment to keep what he called "Arab kosher," cutting out pork products from his diet. He also decided to stop eating shellfish. "It was a big step for me and I was proud to take it."

Art came home that night and told his wife about his epiphany. Even though she was not Jewish, she immediately agreed to join him. Although it created tension with her extended family, Karen remained steadfast in her determination. She saw that other Jewish practices that they had adopted, such as having a Passover Seder, had brought them closer together as a couple, and she was sure this action would be no different.

The commitment to cut out pork and shellfish from their lives launched the Shermans on a journey of growth and exploration. Soon, Art decided to close his store altogether, not being able to handle the contradiction of selling non-kosher sandwiches that he would no longer eat. He and his family moved back to his hometown. They began attending a synagogue around the corner from their house, and he and his wife began taking Jewish classes. Over time they began keeping fully kosher and took on more mitzvos.

Karen attended a class in the synagogue shortly before Shavuos that struck a chord in her.

"Rebbetzin Devorah Weiss, the Rabbi's wife, told the story of Sinai. I felt like there was something really familiar about it. I could actually feel it, visualize it. It was hard to describe, but I felt like I had been there. I finally began to understand the identity of my soul."

With this newfound realization and excitement, Karen continued learning. She and her daughters eventually converted.

When she went before the *beis din* to convert, Karen asked the rabbis if it was possible that her soul had actually been present at Har Sinai. The answer was affirmative.

"That was the most emotional part of my life. It was my beginning, like my birth. That's where I started. It was like a rebirth. I felt like I finally found out who I was."

Since converting, the Sherman family has been on a steady upward growth curve, constantly looking for new mitzvos and practices.

"Keeping Shabbos was one of the most beautiful gifts I have ever gotten," Karen, now Kayla Devorah, said. "Going through all of the different holidays has brought a rhythm to my life."

Art and Kayla Devorah say they still look back in astonishment at the extraordinary source that launched them on their growth. The one comment from the Rastafarian employee, of all people, sent them on an incredible life journey. But the fact that it came from such an unexpected source was a major reason it had the impact that it did.

"I was all ready to defend myself from a religious Jew, but would never expect a gentile to tell me things the rabbis taught," Art said. "I was like a tank. I was fortified, heavily reinforced from the front for a frontal attack, but my armor was not as thick on the side. When you get hit on the side sometimes, boom, the rounds go through. The Rastafarian caught me in the ribs."

Hashem has lots of arrows in His quiver, of all different types, depending on whom He is trying to reach. And you just never know which technique or emissary He will use.

Rashi in *Sanhedrin* 76b describes the essence of a Jew: "Jews are thirsting to fear their Creator and to fulfill His mitzvos." He said this is in contrast to idol worshipers, whose serve their deities insincerely and without a real yearning.

No matter how far a Jew has been flung from Judaism, once properly exposed, he will return like a person parched from dehydration. For Art, it only took a single unexpected comment to send him rushing back home to Judaism.

RETURNING HOME TO MY FATHER'S PALACE

THE SHERMAN FAMILY's life flipped around completely in a single moment due to one concerned comment. For Rachel Friedman*, the process was an up-and-down rollercoaster over several years, aided by many people. Ironically the person who had the greatest impact on her was the one who tried hardest to pull her away.

Rachel grew up in the Five Towns, Long Island. While much of the area is observant, she grew up in a section with a very large Reform community. She had a bas mitzvah ("it was pretty superficial"), and attended the obligatory family Passover Seders and services on the High Holidays. ("It all seemed more cultural than religious.")

In 2007 she went off to college, traveling down south to attend Emory University in Atlanta, Georgia. During her sophomore year she heard about a Birthright trip to Israel over the summer, sponsored in part by Emory Hillel. Excitedly, she applied... and was rejected!

"I think I'm the only person to have ever been rejected from a Birthright trip!"

A few days later she bumped into a friend on campus. She told him about her disappointment over the trip. He told her that he had attended another trip to Israel the previous December through the Atlanta Scholars Kollel (ASK), a local Jewish organization. The trip combined travel through Israel with Jewish courses.

This friend was the first of many people who would serendipitously influence her life over the next few years. Rachel's ears perked up when she heard about the trip. Her friend connected her with the local organizer, Rabbi Yaakov Fleshel from ASK. Even though the program was geared for students in the kollel's campus program, he decided to accept Rachel nonetheless.

Rachel loved the three-week trip. Her group spent the mornings learning at Neve Yerushalayim and the afternoons exploring Israel. She saw elements of Israel and Judaism that she never knew existed.

After arriving back at Emory for her junior year, Rachel was full of energy and inspiration from her trip. She began lighting candles and studying with Rabbi Fleshel once a week. However, over time her enthusiasm slowly began to wane.

"I was trying to make the inspiration of a three-week trip to last two years. It just wasn't enough. By the end, I was hanging on by a thread."

During this time, Rachel began dating a nice Jewish boy named Jared. There was only problem — he was an atheist! And as she was contemplating whether to continue on her religious journey, he was simultaneously trying to pull her down to a path of raw hedonism and a complete denial of Hashem.

Ironically, her boyfriend's cynicism of religion led to Rachel to wonder if she had jumped off the religious train too quickly. Over time, she began to see that the faith and knowledge of G-d's presence that she had developed while in Israel could not fit with her boyfriend's view of the world.

"I couldn't get over the G-d factor. I couldn't accept that he didn't believe in it!"

To grant herself a temporary break from Jared, she decided to spend her Spring Break in Boca Raton, Florida, visiting her grandmother.

One day during her trip, Rachel was relaxing on the beach when her cell phone rang. It was Cynthia, a young woman she had befriended on her Israel trip two years earlier. The two of them had been in touch off and on over the years. Cynthia was also trying to become more religious. The last time they had spoken, Cynthia was living in Argentina working for the U.S. Embassy. Rachel assumed she was still there.

"Rachel, I was sitting on a beach and your name popped into my head. How are you doing?"

"Great. Where are you?" Rachel asked.

"I'm in Boca right now."

"What? Me too!" Rachel screamed.

Cynthia was leaving the country the next day. The two met for dinner that night.

While catching up on the events of the previous two years, Rachel asked Cynthia what she was doing at the end of the year.

"I'm going back to Neve," Cynthia said. "Are you coming too?"

A light bulb went off in Rachel's head.

"Of course I'm going."

That question reignited a spark in her. After she first returned from Neve two years earlier, Rachel had dreamed of returning to learn in seminary after graduation. But over the two years, that dream too had faded. In fact just a few days before her trip, Jared had said to her, "If you keep dating me, there's no way you're going to get yourself to go to seminary after graduation." And so when Cynthia invited Rachel to join her, she realized this was the opportunity she had been waiting for.

Jared had made another chance comment which had unwittingly left an impression on her. During dinner the Friday night shortly before her Florida trip, he called her by a nickname that he knew she abhorred: "Princess."

"He called me 'Princess' all the time. I always told him it bothered me. But that Friday night, I stopped and thought: 'You're right, I am a princess! I'm a daughter of Hashem and this is not the life for me.'"

So therefore, days later, when Cynthia invited Rachel to join her at Neve, she realized it was her ticket to get out.

Shortly after spring break, Rachel broke up with Jared and began planning her post-graduation plan to study in seminary. She left America in May and arrived in Yerushalayim in time for Neve's end-of-the-year banquet.

That night, the nickname that her (now) ex-boyfriend had given her left another unexpected mark on her.

On the table in front of each girl was a pamphlet with quotes from all of the teachers. One quote immediately jumped out at her. It was written by Rebbetzin Yocheved Engel, who has since become a mentor to her: "Only when you realize you're a princess can you begin to grow close to Hashem."

That quote brought tears to Rachel's eyes.

At that moment, the events of the previous two years became clear. She realized that all of the challenges, messages and nudges from random people had brought her back to seminary and to returning to her religious journey.

And it was just like her ex-boyfriend had said — she truly was a Princess. And here she was, back in her Father's palace.

⇨ ⇦

Postscript:

Rachel learned for several months at Neve, becoming fully *shomer Shabbos* and *shomer kashrus*. She then returned to the States to attend law school. She applied herself fully to her studies, but longed to return to seminary to learn further. Unfortunately, she could not foresee any way to take off time and return to Israel without jeopardizing her career.

Rachel's law school routinely brought in professors from abroad to lecture. In the fall of 2013, a professor arrived from Israel, to teach about legal issues of the ongoing Middle East conflicts.

Rachel struck up a friendship with her. The professor told

her about an open six-month position to clerk for the Israel High Court of Justice for the following year. It was the perfect opportunity for Rachel, but as a foreigner with no connections, how could she hope to receive this coveted position over native-born and trained students?

Nevertheless, Rachel applied and davened for help from above. She also asked the professor to write a letter of recommendation.

Fast forward several months. In the interim this particular professor was appointed to become a Justice on the High Court. And on the morning of Rachel's birthday, she received an email that she had been accepted to the clerkship.

"Overnight my life flipped from not knowing how I could get to Israel, to knowing that I'm going."

Rachel spent that year in Israel — but in two worlds. She was exposed to Israeli law first-hand at the highest echelons, and was privileged to spend the other half of her time learning more about her Jewish heritage from some of the top teachers in Israel.

Shortly after our interview, Rachel told me that she was on the verge of getting engaged. While dating, she once went together with her *chasan* to meet his rabbi.

Following the meeting, his rabbi told her *chasan*, "You have a real princess."

Without having heard the story of Jared and the "Princess" nickname, her *chasan* began calling her by that name. But now that she has realized that she is one of Hashem's special children, she loves the name and even appreciates being called by it.

THE JEWISH WRESTLER

GREG HERMAN IS a former professional wrestler. He went by the name Demon Hell Storm and wrestled with everyone from Hulk Hogan to Ricky the Dragon and Sergeant Slaughter. On the mat he was a match for almost every competitor, but outside the ring he had a harder time dealing with them.

Every night he traveled to a different state with his fellow wrestlers, many of whom were former criminals who had become born-again Christians. On bus trips, they taunted him about being Jewish and tried to get him to become Christian too. With plenty of help from Above, and other guides along the way, he was able to fend off their efforts.

Greg was born in 1964 and grew up in Miami, Florida. He always wanted to become a wrestler. He's five-foot-ten and at the height of his career weighed 265 pounds with only three percent body fat. After high school he attended a wrestling school and then signed a contract with the Global Wrestling Federation. Over the next seventeen years he wrestled on TV and for live audiences across the U.S. and around the world.

Greg's mother was one of the top educators in the Reform movement. He grew up proud of his Jewish heritage, but his knowledge of Judaism was insufficient to repel the barbs and challenges of his fellow wrestlers.

"I felt at that point in my life I needed to know who I was so I could rebut their claims," Greg said.

Greg grappled for answers, and spoke over his religious questions with his parents. One day as he was approaching his thirtieth birthday, his parents asked him what gift he wanted. They were shocked at his answer.

"I want a Tanach," Greg told them. "My mom almost had a stroke."

So his parents sent him a copy of an English Tanach and he began poring over it for answers.

In 1996 Greg suffered a career-ending injury: he tore his bicep and pectoral muscles in his right arm in the middle of a match. During his recovery, he fell back on the other trade he knew well: fixing cars. He took a job in a mechanics shop in Florida.

A few months later, a customer came into the shop. He was

dark skinned and something about him stood out. Greg assumed he was a Black Muslim. Greg badgered the man about being Muslim. To his surprise, the man told him he was actually Jewish (he was an Orthodox Jew from Yemen). His name was Ian Norday. The man then gave Greg a ribbing of his own.

"What are you?" Ian asked.

"I'm a Jew," Greg said.

"Then why isn't your head covered?"

"Why should I cover my head?"

"There's a G-d above you," Ian said. "And why aren't you wearing tzitzis?"

"What are those?" Greg asked.

Ian spent fifteen minutes in the store teaching Greg about tzitzis and other fundamental Jewish concepts. As he was leaving, he invited Greg to join him in shul on Shabbos. Greg declined, but accepted Ian's offer to join him in shul on Sunday morning.

Sunday morning came and Greg met the man at his Orthodox shul, the Young Israel of Tamarac, Florida. The members were all aging, straight-laced white-haired men. Greg looked out of place.

"You can imagine what the guys there thought. I showed up at synagogue, driving a jeep with forty-inch tires, a winch on front, all covered in mud. I was wearing a sweatshirt, but they could see my two-hundred-pound frame. My hair was down my back tied in ponytail," Greg recalled. "The guys were scared of me! They didn't even believe I was Jewish."

Despite their initial reactions, the synagogue members quickly welcomed Greg. He began coming every week and soon began to feel at home. He slowly began keeping mitzvos and learning more about his heritage.

During this time he also returned to wrestling. He wrestled for the Sunshine Foundation, a local wrestling foundation, so he did not have to travel.

A few years later, Greg left wrestling for good when he moved to Atlanta and opened the Gann El auto-repair shop, located outside the religious community of Toco Hills. He began learning with a Chabad rabbi, Rabbi Hirshy Minkowicz, and joined a local Orthodox synagogue.

Greg now tries to live a life based on the Jewish values he sees all around him. He goes out of his way to help organizations and private clients in his shop, even when they struggle to pay. He frequently hosts fundraising events for local Jewish charities, including wrestling tournaments.

In the many years since he has been out of the ring, he has been trying to learn a different kind of ropes.

"I've lived the other life — I like this one a lot better. You can have a world full of lunatics that are just out to stab each other in the back, or a world full of people trying to help each other. Which world would you rather live in?

"I don't give myself a label. I just call myself aspiring to be a better person. The more I learn, the more I understand."

Stop in at his repair shop and you'll be greeted with an ear-to-ear smile. The shop is filled with broken cars and the tools to fix them. Tucked away in a back corner is a single hint of his former life — a full-size wrestling ring.

Greg still moves with speed and agility in the ring. Watching him, it's easy to imagine him in his former life. But the *kippah* on his head is an indication that his life is just a little different now.

---

4 Of Life and Love

THE INSTITUTION OF MARRIAGE IS CENTRAL TO JEWISH practice and observance. It is especially important for *ba'alei teshuvah*, as it is often the milestone that cements a Jew's commitment to his growth and demonstrates his seriousness about his new observances. It's also one of the primary vehicles through which he grows and develops as a Jew and a person.

As Rabbi Mendel Weinbach, *zt"l*, Dean of Yeshivas Ohr Somayach jokingly said, "Getting married, that's the final nail in the coffin."

Therefore, due to its importance, it's not surprising to find clear signs of Hashem's Hand bringing people together, often in the most surprising ways.

Boy Meets Girl

THE STORY OF Mandi Biles and Andy Griffin, now Malkah and Meir, is almost the perfect *ba'al teshuvah* love story. They met during college at a Jewish conference — in his tzitzis and *kippah*, he was already well on the journey to becoming observant. Mandi was just beginning to explore Judaism and saw in Andy a role model who could guide her through Jewish rituals and belief.

Oh, and a couple of little details to make the story even more interesting. Did we mention that Andy was not Jewish? And that the conference where they met was not your typical Jewish outreach event? It was actually a weekend for Messianic Jews.

Those little ripples would become major issues of their journeys, as the next five years saw them weaving in and out of Christianity and Judaism while meandering in and out of each other's lives over two continents.

Mandi was raised in northern Georgia by a Jewish mother and Christian father. The family attended a Messianic congregation — her parents each felt comfortable with the inclusion of prayers and beliefs from both of their religions and believed the congregation would offer a strong foundation for their children.

The family's congregation had only a minimal focus on rituals, and Mandi was very curious about authentic Jewish practice. For a few days each December during high school and college, she traveled to Orlando, Florida for the Southeastern Messianic Jewish Alliance of America conference.

During the December 2001 conference, she decided to attend a session about how to observe Shabbos. Most of her friends had gone to a local theme park that day, but she decided to stay behind to attend more classes.

"A tiny minority of the Messianics that I met at the conference were keeping Shabbos, very similar to how we keep Shabbos today. They were keeping kosher. These were things we didn't emphasize where I came from. Because I was drawn to anything Jewish, I gravitated to that."

The session left her filled with many questions, but the presenter had to leave for a lunch appointment afterward, so he was unable to answer her questions. Instead he introduced her to Andy, a young man who had also attended the class and was knowledgeable in the topics.

Andy grew up in the small town of Lenox, deep in the Bible Belt of south Georgia. His parents were Christian but were not very religious. Andy felt a strong need to connect to religious beliefs but was not satisfied by any of the local churches. The only piece of Christianity that really appealed to him was its Jewish roots.

"When I was five years old, a cousin gave me a children's version of the Bible. I basically fell in love with it. Reading the stories from what I then called the Old Testament, the story of Abraham, Isaac, Jacob, the Exodus from Egypt — there was something about these stories that resonated with me."

Andy perceived that Judaism was the source of truth, but there was no one in Lenox who could direct him on how to find it. He therefore bounced from church to church until he found a local Messianic congregation whose use of Jewish themes appealed to him.

Andy was drawn to Jewish rituals and tried to live an outwardly Jewish life while still believing in the Christian messiah. Throughout his adolescence he gobbled up every book and tape he could find about Judaism, including many ArtScroll and Feldheim books and anti-missionary tapes. When he met Mandi at the conference, he was living an outwardly Jewish life despite the fact that he was still Christian.

Andy felt an immediate spark of attraction to her. They spoke throughout the conference and continued the relationship afterward over the phone. She went to visit him several times for Shabbos, staying with a local Messianic family.

Andy had also become connected to families in the Atlanta Orthodox community based around Congregation Beth Jacob and occasionally went there for Shabbos. He once invited Mandi to join him for the whole Shabbos. The experience was the exact opposite of what she had been told to expect from Torah-true Judaism.

"I just remember looking around [in synagogue] and thinking it was very beautiful. I remember crying. Experiencing a real *Kabbalas Shabbos* service — it was very beautiful," Mandi said. "I remember thinking I must have been lied to because I was told that Judaism is a dry, dead religion, and here I was seeing that it wasn't."

That Friday night in the community left Mandi with conflicting emotions. On one hand, she loved the experience and everything she saw and heard; on the other hand, she was intimidated.

She and Andy were invited to Friday night dinner at a home that was a fair distance from synagogue. She walked to the meal in high heels through the pouring rain, arriving drenched and miserable.

"I thought, 'What am I getting myself involved in?' I remember the meal going on and on forever. I think it went till midnight."

Mandi decided not to stay over for lunch the next day. As Andy walked her back to her car, she told him the experience had been too much for her.

Even though she had been overwhelmed by that first Shabbos experience, she still saw the truth and beauty of the traditions of the community. Therefore she decided to return several weeks later to attend the annual community-wide Purim parade and carnival at Beth Jacob.

At the event she met Rick Halpern, who ran an anti-missionary organization. Rick showed her a book he had written called *Choose Life*, which refutes Christian claims about Judaism and the Messiah.

Mandi took the book home, thinking that she could easily challenge its contents, but quickly realized she had no way to respond to the ideas contained inside. Frightened by this realization, she banished the book to a box on a high shelf in her room.

During this time, Andy and Mandi continued dating. They soon became engaged.

It was the perfect *shidduch* — he was a Christian learning more about Judaism, and she was a Jew who was still very much involved in the Christian world!

During this time Andy was growing by leaps and bounds religiously and began contemplating conversion. Each day he was becoming progressively more interested in Judaism and less in the Messianic world. His growth worried Mandi. She was still too much absorbed in her Messianic church to commit to Judaism.

"She thought I was a religious fanatic," Andy said.

Afraid that Andy would soon give up on the Messianic world altogether, and under pressure from her family and friends to end the relationship, Mandi decided to break off the engagement. They each went their separate ways. It was the last they would see of each other, or so they thought.

Their journeys now took parallel but separate paths. Andy soon left the Messianic world and converted to Judaism.

Sometime later Mandi's curiosity got the best of her and she took the anti-missionary book down from the shelf. Every word now made sense to her. The ideas of the book helped answer questions that had nagged her for years, but that she had tried to silence and push deep inside of her.

Based on the ideas she was reading, Mandi began challenging the leaders of her Bible study group. They were unable to provide her with satisfactory answers. She then began contacting Orthodox rabbis involved in anti-missionary work and pounded them with the same questions. She noticed a stark contrast — while all of the rabbis were eager to speak with her and give her answers, her Christian teachers responded with anger and insults. People whom she had known for years suddenly became antagonistic to her.

Over time, Mandi grew in her commitment to Judaism. She

was eventually kicked out of her Messianic Bible study class for asking questions that nobody there knew how to answer. Shortly thereafter, she left the congregation entirely. She began spending more time in the Atlanta community, and eventually she completely dropped her Messianic beliefs and embraced Torah Judaism.

Mandi, now going by her Hebrew name Malkah, had always felt drawn to Israel, and in the middle of 2006 decided to make *aliyah*. She received a job with an American high-tech company in Israel. She loved the lifestyle but felt sad that she had never taken time off to learn in seminary. She confided this to a friend, who told her about the Aish HaTorah Jewel program for women who had become *frum* later in life. However, she saw no way to take off time from her job to attend the program.

Hashem immediately arranged for her to be able to attend. When Malkah arrived at work the next day, she was informed that her division was being shut down and that she was out of a job.

"I said, if that wasn't a sign from G-d, what is?"

Malkah immediately signed up for Jewel.

In December of 2006, four-and-a-half years after breaking up with Andy, she received a surprise email from him. They had not spoken during that time, but Andy, now Meir, had followed events in her life via her blog. He was impressed by her religious growth and her decision to make *aliyah*. Meir said he would be coming to Israel for a two-week trip with Aish HaTorah and wondered if they could meet one night for dinner.

Reading her blog had fanned the flame of his interest in her, but Meir was unsure if she shared the same feelings for him. Meanwhile, she had no idea if he was still connected to the Messianic world. Despite the many doubts and uncertainties that they each had, they decided to meet.

On a snowy evening in Yerushalayim, they met in the Kosel

plaza. Over dinner at a nearby restaurant he told her about his conversion. They compared notes about their simultaneous spiritual journeys and were greatly pleased to hear about each other's growth.

"Something was rekindled in her, but it had never gone out for me," Meir recalled.

However, Meir's trip was soon coming to a close, and he had to return to Atlanta to resume his public-school teaching position. Malkah stayed behind to continue learning in seminary at Neve Yerushalayim and fulfilling her dream of living in Israel. The two did not know if they would see each other again.

Half a year later, right after Shavuos, it was Meir's turn to receive an unexpected call. Malkah had returned to the States for a short visit to see her family. Meir and Malkah met again, and both knew the spark was as strong as ever. They renewed their broken engagement and wed a short time later. This time, Malkah decided to stay in America. They settled into the Beth Jacob community.

"It's amazing how Hashem, after that five-year period, brought us back together," Meir said.

The Gemara (*Kiddushin* 2b) says it is the way of a man to pursue a wife. Just like an owner looks for his lost object, a man is drawn to look for his partner. Rashi explains that the first woman was created from a rib removed from the body of Adam, so it is up to the man to look for his missing piece.

For Meir that quest required copious time and patience. The path of pursuit meandered back and forth for years as he and Malkah each had to grow and change and finally arrive at points in their lives when they could meet again and wed.

They each were looking for religious direction and fulfillment. Once they found that, they were able to find their way back to each other.

The Key That Unlocked His Soul

For the Griffins, their relationship with Hashem and each other took years of development as they grew slowly and finally wed. For Jonathan Kolman*, it just took one evening to change his entire outlook on his religion, meet his wife, and find his way home.

The home in which Jonathan and his younger brother grew up in was Jewish but non-observant. As children, attending their uncle's annual extravagant Xmas holiday party was a bigger hit than any night at home lighting the Chanukah menorah. The other major event of their childhood was their mother's death at a young age.

Both brothers grew up and went off to college. In college, Jonathan's younger brother met a young woman whose mother had also passed away at a young age.

The young couple decided to spend their first year of marriage in Israel on a kibbutz. When they came back observant, Jonathan reacted with surprise, but assumed they had become religious to fill the pain that they each felt.

"I thought that since both had lost their mothers at early ages, this was filling a void for them, acting as a crutch to help them deal with the personal trauma they experienced," Jonathan recalled.

Over the next few years his brother and sister-in-law occasionally encouraged Jonathan to find out more about Judaism, but he always declined. To him it was still an archaic emotional support system for people weaker than him.

"I was always a spiritual-type person. I liked philosophy and spirituality, but religion and G-d were not things I was particularly interested in. I still thought those things were for people looking for something to lean on."

However, one day they gave him an invitation that was right up his alley.

"My sister-in-law called me up and told me that her favorite rabbi from Israel, Rabbi Dovid Gottlieb, was coming to the U.S. for a speaking tour and would be stopping in New York. What hooked me was when she told me that he had been a former Philosophy Professor at Johns Hopkins and had given it up to become a rabbi. I thought it would be fascinating to hear someone who had been in academia and had given it up to become religious."

Rabbi Gottlieb was speaking that night on the topic of relationships, in a synagogue in Manhattan. Jonathan arrived at the synagogue in time for the lecture, but then froze at the door.

"I walked to the front door of the shul and hesitated. I didn't know the protocol. I had thought that this might be a very religious synagogue, but I had no idea about separate seating."

Jonathan chose a seat on a bench next to a woman, who would become his wife.

"I had never been to a shul unless it was a wedding or a bar mitzvah. It was pretty clear to me that it was Divine intervention. I didn't realize it at the time, but looking back it was too much of a coincidence."

Jonathan and Susan hit it off immediately. She had studied at Neve and had attended classes with Rabbi Gottlieb. She loved his material so decided to come listen to him that night. She had actually brought her parents with her that night too. Much to Jonathan's embarrassment, they were sitting in the row behind Jonathan and Susan, getting a firsthand view of the budding romance.

"I didn't even know they were there until they invited me to go out for ice cream afterward."

A friend of Susan's had also joined them. At one point during the evening she whispered into Susan's ear, "Marry him."

Despite having attended Neve, Susan was not religiously committed. Jonathan and Susan began dating, and decided to attend an Aish Discovery Seminar together. A year later they were married. After their wedding, they attended a full Discovery Weekend that opened Jonathan's eyes to the truth of the Torah.

"It was at that weekend that I learned certain things about the Torah that I found fascinating. We decided that weekend to become *shomer Shabbos*. After that I started going to shul on Shabbos."

Jonathan's journey to Orthodoxy started at that Discovery weekend, but he did not grow much past it. He and his family moved to a *frum* community in Queens so he could be within walking distance of shul. He went to synagogue every Shabbos morning and occasionally on Friday night, but mainly for the social environment. He never davened during the week. For close to twenty years his observance continued at this pace: he donned his *kippah* and observance for Shabbos, but there was little of it during the week. Even Torah learning was non-existent in his life.

Jonathan's brother and family were living in Chicago. One year, they invited the Kolmans to come for Pesach. For Jonathan and his family, it was a chance to spend time in a fully religious home and environment.

Their trip to Chicago was originally planned for seven days, but they were having such a good time that they decided to extend their trip for another five. The two weeks in Chicago showed Jonathan and his family an entirely different level of observance. It was a week of davening three times a day, learning together, and exploring more of the *ruchniyus* of Judaism.

"By time the twelve days were up, I was in a state of — I don't know what to call it — a state of bliss, of feeling so wonderful being with my family. I can't explain the feeling. It was a feeling of being elevated... a spiritual feeling," Jonathan explained. "When we got back to New York I decided I had to do something to maintain this experience, this feeling. The only thing I could think of to do was to start davening every day.

"I started doing it and enjoyed it. The more I did it, the more I felt like I was getting value out of it — becoming more connected to Hashem. This was when my spirituality was really born. Coming back home after that Pesach, starting to daven every day, that's when I really became religious. Until then I was just following a routine."

As he started davening everyday, the experience took on a new, greater meaning. The prayers were not just words on a page he would mumble, but each *tefillah* was a new way to connect to Hashem. He felt his *emunah* growing and began noticing Hashem's Hand in his life.

Once he made Judaism part of his daily routine, he saw his entire life transformed. The religion that he had once called a crutch was quickly shaping his life into one of mission and substance.

"I've become much more focused on people, contributing to them, supporting them, and helping them. My relationship with my children and spouse has changed a great deal. Before my religious transformation, I had a much more difficult time controlling my anger and emotions," Jonathan said. "I have completely transformed in that area. I used to get annoyed more quickly and triggered more easily; I was an angry person and I didn't even know it. I've really turned that around. I've learned a lot of *mussar* and and am now more knowledgeable in other areas that relate to my religion."

For Jonathan, the biggest message of his journey was finding greater fulfillment in his connection with Hashem and his relationships with others.

And where did it all begin? In a class on the very topic of relationships.

YEARS IN THE MAKING

AKIVA FRANKEL* GREW up in a marginally observant home in New York but was always fascinated by Jewish ritual. He attended college in upstate New York, where he met Allyson*, who had grown up in a similar background and was already trying to become *shomer Shabbos*. The process was slower for him, and when he graduated college a few months later, he was still interested and growing but was not yet committed to becoming fully religious.

Akiva and Allyson went their separate ways after graduation but remained in touch. He stayed in the Northeast for medical school while she headed west for graduate school. He continued to grow steadily.

Several years later, they met again and decided to finally seal the bond and get married.

Soon after, they saw a clear sign that reinforced what they already had figured out — that they had been predestined for each other.

Growing up, Akiva had a metal *tzedakah* box on the desk in his bedroom. He had always been fascinated with the lock mechanism on the bottom and was curious where it had been made. The only clue was an address in Fairlawn, New Jersey.

When Allyson first saw the box on his desk she said matter-of-factly, "Oh, my father made those. That was his business."

"Really? My whole life I was wondering what was at that address."

Akiva said he loves seeing the Hand of Hashem in the story when he tells it over.

"It's hard enough making a *shidduch*, but for two people to grow up not *frum*, and reach a point in their lives where they're equally open to spiritual growth and can grow together, is truly *bashert*."

As the Gemara teaches, forty days before a baby boy is born, it is already decided whom he will marry (*Sotah* 2a). Akiva and Allyson clearly saw this in their journey.

HASHEM HAS A SENSE OF HUMOR

THROUGHOUT ADELE AND Jack Kaufman's lives, they have repeatedly felt Hashem's Hand guiding them toward Jewish growth and observance. However, the ways He has chosen to do so have been comical: their *teshuvah* journey began at a Christian "Marriage Encounter" weekend, and a major turning point in their lives was influenced by a simple inspirational button.

Adele was raised in a Modern Orthodox home. Her parents attended a local Young Israel synagogue. They and the people around her had simple faith but limited knowledge of the Torah and the intricacies of Jewish belief. Therefore, when she was bothered by challenging questions on Judaism, she had nowhere to turn.

Adele grew up, married Jack, and the couple settled on Long Island. They joined a Conservative synagogue and raised a family. They felt like their life was perfect.

"It was a wonderful life. We were very happy. If anyone would have told me we would become *ba'alei teshuvah*, I would have laughed," Adele said.

Though they had a successful marriage, the Kaufmans accepted a friend's offer to find ways to make it even better by attending a Christian "Marriage Encounter" weekend. The weekends, organized by a local church, tried to teach couples better communication techniques and other strategies to help them improve their marriages through Christian teachings.

The weekend concluded with a Mass service. The Kaufmans and the few other Jewish couples sat in the back of the room and watched the service, feeling out of place.

A few weeks later, a friend suggested they start a Jewish "Marriage Encounter" weekend. A few couples got together and started one. Adele and Jack went on the Jewish "Marriage Encounter" weekend and learned how holy a Jewish marriage is, and that it consists of husband, wife, and Hashem.

Also attending the weekend was a local Chabad rabbi and rebbetzin, who wanted to find out what the weekend was about. After the weekend, the Chabad couple offered to start monthly Jewish groups in local homes. Adele and Jack decided to host the groups in their house. In addition to marriage, the classes covered *kashrus*, Shabbos, and Jewish holidays. Adele was finally getting answers to her questions.

One week, the Chabad rebbetzin asked Adele if she lit candles every Friday night.

"I said no, since I work all week and we go out to eat on Friday night," Adele said. "The rebbetzin explained that the mitzvah of lighting candles is not erased by going out to eat. 'Try lighting candles, and don't tell me what you do afterward. Bring the light and beauty of Shabbos into your home.'"

Adele took her up on her offer and began lighting candles at home. After a few months, she decided to start making Shabbos dinners at home each week.

"I said to my husband, 'Why go out? Let's make a Shabbos meal so we can enjoy the beautiful Shabbos candles.'"

From there, Adele and Jack began bringing other small observances into their home. For the first time they decided to *kasher* their home for Passover. Adele made a full-blown Passover Seder in their newly kosher home.

One day, Adele decided that it was time for her husband to start putting on tefillin each morning. He owned a pair, but did not put them on regularly. So Adele began dropping subtle hints and suggestions to get him to start using them, but she soon saw that a stronger approach was needed.

"What does a wife do when she wants her husband to do something? She nags. I asked him to put on tefillin again and again," Adele said. "Finally he told me to stop nagging. I decided my marriage was more important and so did not mention it anymore."

Hashem had different plans.

A few days later, a friend called Adele. She had visited Crown Heights for the day, and in a store window saw a sign that read "Buy one bag of buttons, get the second bag FREE!" So her friend bought two bags, and was calling to ask Adele if she wanted one.

"I didn't want to hurt her. I'm not a button person, but I said, 'Sure, come over.'"

Adele was in for a surprise when she opened the bag.

"The first button I saw when I opened my bag read 'Have You Put on Tefillin Today?'"

Adele dropped the button in shock. She could not believe the wording on the button, but now had a dilemma: She had promised her husband that she would no longer nag him, so what to do with the button?

"I said, 'Hashem what should I do?' I decided if it doesn't come out of my mouth, it's okay," Adele said. "I decided to put it in his underwear drawer so he would notice it when he showered. I was very nervous. He would either laugh or get upset.

"I was sitting in the kitchen. He went upstairs to shower. The next thing I knew, I heard him laughing so hard."

The following morning Adele came downstairs for breakfast, and there was her husband, praying and wearing tefillin. For him it was a major step, one of many more that have come since.

The act of marriage not only shows a person's commitment to Judaism, but is one of the primary tools through which he continues to grow in his service of Hashem. The Maharal teaches that the number three is associated with potential, and the number four with the development of that potential. He explains that the three patriarchs — Avraham, Yitzchak, and Yaakov — created the potential of the Jewish people, but it was only their four wives, the matriarchs — Sarah,

Rivkah, Rachel and Leah — who nurtured the nation and brought it to fruition.

A man may have an initial idea and inspiration, but it is his/the wife who molds it, channels his energy, and helps him reach his full potential. That's what Adele was able to achieve, with the help of a simple button.

A Book and a *Berachah*

Like many families in Manchester, England, the Greens* family attended a local Orthodox synagogue, and although they themselves were not observant. However, the parents had tried to instill in their three sons an appreciation of their religion and a minimal observance of the mitzvos. In 2004, a series of seemingly unconnected events across three continents converged suddenly to shape the religious observance of their family.

Richard, the youngest son, began becoming observant on his own in 2002. In November, 2003, he went off to Yerushalayim to learn at Aish HaTorah.

While in yeshivah, Richard tried teaching his father over the phone some of the religious concepts he was learning. Mr. Green was interested, but noncommittal.

In the early summer of 2004, Richard decided to send his father a copy of *What the Angel Taught You*, a book by Rabbi Noach Weinberg, the founder of Aish HaTorah.

The timing was advantageous: his parents were leaving shortly for a month-long cruise and he knew his father would have plenty of time to read the book. On the other hand, however, it could be read and forgotten. Richard visited a prominent Chassidic rabbi in Yerushalayim, the Hornosteipler Rebbe, for advice. The Rebbe gave him a blessing that the book should be inspiring to his family.

Richard decided to order the book from a store in Manchester so it would be easy for Mr. Green to receive it. However, ordering it was not as easy as it would seem. First, Richard didn't have sufficient money in his British bank account to pay for the book, and it inexplicably took several days to transfer money into the account. Then, when he called a Jewish bookstore near his parents' house, they told him they were unable to order it.

He called another store, and although it was not in stock, they said they could order it. Richard was ecstatic. There were still a few days until his parents sailed, plenty of time to get them the book.

Richard called the store a few days later to check on his order. A different sales clerk answered the phone. To his surprise and disappointment, she told him that the book had actually not been ordered and in fact they would not be able to get it for him.

A few days later, the elder Greens left for their cruise, without the book. Richard was crestfallen. He could not understand why his hopes to send the book to his father had fallen apart so completely.

He still remembered the Rebbe's *berachah*, but was now unsure of what it had meant. He tried to remind himself that Hashem was in charge and whatever He wanted would happen.

Stage two of the Green family saga was already in progress. Richard's older brother Matt had been seriously dating a Chinese-English girl named Angie for several years. Early on in the relationship, Mr. Green had given him an ultimatum: either Angie converts to Judaism or he had to break up with her. Matt and Angie took the former option, deciding that she would convert under Orthodox auspices through the London *Beis Din*.

Over the next two-and-a-half years, Matt and Angie continued to date as she attended conversion classes. As part of the process, Matt was required to also learn about Judaism and attend shul. Together they decided that they wanted to raise their children in a Jewish home.

As the conversion date approached, Richard visited the Hornosteipler Rebbe again, asking for a *berachah* on his brother's behalf. He asked for a blessing that Angie's conversion should progress smoothly and be finished soon. The Rebbe issued a simple, but surprising *berachah*: whatever Hashem wants, exactly that should happen.

Richard relayed the Rabbi's blessing to his brother and parents. They were surprised at the words, but accepted them nonetheless.

Soon afterward, the pieces of Matt and Angie's life together began to suddenly crumble, and soon all of their plans spiraled out of control.

In the summer of 2004, shortly before her conversion, Angie decided to go to Australia for a month to visit her parents who had just moved there.

A few days after she left, Matt arrived at work one morning and was informed that he had been fired from his job, effective immediately. There had been no warning signs, and he was offered neither recourse nor severance pay.

With Angie's conversion date approaching and their wedding being planned, Matt began to panic. He knew he would soon be broke. He didn't know where else he could find a job in time. Plus, with his girlfriend on the other side of the world and his parents away, he felt alone. It was enough to be out of a job, but without compassionate shoulders to cry on, he felt hopeless.

On the way home that day, he stopped at a local Jewish bookstore to try to find a book that could give him encouragement or guidance for his worries.

He happened to enter the second bookstore that his brother Richard had called just a week earlier. The sales clerk asked him, "Are you here to pick up the book for your brother?" Even though the clerk had told Richard that they would not be able to order the book from the publisher, they had indeed ordered and received it.

Shocked at the seeming coincidence and thinking it must be a sign from Heaven, Matt purchased *What the Angel Taught You* for himself. With its message about basic Jewish beliefs, faith, and overcoming struggles, it was exactly the balm he needed for his wounds.

He finished the book within a few days. He felt like he could now pick up the pieces and get on with his life again. But the book also made him realize that the little he had been learning in the conversion classes with Angie was insufficient. He immediately called Richard in Yerushalayim to tell him about the book and his need to learn more.

Matt decided to fly to Yerushalayim that week to join his brother at Aish HaTorah. He spent several weeks there. He loved everything he was learning and found his soul soaring.

Shortly before leaving Israel to return back home to England, Matt decided to visit the Hornosteipler Rebbe and speak to him personally about his life, job search, and the upcoming conversion and wedding.

They spoke for thirty minutes. In the middle of the conversation the Rebbe mentioned a seemingly unrelated story of a woman who had run away on the morning of her wedding.

Matt was surprised by the story and unsure how it related to his current situation, but did not question it.

He left Israel and arrived back in Manchester a day before Angie returned. The next day he picked her up at the airport. During the drive home, she dropped a bombshell. She told him that she had done a lot of thinking while she was away and came to the realization that she had moved too quickly toward conversion. She felt like she was not ready to take the plunge.

The next week was spent in heartfelt and heart-wrenching discussions. Finally, at the end of the week, she told Matt that she had decided to drop out of the conversion program altogether. Not only that, but she had decided to break up with him as well!

Now with neither a job nor a marriage in his near future, Matt felt even emptier than he had felt before. However instead of getting depressed, he saw the events as an opportunity. He decided to immediately return to Yerushalayim. He spent seven months learning at Aish and became fully observant.

Matt eventually moved back to Manchester and got married, to none other than the woman in the bookstore who had helped him.

And what about their father? Over the years as he watched his sons grow and become *frum*, Mr. Green followed suit.

And it was exactly as the Rebbe had said — whatever Hashem wanted, happened.

5 Returning Home, Together

A PERSON'S RETURN TO JUDAISM OFTEN HAS RIPPLE EFfects far beyond his own life. A single person's *teshuvah* journey can uplift and inspire those around him. Children bring their parents back to Judaism, brothers and sisters grow together, and three or four generations can be inspired by a single person's growth.

THE LONG SHOT

MARC STRAUSBERG* AND his sister Nicole* grew up in a family in New Jersey that was Conservative but deeply committed to its Jewish identity. Marc began to become *frum* in college, and hoped that after graduation in 1999 he would be able to learn in yeshivah in Israel. He planned that his sister Nicole, who was two years younger and was also becoming *frum*, would spend the summer with an Aish HaTorah women's trip.

Marc and Nicole wanted their father's approval for their decision to attend the programs, but he was opposed to it. After a long conversation, their father Robert, a physician, became more open to Marc going, but his answer was still an absolute no for Nicole.

He was concerned about her as a young, single female spending time abroad.

"I was lobbying as hard as I could that we should both be allowed to go — for me it was a 50–50 shot. For Nicole, it was 0," Marc recalled.

Marc continued the pressure. He tried to hit every angle — she would grow spiritually, get to travel and maybe even meet her husband in Israel. Nothing worked.

"He wasn't budging with Nicole. I was about to throw my hands up in the air, when I did the equivalent of a half-court shot in basketball. I tried the most long-shot, the argument least-likely to succeed.

"I blurted out, and I don't even know why I said it, 'Dad — if you let Nicole go, she'll meet and become very connected to a big rabbi at Aish.'"

Marc hoped that his father, who was very connected in Jewish circles in New Jersey, might be impressed by the connection.

"Who?" Dr. Strausberg asked.

Marc had not expected him to take the bait, and now didn't know what to tell him.

"Who? Never mind, you wouldn't know."

"No, who, I want to know."

"No, really, you won't know him," Marc replied, the whole time thinking, "What am I going to tell him?"

"Who?"

Finally Marc said, "Rabbi Noach Weinberg."

Dr. Strausberg's face lit up. "I know him — we're good friends."

Marc was shocked. He had never heard Rabbi Weinberg's name in their house. Plus he could not fathom how his father would have come in contact with him, let alone have a close connection.

"Nicole, Marc. Sit down. I want to tell you a story."

Dr. Strausberg told his children that in 1973 he was attending medical school in Spain when the Yom Kippur War broke out in the Middle East. At the same time the faculty of his medical school went on strike, so he took the opportunity to travel to Israel to volunteer his services. He was close to becoming a physician, so he hoped he would be able to help out behind the front lines in Israel.

He was placed on a kibbutz and assisted where he could. However the war ended soon after he arrived so there was little he could do.

One day during his trip he went to Yerushalayim and visited the Kosel. There he met a couple of twenty-something year-old guys from America from a similar background who had become *frum*. They were attending a local yeshivah named Shema Yisrael (which had been founded by Rabbi Weinberg before Aish HaTorah) and invited him to come for a meal in the yeshivah that Friday night. He jumped at the chance to have some real food and a positive Jewish experience.

He stayed for a few weeks and alternated between attending classes in the yeshivah and traveling around the country. During his short time in the yeshivah he became close to Rabbi Weinberg.

With the war in the Middle East over and the medical school strike coming to a close, Dr. Strausberg packed up his bags and returned to Spain. He never mentioned the experience of having studied in Yerushalayim to his children.

Now Dr. Strausberg turned to his children.

"If you want to go to Israel to be with people like Rabbi Noach Weinberg, you have my blessing to go."

Both of their jaws dropped. The warm impression that Rabbi Weinberg had made on their father had remained with him for more than two decades, and now paved the way for them to study in Israel.

When Marc arrived in Yerushalayim a few months later, he told Rabbi Weinberg the story.

"Tell your father I love him," Rabbi Weinberg said.

Marc then suggested a point, which Rabbi Weinberg agreed

to: "Sometimes a person can plant a seed and never know when it will sprout. Some guys enter and five years later it works. For my dad it was twenty-six years. That's when the seed sprouted.

"It was out-of-the-blue, a half-court shot that I did. As soon as I blurted it out I thought it would fail, but it worked. Hashem took care of those seeds."

Marc has since become a rabbi himself and is involved in outreach and community work. His sister Nicole also became fully observant and has also worked in *kiruv*. The message they both learned from their father and Rabbi Weinberg has stayed with them ever since.

As Rabbi Tarfon said, "The day is short, the task is abundant ... You are not required to complete the task, yet you are not free to withdraw from it" (*Pirkei Avos* 2:20–21).

Our job is to do as much as we can with the tools that Hashem gives us. We do our part, plant the seeds that we can, and then leave it to Hashem to water the seeds and nurture them, bringing forth beautiful fruits at just the right time.

Family Ties

TESHUVAH IS CONTAGIOUS. Often when a person becomes observant, his siblings follow suit. One *ba'al teshuvah* told me that he and all four of his brothers had become *frum*, and subsequently all attended the same yeshivah. By the time the youngest brother began to show his own interest in the religious path, his parents knew well what to expect and just watched and let him grow.

It took Eliahu Levenson several years, but eventually he followed his sister into observance. But he only found out later just how similar their religious journeys were.

Eliahu embarked on his path to religious observance in 1984. He had grown up in a non-observant household and had little connection or interest in Judaism. In fact, when his sister had become observant four years earlier, he viewed the event like a disinterested spectator from the sidelines. He was so removed from Judaism that the event had no conscious impact on his life.

Eliahu's own journey began when he was invited by friends to attend a local Orthodox synagogue on Shabbos in Venice, California. He was totally shocked by the experience. He had always thought that Judaism was based solely on blind faith with no room for intellectualism or rationality. Yet in synagogue on that Shabbos he heard a sermon by Rabbi Daniel Lapin that challenged everything he thought he knew about Judaism.

"After hearing him speak, my life changed overnight. For the first time, I heard a religious discussion that was based on logic and intellect, and not on blind faith. I was stunned. I never imaged there could be anything 'logical' about religious doctrine," Eliahu said.

From that moment, Eliahu was hooked. He engaged Rabbi Lapin in theological discussions and every answer he heard penetrated his soul. He began returning to the community week after week and went to the rabbi and other families for Shabbos meals. He eventually became fully observant.

A few months after beginning his own religious journey, Eliahu asked his sister how she had become observant. She told him that she had heard a rabbi speaking on a radio program and was extremely impressed with how he presented Judaism. She was so drawn to what he said that she went to meet him in person afterward, and she eventually became observant through his help.

That rabbi was none other than — Rabbi Daniel Lapin! The messages that he presented were the key to bringing both Eliahu and his sister back to Yiddishkeit.

The concept of *emes*, truth, is the foundation of the world. Many synagogues recite the *An'im Zemiros* prayer at the end of Shabbos morning davening. There we say "*Rosh devarecha emes koreh m'rosh* — the very beginning of Your word is truth. One reads it from the Torah's start."

The words of this line refer to the initial three words of the Torah: "*Bereishis Bara Elokim* — in the beginning of Hashem creating [the world]." The last three letters of the words spell "*emes*."

Emes is not only the foundation of the world but is also the signature of Hashem (*Shabbos* 55a). Eliahu and his sister were both drawn to Judaism by the truth they saw in it. It was real, it was meaningful, but most of all, it was true.

Parents are traditionally the teachers of their children, but in a role reversal, over the last several decades it has been the children who often bring their parents with them back to Judaism. Through their excitement and love of mitzvos and Torah, children can inspire their families to embrace Judaism.

This was predicted by the prophet Malachi. Before his passing he foresaw that the prophet Eliyahu will arrive before the Mashiach and: "He will turn back the hearts of fathers with sons and the hearts of sons with their fathers" (*Malachi* 3:24).

How will this happen? Rashi writes that the fathers will return to Hashem and Judaism *through* their children, due to their influence. It is the children who will cause their parents to become observant and to "grab onto the ways of Hashem."

Parent-Raising

THE POWER OF children to bring their parents to observance is crystal-clear in the story of Yehoshua (Harry) and Debbie Looks.

Harry was a high-powered corporate executive. He had a clear direction of where he wanted to go in life and worked hard to achieve it. But when his equally persistent six-year-old son asked him pointed questions about their family's religious observance, life for their family took a completely unexpected turn.

Yehoshua had grown up in a loosely affiliated Reconstructionist house, while his wife Debbie was raised in a strongly committed Reform home. Debbie's mother lit candles every Friday night and the family had Shabbos dinner every week and followed some laws of *kashrus*.

"Friday night was always important for me, but it was not until I was a teenager that I knew that Shabbos extended until Saturday," Debbie said.

After their marriage and a MBA from Harvard University, Yehoshua and Debbie moved to St. Louis, Missouri, and then to Baltimore, Maryland, as Yehoshua rose in the corporate ranks of Edison Brothers. He eventually became president of the company's international division. The family was also on the move spiritually — they floated between different synagogues. (At one point in their journey they even had memberships in synagogues of four different levels of observance!)

In Baltimore, many of their friends from their Conservative Synagogue sent their children to a local Solomon Schechter school and the Looks family felt it was the right place for them as well. The school was affiliated with the Conservative movement and taught a background of basic mitzvah observance.

After moving back to St. Louis, they enrolled their oldest son Moshe in the first grade, again at Schechter. Moshe soon began noticing discrepancies between the religious practices he was learning in school and the family's observance at home.

"As Moshe learned more, he started coming home with questions. One day he asked, out of the blue, 'Why don't we keep kosher?' I had never kept kosher growing up. My family belonged to

[a] Reconstructionist congregation. I was aware of kashrus but it was a foreign concept," Yehoshua said. "I said, 'Let me think about it,' but it really was a way to put off the decision.

"The next day Moshe asked, 'So?' We decided then to do it."

Moshe's questions became the impetus for the family's decision, and within a short time the kitchen was *kashered*. But it was only one of many times they did it — the family *kashered* their kitchen three or four times over the next few years as they became more observant.

The more he learned in school, the more questions Moshe brought home. Ironically for Yehoshua the questions came at an opportune time in his life.

"As the questions got stronger for me, I was also approaching my midlife crisis. Instead of buying a sports car, I got into religion."

Around this time, a new Conservative rabbi came to town. Yeshoshua was drawn to him and the two men began learning Talmud and other sources together. From then on, Yehoshua's journey took off like a lightning bolt. He traded his daily 5:30 A.M. racquetball game for a Daf Yomi *shiur* and began carting his Gemaras and canned food with him on his business trips to the Far East.

Back home, the journey was slower for Debbie. Yehoshua jumped into many commitments earlier than her and he needed to learn patience, something hard for him, until Debbie and their children found their own path. The family still belonged to a Conservative synagogue but lived far from it. Once Yehoshua stopped driving on Shabbos, the distance became a challenge.

During one of Yehoshua's many business trips, Debbie was at home with their children. They had not been to the Conservative synagogue in a while and Debbie missed the social aspects. That Shabbos, the Rabbi's wife had invited Debbie and her children to come for Shabbos lunch. Debbie was still driving on Shabbos, so she buckled the children in the car and was about to pull out of the driveway. This time it was their six-year-old daughter Elka's turn to make a statement that would change the religious direction of the family.

"I looked in the back and Elka was in her seat crying uncontrollably. I looked at her and she said to me, 'You wouldn't even let me keep the mitzvah of Shabbos!' I said, 'Sweetie, this will be the last time' — and it was," Debbie said. "You have to take this seriously. You can't say one thing to your kids and then do something else."

That was the last time the family attended the Conservative synagogue on Shabbos. They next joined a local Orthodox shul which was warm and welcoming. When Moshe graduated from Solomon Schechter and parents of the other students enrolled their children in public school, the Looks family decided to send him to the Orthodox day school instead.

Next came a ten-day family trip to Israel in 1994, which solidified the religious direction in which they were headed. Again it was the inspiration of the children — after seeing and living a fully religious life during their stay in Israel, they pushed their family to even higher levels of commitments.

As the trip came to a close, Yehoshua, Debbie, and their three children also agreed that they wanted to go back to Israel one day.

That day came much faster than they had expected. In November of 1995, Edison Brothers declared bankruptcy. In April 1996, the company bought out Yehoshua's contract and he was left with a severance package commensurate with his fifteen years experience at the company.

With their future now wide open, Debbie suggested the family take a one-year sabbatical in Israel. They sold their house and cars and moved to Yerushalayim. One year became two, and they decided to make Israel their home. Yehoshua eventually became a rabbi. Since then he has worked in outreach and Jewish education in Israel and America, using his years of business experience to help manage Jewish organizations.

The Looks children are all grown up now. All the members of the family are still on paths of growth, but they are now pushing each other.

As the Torah records (*Devarim* 30:6), if a person attempts to make a spiritual change in his life, Hashem aids not only him, but his children, in maintaining the lifestyle. The verse says: "Hashem will circumcise your heart and the heart of your children." When the verse refers to "circumcision," it means that Hashem helps remove the spiritual barriers that stand in the way of a person's growth.

The Sfas Emes said the verse teaches the amazing impact of a person returning in *teshuvah*. Hashem doesn't only help him, but gives assistance to his descendants to continue to grow and develop their own religious determination.

Taking It Slowly

When a jew becomes observant, the experience is new for him and for those around him. As much as possible, it's essential for the *ba'al teshuvah* to continue to show respect and warmth to those around him in order to maintain his strong bonds with them and to show them the beauty of his new observances.

Baruch Price grew up in South Africa. His Lithuanian-born grandparents were *frum* and continued their observance after immigrating to South Africa. Baruch's parents officially maintained a *frum* home, but were less observant than their own parents. However, Baruch had a close connection with his grandparents during his childhood, and was raised on a steady diet of stories from pre-war European Jewish life. He desired to return to that level of observance himself.

Over time, Baruch became closer to his roots. He went to university and received a degree to become a veterinarian. However, he felt like he wanted to leave a mark on the larger Jewish world, and so decided to receive *semichah* and entered *kiruv*, eventually becoming the director of the Jewish Learning Experience of Teaneck, New Jersey.

"As I looked around and saw Jews who were losing their Jewish identity and going off the path, I thought very strongly what was the point in surviving the Holocaust and maintaining one's Jewish identity if it was totally meaningless? I felt very passionately that I wanted to get involved to maintain the Jewish people in one way or another, to contribute my little part."

His advice for children who are becoming observant: tread carefully and always show respect to parents.

"If a child works on his relationship with his parents and emphasizes that the effort he's making is due to the mitzvah of *kibud av va'eim*, and he really expresses this in action, the parents will realize that the Torah is not their enemy. The Torah is there to make their relationship better."

Rabbi Price says the key to achieving this is by appreciating that Hashem Himself chose to place the *ba'al teshuvah* into his particular family.

"The family into which one is born, the circumstances one lived in before becoming *frum*, all that is there to help make you what you are. ... People should build on what they had before, rather than destroy it and start anew."

⇨ ⇦

Dan Fried and his family received similar advice during their journey toward becoming observant. It was Dan's concern for the religious wellbeing of his children that initially led his family to discover Orthodoxy. His children then took over, leading the way in shaping their family's identity. Throughout the years of growth, all members of the family were careful to maintain the peace in their home. This attention preserved the family's structure and made the process smooth for everyone.

Dan grew up in a Conservative Jewish home in Fairfield, Connecticut. After his marriage in 1984, he and his wife Marge first joined a Reform synagogue and then a Conservative synagogue. Both felt spiritually empty. They weren't looking for religion necessarily; they just wanted something that would give them a path in life.

One day in December 1998, their daughter Rachael — who was in the third grade in a local public school — came home from school singing songs about Xmas. She said the kids were practicing songs every day for their school's Xmas concert a few weeks later.

Dan's wife was outraged, but Dan shrugged it off. Marge told Dan that he needed to speak to the school principal and insist that the concert not include Christian holiday songs. Dan reluctantly agreed.

"I was the last guy you should call when my daughter is singing about Christianity. I was the bottom of the list to defend my daughter's and my family's Yiddishkeit."

Dan had a close relationship with the principal so he expected that she would be receptive to his appeal. He was dead wrong. She belittled his request and refused to change the concert.

Dan researched legal precedent and returned to the principal with court decisions that supported the separation of church and state in cases similar to his. Again she refused to listen.

The school had a high number of non-observant Jewish students, so Dan turned to their parents to garner support for his efforts. They all refused to help, saying they did not want to cause problems.

Around this time Dan received tickets to go see a Yankees

game on a Sunday. He told Rachael and her fifth-grade sister Leah that they could skip their Sunday Hebrew School that morning. Recalling his own childhood experience dreading Sunday school each week, he was shocked when they said they loved Sunday school and would not miss it for a baseball game.

"That's when I realized that I was fighting a real fight. My daughters had a genuine built-in connection to Judaism."

His daughters' reaction gave new fuel to Dan's one-man fight. He threatened the school with a lawsuit and began calling local media outlets. The school still refused to listen and said it would proceed with the concert.

The evening of the concert arrived. The Frieds arrived at the school and were greeted by local news outlets. The school's principal welcomed Dan with a warm smile as if nothing had happened, but Dan maintained a stern demeanor. He had a camcorder around his neck to record the event. This was the culmination of weeks of preparation and he was prepared for the coming fight.

The students took their place on the stage as all parents sat on the edges of their seats awaiting the confrontation. Who would back down — the school or Mr. Fried? Would he really make a scene?

The students began singing several general holiday songs. Dan's stomach turned in knots as they began a song about Xmas. They sang several stanzas and then the choir conductor told them to stop. He announced that he had wanted to demonstrate how the students could sing harmonies, but the school decided not to sing the specific religious song containing the name of the founder of Christianity. Dan had won!

The concert ended and the Frieds walked out of the room. The other Jewish families tried to pat Dan on his back as he went. He tried to avoid them. He was ecstatic that the school had backed down, but was disappointed at the other families for not supporting him.

Dan's fight against the concert was a pivotal moment. He had discovered that his Judaism had meaning for him and his family and that he was prepared to fight for it.

Hashem saw Dan's drive and eagerness and therefore sent him messengers to help guide him to learn more about his Judaism.

During the year before the concert, a *frum* family had moved next door to the Frieds. The Frieds watched them with curiosity as they walked to synagogue each Shabbos in the snow. One week in the cold Connecticut autumn Dan watched as the new family inexplicably built a small hut outside their home, and then proceeded to eat their meals in it over the next seven days!

Another time, the family next door invited the Frieds for Shabbos dinner. When the father put his hands on his children's heads to bless them, Dan began to cry.

"I had never seen such a beautiful thing," Dan said. "I asked him what he was doing. He told me that every Friday night he blesses his children. I read the words of the blessing and tears came to my eyes. I knew this was what I wanted."

Dan and Marge began learning more about Orthodoxy. They soon pulled their daughters out of public school and enrolled them in a local Orthodox day school, the Hillel Academy. With their daughters taking the lead, the entire family fell in love with Orthodoxy and became observant.

Like a rain-starved seed that grows quickly when watered, the girls began soaking up everything they heard in school and wanted to start keeping every mitzvah and observance at once. This posed a challenge for their parents who wanted to take it slower.

"Our daughters were so in love with it they wanted to become super-*frum* immediately. They wanted to become Super Jews the first week."

That night Dan called Rabbi Shalom Baum, a local rabbi and teacher, for help. He said he would be right over.

"Girls, you get in that corner, parents in that corner," the rabbi said, acting like a referee at a wrestling match.

"Girls, you got to take it easy. Your parents understand what you're asking of them, what they need to do, but you need to let them take it easy and evolve at their pace." The girls agreed.

Then he turned to Dan and Marge:

"Parents, step on it!"

Dan said that one conversation made all the difference in their family's religious growth.

"It was amazing, that one interaction from the rabbi changed our fate. We all saw the humor in it. Everyone felt good about it because this one rabbi cared."

The strength of the Fried daughters had another beautiful impact on how their entire family viewed life.

One year early on in their *teshuvah* journey, the daughters begged their parents to build their own sukkah outside the house.

"It was cold and miserable outside," Dan recalled. "We were shivering. I was miserable. Finally I said, 'Girls, this is ridiculous.' They both stood up and said, 'We do this to remind us that everything in this world is temporary. The only thing that matters is the mitzvos that we do.'"

Dan said he felt the same way as he did when he had received the Yankees tickets — his daughters were correct and had put him in his place.

That message from his daughters stayed with him and it had an impact on yet another member of their family, in a way that no one could have expected. The Frieds lived near Dan's elderly grandmother, and the years were beginning to show on her. One day Dan had the daunting task of having to tell her that she could no longer live by herself in her own house anymore. It was one of the hardest things he ever had to do.

"It was the first time I had ever seen her cry. She said, 'You're taking away my home; that's how I define myself.'"

Dan didn't know how to respond. He knew that she needed to move to a nursing home, but he couldn't bear to take away her independence. He left her house and went home feeling despondent.

The next night when visiting his grandmother again, Dan recalled the story of his girls in the sukkah and told it to her. Something immediately changed. She broke out in a smile from ear to ear and told Dan that she was now ready to move.

What had changed? It was the message of the story and the words of her great-granddaughters. They were correct — this world is only temporary. In a temporary world, the physical place in which one lives does not make a big difference.

Soon after she moved to a nursing home and began calling it her "sukkah." She would tell Dan: "This sukkah is not so bad."

The family had to move her several times from one home to another, and she found a way to be positive about each one. "Wow, this sukkah is nicer than the last one," she would say.

"It was riveting to see how my grandmother, in pain, could forget the problem she had. She actually rejoiced! I was so happy I could relieve her pain through my daughters' story."

This world is only temporary, and our lives in it pass by in a matter of only a few years. However, after a person leaves this world, his *neshamah* ascends to the heavenly spheres, and eventually to the World to Come at the time of Mashiach. Those time periods are eternal and the reward in them is without comprehension. In comparison, this world and its pleasures are only temporary.

We learn in the ninth chapter of *Mesillas Yesharim* that a person should strive to make himself *"Ar'ai,"* temporary, without permanent roots in this world, and rooted instead in the service of Hashem. It is too easy to do the opposite, and people focus most of their energies on trying to build comfortable lives in this world.

The currency of the Next World is the *mitzvos* and Torah study that we performed in this world. By immersing ourselves in these, and by constantly reminding ourselves that our lives in this world are only transient, we can succeed in preparing for the afterlife.

The sukkah is a *dirat ar'ai*, a non-permanent building. We build the sukkah and live in it for a week at the beginning of each year, just after the holidays of Rosh Hashanah and Yom Kippur. Its placement at the beginning of the year helps to remind us of the fleeting nature of this world.

This message was clear to Rachael and Leah. And to their great-grandmother too. The message helped to ease her transition into each new nursing home she entered, no matter how fancy and permanent it appeared to be.

BEHIND THE SCENES

FOR THE FRIED family, change started from the children and spread upwards to their parents. Doreen and Burt Wittenberg of Atlanta took a more subtle approach, leading their children, often without their knowledge.

As they were becoming observant, Doreen volunteered for the Atlanta Scholars Kollel outreach organization. She heard about a two-week trip through the kollel for young men to learn at Yeshivas Ohr Somayach in Yerushalayim. The trip sounded like a perfect opportunity for her son Josh, who was not religiously committed. However, she knew that if she suggested it, he would not go.

The Wittenbergs decided to donate money to the kollel for the creation of a single "scholarship" for one young man to go on the trip. They asked one of the rabbis who knew Josh to tell him about the scholarship. Josh went on the trip and fell in love with the observant lifestyle, only finding out much later that the "scholarship" was straight from his parents.

Doreen's behind-the-scenes work even found Josh his wife. Doreen was attending a women's class on Judaism with a young woman named Jodi. Doreen would tell her, "*Frum* up and I have a guy for you."

Some time later, at a Shabbaton in the community, Jodi noticed the whole Wittenberg family sitting together at a table. Doreen remarked to her, "See that, it can all be yours."

A short time later, Josh and Jodi were married and Jodi became a member of the family.

"She told me later that she had always wanted to marry a family."

A Prayer from the Heart

Jonathan Levenstein's* return to Judaism occurred through his son, but not in the way one would expect. When his wife was in labor and encountered fetal distress, Jonathan made a vow to Hashem that if everything went smoothly, he would try to teach his son to know Hashem. Hashem listened, and now it was up to Jonathan to uphold his part of the deal. He just had no idea how he would do it.

Jonathan grew up in Canada. Both sets of his grandparents had emigrated from Europe and held on to their religious lifestyle even in their new country. One grandfather was the gabbai of his synagogue, and Jonathan can still picture him walking around the synagogue on Shabbos morning, his tallis flowing behind him as he gave out aliyot. Jonathan has clear memories of his other grandfather putting on tefillin in his bedroom each morning.

The tenacity through which Jonathan's grandparents retained their religion left an indelible impression on him. Even as his parents strayed from religion observance and moved to the suburbs far away from any Jewish community, Jonathan held on to the prayers of his grandparents.

"Since I was eight or nine years old I have prayed to Hashem at night, the first, second and third paragraphs of the Shema. As events unfolded in our lives, I never missed a night of davening, no matter where I was," Jonathan recalled. Every night he recited the formal prayers of the Shema, followed by his own requests from deep within his heart.

Jonathan grew up, and while not religious, continued his nightly pleas to Hashem. When his sister was diagnosed with multiple sclerosis, Jonathan's davening increased in intensity. He prayed that Hashem would make everything right.

Jonathan married his wife Barbara. They dreamed about settling down and raising a beautiful Jewish family. By 1974, they were expecting their first child. After an uneventful, normal pregnancy Barbara went into labor. Their baby suffered fetal distress and the doctor was unprepared. The baby's umbilical cord was wrapped around his neck and was strangling him. The doctors were unable to take him out.

The OB-GYN approached Jonathan and said the baby had already lost oxygen and his heart had stopped. There was not enough time to take X-rays and there was no option but to do an emergency C-section and hope for the best.

"I went into a little room and davened to Hashem. That felt like the natural thing to do. I promised Hashem that if he saved my son and he came out alive, my son would know Hashem."

Jonathan prayed like he had never done before. The tears flowed freely. Jonathan always knew that Hashem listened to his prayers, but that day in the hospital the power of tefilah became clear. As the doctors tried every medical procedure in the operating room, Jonathan used every ounce of strength to plead and cry before Hashem.

After what felt like an eternity the doctor found Jonathan. He reported that after a difficult C-section the baby was out and alive, but had lost oxygen for extended periods and would have many health problems.

Jonathan was unconcerned. The fact that his son was alive was all that mattered. He was euphoric! Jonathan knew that with Hashem's help they would get through his challenges.

"I knew I had made a vow to Hashem and He had brought him out alive. I knew I had obligation to do my best for my son to help him know Hashem."

Putting the goal into practice proved to be very difficult. The child, whom they named Alex, had many health challenges, including language delays.

School was another challenge. The blood loss had scarred his brain development, leaving him with learning challenges and social problems that took years to overcome. His mannerisms were different and he had difficulty fitting in.

Jonathan tried to teach him about the Jewish rituals and stories he remembered from his own youth. He brought him to synagogue most Shabbos mornings, but nothing seemed to sink in.

"I tried to teach him. I tried to get him to sit, but he always went away from us. I would look back and he would have his siddur upside down with an Archie comic book inside."

In high school another young Jewish boy struck up a friendship with Alex. He was able to look beyond Alex's external quirks to find his sweet inner core. He invited Alex to join him one Shabbos as he went to a local Chabad House.

The two young men started attending every week. Alex found the synagogue to be warm and accepting. Over time he began putting on tefillin and took on other mitzvos. He later attended a six-week Aish HaTorah learning program in Israel and came back fired up. Now Alex led the way for his father in recognizing Hashem.

"As he got involved, I started taking more of an interest in it. I had wanted him to see me model it, but he became a role model for me!" Jonathan said. "I had to keep up to him."

Jonathan, who had exerted himself to find ways to inspire his son to love Judaism, now sat back and watched as he developed his own love for his religion.

"I walked around and said, 'Thank You, Hashem! How could it be that you helped me fulfill my vow?' For me it was a miracle."

Alex began attending other Orthodox synagogues in the area and spent Shabbosos and Yamim Tovim with many local families. The embrace he received from local families was heartwarming.

"Nobody looked down on him because he wasn't *frum* from birth. No one said anything about his different mannerisms," Jonathan recalled. "The community was so very warm and accepting; they were like another family."

Jonathan also began putting on tefillin and took on many mitzvos himself. He became *shomer Shabbos* and he and Barbara eventually *kashered* their kitchen and joined a local Orthodox synagogue. After a very successful law career, Jonathan retired at age fifty and now spends much of his time learning Torah.

Alex moved to New York, and through a *shadchan* found a sweet young woman, a social worker. They are now raising a family in Israel.

Jonathan said he still looks back on his life and marvels at the amazing interventions time and again by the Hand of Hashem.

"The fact that He brought my son into the world when the doctors said there was a fifty-fifty chance he would die, and then brought him to be a *frum* Jew, it's incredible," he said. "I attribute it all to help from Hashem. He knows I want to get closer. He helps me every day."

Jonathan, who once wondered how he would ever get his son close to Hashem, now knows he wasn't the only one who wanted it. Hashem had an interest in it as well, and He made it all come together.

The *mishnah* at the end of *Sotah* reminds us several times: "Whom do we have to rely on? Only our Father in Heaven." For Jonathan, that message was clear. When faced with the most difficult moments, both in ensuring that his son stayed alive physically and later religiously, he knew that he could turn to no one but Hashem.

---

6 Planting a Seed

THE SEED OF A PLANT CAN LIE DORMANT FOR YEARS, until one day it is placed in dirt and watered. It can then grow into a beautiful flower. So, too, a seed of inspiration can be planted deep inside a person's soul and sit for years or even decades until it comes out to help bring him back to Judaism.

A Message from the Past

BECOMING OBSERVANT OFTEN requires a person to make radical changes in his life as he takes on new observances and practices. The changes can be daunting. But for David Wachtfungel*, an unexpected encounter with the memory of a deceased great-grandfather helped him overcome these hurdles.

David grew up in Michigan and was a typical all-American. He rarely attended synagogue, dated non-Jewish girls, and played varsity football in high school. One year a big game fell on a Jewish holiday and though it was eventually rescheduled, David had no qualms about missing the holiday to play. "I was more committed to my friends than the holiday. It didn't have a whole lot of relevancy for me."

During college David explored his Judaism a bit more. He began attending Hillel and joined a Jewish fraternity. At this time he began realizing how important it was to be able to pass Judaism onto his children. David's parents had gotten divorced years earlier, and his father had remarried a non-Jewish woman and had non-Jewish children with her. David's brother married out of the religion. His sister followed suit and did not raise her children Jewish. David recognized that the future of any hint of Judaism in his family was up to him.

"I realized I was going to be the last one to carry on the Jewish tradition in the family. I felt I owed it to myself to start asking questions about my Judaism," David said. "I realized it's ending with me, this Reform Jew. I didn't have a clue about Shabbos and Judaism. I had to make an educated decision. I needed to know why [I should be Jewish]. The more I learned, the more I realized this is who I am."

David went to Israel after college, not to become observant, but to increase his knowledge of Jewish culture and history. To him, all elements of the religion — from Shabbos to kosher eating — were only cultural components.

He spent two years there, first in a Hebrew course, and then in Marvah, a program that lets foreigners serve in the Israeli army. He loved it and was all set to make *aliyah* when he hurt his ankle in training and returned to the United States for treatment.

A doctor in Detroit examined his leg and found that he had torn two ligaments in his ankle and needed surgery. After the surgery he spent a few months in Michigan recovering. All through the recuperation his heart ached to return to Israel. Even though he still knew very little about his religion, he had felt the most connected to it there.

While in Michigan, he met several Orthodox Jews and began

learning more about Judaism from them. He soon realized that it wasn't the country of Israel that he missed, but the religious feelings he had experienced there.

David began working for a small company in Michigan owned by Shimon Traeger*, who himself had become observant a few years earlier. During work the two men often discussed Judaism and Shimon tried answering David's many questions.

After a few months working together, Shimon invited David to spend Shabbos with him and his family. He came and had a beautiful time. Still, David had many doubts about Orthodoxy. He loved the deep intellectual traditions of Judaism and learning the reasons for the commandments, but he could not take the leap to accept Judaism as a way of life. He felt like it was still too foreign to his lifestyle and to how his family practiced the religion.

On Shabbos afternoon, Shimon and David went to a small Chassidic synagogue for Minchah. Shimon occasionally prayed there and enjoyed the synagogue's small size and quaint feel. After the service, Shimon introduced David to the Rabbi of the synagogue, Rabbi Stein. He was a middle-aged man and the son of the founding rabbi of the synagogue who had passed away years earlier. The younger Rabbi Stein was officially the Rabbi of the synagogue, but lived in New York and traveled to Michigan only a few times a year for the Jewish holidays and an occasional Shabbos.

"Rabbi, this is my friend David Wachtfungel," Shimon said.

The Rabbi stood in shock for a second.

"David Wachtfungel?" the Rabbi replied. "Was your grandfather Ira Wachtfungel?"

David nodded, shocked to hear his grandfather's name.

"Stand right here. I have something for you."

The Rabbi returned a minute later holding two dusty plaques. They were acknowledgments of contributions made many years earlier to the synagogue, and inscribed on them were the names of David's grandfather, great-grandfather, and great-grandmother! The Rabbi said that David's great-grandparents, who were Orthodox, had been active members of the synagogue in its early days.

One plaque was from David's great-grandfather in memory of his wife, and the other was from David's grandfather in memory of his father. David's grandfather was not Orthodox but he knew how much his father loved the synagogue and had thus given a significant donation in his memory. The plaques had been sitting untouched in the synagogue for thirty years.

David's great-grandfather passed away when David was very young. When he was five, David remembers visiting his great-grandfather and receiving a kiss from him on his forehead. His great-grandfather said something to him, and while David doesn't remember what it was, he thinks it was a blessing or a prayer for him.

"That memory has always remained with me. Even though I was not close with him, I have always felt a connection to him as if he were watching over me. [In our dining room] I have a picture of him kissing me on my forehead, probably from that same visit," David said. "Whenever I look at it and see him in his big *kippah*, I can't help but feel grateful to him and those words he said to me. I truly believe that he is a big part of why I was worthy of becoming *frum*."

The rabbi knew David's great-grandfather well and still remembered him from years earlier. He described his piety and his great love for the synagogue. Later David spoke to elderly members of the synagogue who remembered his great-grandparents and were able to fill in more details about their personalities.

For David, finding his great-grandfather's plaques was the key he was missing. His biggest hurdle was trying to understand Judaism as a way of life with a code of behaviors we must follow every day. Yet here were members of his own family who lived based on those principles. Judaism was not just about old, dusty customs, but behaviors with eternal relevance for our lives.

David began spending more time in the Orthodox community, attended classes and eventually enrolled in a yeshivah. He wanted to understand what his great-grandparents found so significant in Judaism. The more he learned about their observance, the more he understood and believed in Judaism as a religion and saw his role in it.

"I realized these were my roots. I realized this is not a cultural thing, but this is my family," David said. "That was a big turning point. For so many years I was interested in Judaism, but the gap seemed too large. It always appeared like two different worlds. How do you bridge that gap? That was a big breakthrough when I saw that my great-grandfather was religious."

David had also been hesitant to adopt an observant lifestyle because he felt like doing so would cut off his family. He didn't want to anger them by taking on new observances. But once he learned that his great-grandparents had been Orthodox, he realized that he wasn't breaking with his family but was actually returning to their traditions.

"Going into that shul, seeing my family, I had family that was religious, I felt at home," David said. "I realized I'm not changing, I'm coming back. I'm being consistent with how my family lived for who knows how many generations."

The guiding Hand of Hashem is clear in David's story. David and Shimon just happened to go into the synagogue, the rabbi just happened to be there that Shabbos and the plaques just happened to still be sitting there after thirty years. But in reality, nothing in this world happens without G-d's involvement. G-d arranged the events behind the scenes in precisely the order that David needed to help him return.

David's story also proves that you never know the result of a good deed. Hashem takes note of each and every kindness that we do, and remembers them all. The results may be seen only generations later. For the charity of David's grandfather, the outcome was long in coming but the rewards were tremendous.

When Rabbi Elazar Meisels, who is affiliated with several outreach organizations, heard the story from David he told him, "Your grandfather thought he was helping the rabbi when he gave him the money. What he didn't realize is this money that he gave was going to ensure that his family would continue, because it's only from you that he would have Jewish offspring who would adhere to Judaism."

"YOU'RE ACCEPTED!"

THE IVORY TOWERS of Columbia University attract some of the country's brightest and most motivated students each year, promising to help them find their path to the lucrative American dream. For one young Jewish woman, the school helped her decipher her grandfather's cryptic last words, which in turn sent her on a religious journey of self-exploration.

Rebecca Rubenstein* grew up on Long Island, New York, in a home devoid of Jewish content. Yom Kippur was spent eating out in non-kosher restaurants, and she never attended Hebrew School or experienced any of the practices of Shabbos.

The Hillel House at Columbia hosts a yearly fair every September to introduce students to the programs offered on campus by various Jewish organizations. At the beginning of her sophomore year, Rebecca was walking in the area of the fair when she was approached by Ariella Cohen*, the director of operations for a local Jewish outreach program.

"I was randomly going up to students, telling them about programs on campus," Ariella said. "[Rebecca] looked like a warm, friendly person. She looked lost and very disconnected, but yearning, wanting to know what was going on."

Ariella told her about the courses being offered on campus by her organization and encouraged her to apply. A few days later the office received her application and set up an interview for her with the director, Rabbi Shlomo Linder*.

Rabbi Linder described the program to Rebecca, and she said she was very eager to join. She had gone to Israel on a Birthright trip the previous winter. It was her first time there, and she had felt something stir inside of her. She couldn't put her finger on it, but she felt a desire to learn more.

She also recounted to Rabbi Linder one tragic event of the trip: while standing atop Massada early one morning, she received a phone call that her maternal grandfather had just passed away.

Rebecca had been very close to him, even though he had little relationship with other members of the family. He had been very Zionistic and had even made *aliyah* in the early years of the State and took great pride in the work he had done then. She thought that perhaps she had inherited his love of Eretz Yisrael and this was the origin of the spark she was feeling. However she felt that there had to be more to the feeling of Jewish pride stirring inside her and wanted to find out.

Rabbi Linder told her that even though she was a strong applicant, unfortunately he would have to reject her application until a subsequent year. He explained that the organizers tried to only accept students in their junior or senior years, as they typically displayed more maturity and were already thinking seriously about their post-college lives. She accepted the news, albeit a bit sadly.

As the interview was ending, Rabbi Linder asked her if she had any questions about Judaism or life in general that he could answer. She said that in fact there was one question which was bothering her.

"Have you ever heard of the Genius of Vilna?" she asked.

"Do you mean the Vilna Gaon?" he replied, curious as to how a non-observant student would have heard of him.

"Yes, him."

"Of course, he's one of the greatest rabbis of all time."

Rebecca's face lit up. She told Rabbi Linder that shortly before leaving for the Birthright trip, she had visited her grandfather in the hospital. He was very sick, and she thought it might be the last time she would see him.

When it was time to leave his side, she gave him a kiss. He held her hand and would not let go. He looked her in the eyes and said, "Don't forget, Rebecca — you are a descendant of the Genius of Vilna, one of the greatest rabbis."

It was the first time her grandfather had ever told any member of the family about the connection. His words were engraved on her mind.

"Rabbi Linder, I'm a descendant of his. Can we learn about this rabbi together?"

On the spot, Rabbi Linder changed his mind and immediately accepted her into the program.

Following that fateful conversation, Rebecca grew tremendously — first in the local program at Columbia, and then during trips to Israel and Poland. She later studied in a seminary in Eretz Yisrael, got married and is now living a Torah-true life in Far Rockaway, New York.

Rabbi Linder's decision to accept Rebecca was two-fold. Firstly, it would have been inconceivable to let a descendant of the Vilna Gaon be lost again to Judaism. The Jewish world of the last two centuries owes tremendous gratitude to him for his leadership, teaching and his ongoing influence. Rabbi Linder had the opportunity to show our collective indebtedness by rescuing one of his descendants.

But the deeper message is that it was the merits of the Vilna Gaon that brought Rebecca back to Judaism. It was not the brief deathbed comment that led to her return, but the tremendous merits of the Vilna Gaon that had accrued over the many years and caused Rebecca's grandfather to tell her of the connection. It was those merits that also allowed his comment to penetrate her and make an imprint on her soul.

No Dry Eyes

How many tears have been shed over the last two hundred years as Jews watched their children turn away from Judaism? Hashem gathered up all the tears, and these tears are helping to bring their descendants back to Judaism.

This phenomenon was predicted in 1908 by Rabbi Avraham Yitzhak HaCohen Kook, who became the first Ashkenazi Chief Rabbi of the British Mandate of Palestine. A rabbi from Europe wrote to Rav Kook to ask how he should respond to his children who were turning away from Orthodoxy. Rav Kook responded that if we try to influence these Jews to return, and cry out and pray to Hashem for help, they or their descendants will come back.

"Those children who have strayed from the ways of the Torah and religious faith, having been carried away by the raging currents of the time. ...[there is] hope for all of them. The inner essence of Jewish holiness remains hidden in their hearts," Rav Kook wrote. He advised the rabbi that if we continue to show love to those Jews who have strayed from religious observance, Hashem will hear our prayers and help them return.

"As a result of this, future generations will be influenced to rise to a very high level, holding firmly to the glory of Israel and to the light of G-d that shines in them so brightly," he wrote.

That is the time period we're living in now, when thousands

of Jews each year are rising up to return to Torah-true Judaism. They're hearing a call from deep within their souls, a call placed there by the tears of their grandparents.

My wife and I observed this first-hand. Both of us became observant separately during college and met and married soon after. My wife has a second cousin named Ari Heitner who was becoming religious at the same time, though our paths did not cross.

In 2009 my wife, children, and I made *aliyah* and moved to Ramat Beit Shemesh Alef. Four years later, we heard that Ari and his family were also making *aliyah*, so we made contact with them.

They decided to move to a home just a block away from us and joined us for dinner the night they arrived. Three or four generations ago, our families had been *frum*, and the family tree included several prominent rabbis. During dinner, we all commented on the *nachas* that our great-grandparents were getting from looking down on us from above, seeing how we have returned to the religious roots and observances that they had so carefully maintained.

A Bar Mitzvah in the Frozen Tundra

ONE NEVER KNOWS where or when his prayers and tears will have an effect. For one family, the tears shed by ancestors long ago were even able to melt the ice and give life to a seed in the frozen hinterlands of Alaska.

In Alaska there is an abundance of snow and moose but few Jews. There are less than 6,000 Jews in the entire state. Half of the Jews live in the city of Anchorage, so when Rabbi Yosef and Esther Greenberg arrived in Alaska in 1991 they set up the

Chabad-Lubavitch Jewish Center of Alaska there. Handfuls of Jews also live in remote towns and cities such as Sitka, Kenai, Ketchikan, and Kotzubue. Rabbi Greenberg flies to these areas, sometimes in a seaplane, to prepare boys for their bar mitzvahs, put up mezuzahs, and teach Jewish classes.

The Greenberg's annual Chanukkah party has always been their most popular event. At the 1993 party, Rabbi Greenberg noticed a new couple among the many familiar faces. He introduced himself and spoke to them for a few minutes but did not expect to see them again.

A few months later the wife called Rabbi Greenberg and asked him if he could train their son for his upcoming bar mitzvah. Their son had never been to Hebrew school and could not read Hebrew. His family had not even planned to make a bar mitzvah. However, the boy's elderly grandmother from Los Angeles was persistent that her grandson have one, so to make her happy the couple was now turning to Rabbi Greenberg for help in preparing for it.

Rabbi Greenberg tutored the boy, teaching him Hebrew and training him to say the blessings on the Torah. Finally, the Shabbos of the bar mitzvah arrived and the boy's extended family flew in from all over the United States.

The bar mitzvah was beautiful. The boy read the blessings, and Rabbi Greenberg chanted the Torah portion and Haftarah.

During lunch in the synagogue after services, the boy's grandmother asked for permission to speak. She stood up and explained why it was so important that her grandson have a bar mitzvah.

First, she was worried that living in Alaska, he would grow up without a Jewish identity. Therefore she wanted to make sure he would at least have a bar mitzvah.

Second, the grandmother related that she had moved to the United States from Russia many years earlier. She rarely attended synagogue, but fondly remembered receiving a strong Jewish education in her youth. She grew up in the town of Berditchev, and a private teacher had come to her house every day to teach her and her siblings Jewish subjects. When Jewish observance was banned after the Russian Revolution of 1917, her religious education ceased.

Why did her parents value Jewish education so much, and why had she pushed so fervently for her grandson to have a bar mitzvah?

"It was very important to me to make this bar mitzvah because of my family tree," she continued, now looking directly at Rabbi Greenberg. "My family, we come from a big rabbi. Maybe you've heard of him. His name was Rabbi Yisrael Baal Shem Tov."

Rabbi Greenberg's jaw dropped. The Baal Shem Tov founded the Chassidic movement in the 1700s, of which Chabad-Lubavitch is a part. Two hundred years later the Baal Shem Tov's efforts helped provide his descendants in Alaska with an authentic Jewish experience and a point of entry to return to Jewish observance.

After lunch Rabbi Greenberg approached the grandmother and said he had a piece to add to her story. Rabbi Greenberg said he himself is a ninth-generation descendant of the Maggid of Mezritch, who was the foremost student and successor of the Ba'al Shem Tov. So here in Alaska was a descendant of the Maggid of Mezritch helping to bring back a descendant of his teacher the Ba'al Shem Tov.

In the years since the bar mitzvah, the young man and his family have become more observant. Hashem specifically sent Rabbi Greenberg to Alaska because He knew that the deep relationship between the Ba'al Shem Tov and his student would help his descendants return. Additionally, G-d knew that the many merits of the Baal Shem Tov would remain in the family and be a spiritual catalyst to bring them back.

"All Jewish children running around world are the grandchildren of *tzaddikim* and *tzidkaniyos*," Rabbi Greenberg said. "If your child or grandchild was going away from Judaism, wouldn't you fight to get him back? The Baal Shem Tov was crying in heaven."

Those tears from the Baal Shem Tov were the exact stream needed to sustain and rejuvenate the seeds of Yiddishkeit in the family.

7 Living in the Palace of the King

THE LAND OF ISRAEL IS THE THRESHOLD TO HEAVEN, THE point where the physical and spiritual worlds meet. Its air, fruit, and vegetables — and even its dirt — are all holy. While Hashem deals with other countries through angelic messengers, He acts toward the land and the people of Israel directly. His eyes are constantly turned toward the land.

"A land that Hashem, your G-d seeks out; the eyes of Hashem, your G-d are always upon it, from the beginning of the year to year's end." (*Devarim* 11:12)

In *Sifsei Chaim* (*Mo'adim*, Volume 3, p. 34), Rabbi Chaim Friedlander explains the verse: no place offers a greater potential for connection with Hashem than the land of Israel.

G-d is constantly influencing and directing events in the land, both subtly and overtly. Eretz Yisrael is the place that is easiest to see His constant miracles and direct control, as long as a person looks for them.

Rabbi Friedlander notes that the forty years the Jews spent in the desert before entering the land were a preparation for this. For those years they were fed manna directly from Heaven and thus had a constant awareness of the Divine source of all of their support. This trained them to be able to see Hashem's Hand in their lives once they entered the land.

Hashem's Hand is apparent everywhere throughout the land, gently pulling people to return to Him.

The Dreamer

JEFF BERGER* RAN *in terror. The gigantic dog was gaining on him and he had nowhere to hide. He knew that within seconds it would sink its razor-sharp sharp teeth into him. And then suddenly, the dog lunged at somebody else and Jeff got away.*

Jeff awoke in a cold sweat. He couldn't shake the nightmares. The dreams about wild dogs and other savage animals had filled his sleep every night since he had arrived in Eilat.

Jeff had grown up in a non-observant home in New Jersey and spent his high school years enmeshed in a counter-culture lifestyle, complete with long hair and a pierced lip. He searched desperately for meaning and substance to life, but felt only frustration at the inability of the world to provide serious answers to his existential questions. After he finished his freshman year at Emory University in Atlanta, Georgia, in May 1996, Jeff decided not to return for a second year. Instead he set off to travel to try to find his place in the world.

His journeys took him all the way up to the frigid waters of Alaska, where he worked around the clock on a fishing boat, and down to the sandy beaches of Key West. He thought he would relish the freedom and independence, but he had never felt so alone and frustrated in his life.

In the midst of his journeys his mother offered to pay for him to fly to Israel to record a video of his great-aunt speaking about how their family had survived the Holocaust in Hungary. Jeff flew to Israel, recorded the video, and then set off for a ten-day vacation across the country.

Jeff spent the first few days in Yerushalayim with an observant cousin named Asher and his wife Yehudit. They asked him if he would be interested in attending a series of classes on Judaism at Yeshivas Aish HaTorah. He found the classes to be interesting but not life-changing.

He then traveled south for three days to Eilat. It was there that his nightmares began. The first night he dreamt that he was being attacked by savage, monstrous creatures and skeletons of wild animals. The next night he dreamt about the dog. After three days in Eilat, Jeff traveled to Tel Aviv.

His nightmares became progressively more vivid and terrifying each night. In Tel Aviv he befriended a Druze man who called himself "Steve" and told him about the dreams. Steve suggested that perhaps G-d was trying to send him a message. Jeff initially doubted the thought but eventually considered it.

"The idea of G-d trying to give me a message was completely different from my concept of G-d," Jeff said. "My concept of G-d was that it was some kind of impersonal force that doesn't have a will of its own, but in my dreams someone was trying to send me a message."

Despite the utter terror the dreams were causing him, he actually began to experience a feeling of solace from them. The fact that some power was trying to communicate with him stood in contrast to the deep loneliness he was feeling. He felt comforted by the thought of a Divine force looking out for him.

One evening Jeff took a walk through downtown Tel Aviv, trying to find answers to the chaotic thoughts running through his head. But then suddenly, in the middle of Dizengoff Square in a pouring rainstorm, everything began to become clear.

"I had this whole idea through high school of being invincible, that I was the center of things," Jeff recalled. He had never been egotistical, but simply believed that he was always correct and the rest of the world was wrong. "After all these dreams, I had a moment of internal reckoning. None of this is working. I have to make a change. G-d wants me to change."

Once he made room for G-d in his life, Jeff felt extraordinarily happy. He realized that he needed to learn more about G-d and the messages that He was sending. He knew that he needed to return to Yerushalayim to do so.

That night he had only good dreams.

The next day he arrived back in Yerushalayim. He decided not to call his cousin. He still wanted to find answers on his own.

He had a list of several hostels in the Arab quarter of the Old City. In the pouring rain he tried in vain to find a place to stay. One hostel was closed, another was being renovated, and he couldn't find the third location. Finally recognizing the forces that were pushing against him, he admitted defeat and returned to Asher's apartment.

Jeff told Asher and Yehudit about his dreams, especially the one about the vicious dog. Asher told him that when people have nightmares about dogs, it is customary to read the verse in the Torah that recalls that the dogs of Egypt did not bark when the Jews departed in the Exodus: "But against all the Children of Israel, no dog shall whet its tongue, against neither man nor beast, so that you shall know that Hashem will have differentiated between Egypt and Israel" (*Shemos* 11:7).

Jeff said he never understood why G-d would distinguish between Jews and non-Jews. But in the verse and in his dream he saw that even dogs knew the difference. The dog in his dream only attacked the other man. In fact the man appeared dark-skinned, much like an Egyptian.

Reading the verse and learning its lesson helped Jeff realize that Hashem also could differentiate between people.

"I thought, 'If He's the G-d of all humanity, why does it matter who I am?' But He was telling me, 'You're a Jew and I care,'" Jeff said. "When I realized I was a Jew, I knew that Jews and G-d have a certain relationship. I had to find out about that."

The next day Jeff went back to Aish HaTorah. He skipped the introductory classes and signed right up for classes on practical Judaism and mitzvos. Within a very short time he became observant.

⇨ ⇦

The Gemara (*Berachos* 55a-57b) discusses the interpretation of dreams. Toward the beginning, Rav Chisda states: "A negative dream is worse than [receiving] a lashing."

Rashi explains: a bad dream frightens a person and causes him to become humbled and return to Hashem.

Jeff's dreams were a clear sign that Hashem was calling him to return. Thankfully, he was able to push aside his previous misconceptions and listen to the call. And living in the spiritually fertile atmosphere of Israel, it was a very quick road to becoming religious.

He spent the next six weeks studying at Aish and Ohr Somayach and then returned to America. He now felt much more confident about the value of the world and his place in it. He finished Emory, and soon after returned to Israel. He now goes by the name Yitzchak and lives with his wife and children in Yerushalayim.

⇨ ⇦

Epilogue: While in Atlanta after his return to America, Jeff was at synagogue one Shabbos morning and received an *aliyah* to the Torah (which was a very rare occurrence, as the *aliyos* were usually given to older members of the synagogue). It was in the Torah portion of *Bo*. His jaw dropped when he realized that his *aliyah* included the very verse about the dogs that he had recited in his cousin's house in Yerushalayim.

"It was like G-d was keeping an eye on me. It was like He was saying, 'Are you sticking with the plan here?' It was kind of scary," Jeff said.

Once again, Jeff realized that Hashem was looking out for him.

Standing Outside the Ari Mikveh

The Ari mikveh in Tzefas is the birthplace of many *ba'alei teshuvah*'s religious journeys. It was used hundreds of years ago by the Arizal himself, and he gave a *berachah* that its waters should lead people to *teshuvah*. The mikveh's frigid waters come from a spring flowing directly out of a mountain, and have been known to awaken both body and soul. Joe and Evelyn Cooper* didn't even have to enter the mikveh to be forever changed by its holy waters. Just standing outside was enough for them.

Joe and Evelyn grew up in the Conservative movement in America. When they were in their twenties and their first child was born, they began contemplating the level of religious observance they wanted for their family. This discussion took on new light during a trip to Israel in the late 1980s.

Joe had always been intrigued by the Ari mikveh. The mikveh is in a cave next to the Tzefas cemetery. Today a wide, easily navigable road leads to it, but at the time it was accessible by only a small path.

Joe had tried to visit the mikveh on several occasions but had never made it. One time he missed his bus to Tzefas. On another occasion he and a friend stopped at the cemetery on their way to the mikveh and became so absorbed by the graves they forgot about the mikveh. He heard years later from a Chassid that impure spiritual forces try to keep people away from the mikveh.

During their trip Joe and Evelyn were driving in the area of Tzefas with a friend. Out of the blue, their friend suggested they take a detour to the Ari mikveh. Joe jumped at the chance to finally try to put a foot inside it.

When they arrived and walked down the path, they found the mikveh empty. Joe told his wife to go inside to see what it was like while he and their friend waited outside.

The two men were standing leaning on the outer wall of the cave looking down into the valley when out of nowhere a short man in a white shirt, black suit and beard walked up to them.

"Let me tell you about Judaism," he said.

"Sure, tell us," Joe said, a tad sarcastically, as if the two of them had been waiting all day for him to show up and teach them about Judaism. The man started a speech about putting on tefillin and learning Torah. He then handed a small book to Joe, but gave nothing to his friend.

"This is for you; you have to read this."

"Sure, I'll read it," Joe said in a clearly noncommittal tone.

"No, you really have to read it."

Joe put the book in his pocket and then turned away from the man. He and his friend began talking for a few seconds and then turned back to the man. He was nowhere to be seen. Even the path leading back up the mountain was vacant.

Though perplexed by the incident, Joe quickly put it into the back of his mind.

A few weeks later after they returned to America, Joe was thinking more about the religious direction of their family. It was a Sunday morning and as he was putting on a pair of pants he felt a lump inside.

"I felt something in the back pocket. Oh my G-d — it was that little book the guy had given me a couple of weeks ago in Israel."

The book was a pamphlet called Patience containing quotes from Rabbi Nachman of Breslov and other Jewish sources.

"For some reason this book spoke to me. I mean it really spoke to me. It was written in a very personal way: 'My dear friend, I'm writing this book for you, if you want to find Hashem, you need patience.' This book really struck me. No question in my mind that it was a huge turning point.

"I became very enthusiastic about the book. I said, if I'm looking for a way to go, I'm going to start looking into my religion. I want to start looking in before looking out."

Joe spoke to a few Jewish friends in his office and suggested they form a group to learn more about Judaism. He contacted a local Chabad rabbi and asked him to come teach them.

"I said, 'Rabbi we want to learn.'"

"He said 'Great!'"

"We want to learn downtown in our building."

"Great."

"Before work."

"Fine."

("It was a little disconcerting. He wasn't saying much.")

"You haven't asked anything about money," Joe said.

"You're right. There's no fee."

The rabbi began teaching a class on *Pirkei Avos*. Joe was hooked. Within a month he began going to the rabbi's Chabad House in Lauder Hill, Florida, on Shabbos. His wife soon began coming too. From there their journey took off like a rocket.

They initially drove to shul each Shabbos, but as they became more involved they longed to move closer to be able to walk. However, at the time the Florida real estate market was in a slump and they were unable to find a buyer for their home.

Their religious journey progressed. On a trip to see family in New York, they visited the leader of Chabad, Rabbi Menachem Mendel Schneerson, for a blessing. At the time, their oldest son was five and they had been debating whether to send him to a Chabad school a few towns away. It would require driving him forty minutes each way, but after returning from New York they decided it was an important move for their Jewish growth.

One day Evelyn drove to the school to drop off a registration check. When she arrived home, she found a note in their mailbox from a realtor who had a buyer looking for a home in their neighborhood!

Soon after they sold their home and moved near the Chabad House. They now could walk to shul and were only twenty minutes away from the school. Not only did their three children attend the school as they became old enough, but Evelyn also ended up getting a job in the school, which eventually led to a whole new career for her.

For Joe, the family's entire journey has been a clear path leading from that first meeting with the mysterious man outside the mikveh in Tzefas.

"I can trace our whole development as *ba'alei teshuvah* from that one moment. It all started by being given a book by a little man in a place I felt was significant. He did not give it to my friend; he said it was for me," Joe said. "Hashem knew that I was searching. He said, 'Let's give a nudge in the right direction.'"

A mikveh's waters can purify a person in many ways. Standing outside the mikveh so many years ago, the Coopers found their own unique way to be purified by it.

HASHEM'S COMMANDO: THE JOURNEY OF RABBI LAZER BRODY

HASHEM'S HAND IS apparent daily on the streets of Israel. Jews who have fought in Israel's war report seeing His miracles on a nearly minute-by-minute basis.

Rabbi Lazer Brody, fondly known as Reb Lazer, was born

in 1949 and grew up in a non-observant home in Silver Spring, Maryland. He made *aliyah* in 1970 and joined the IDF, where he was placed in an elite Special Forces unit. He participated in several daring missions during and after the 1973 Yom Kippur War. When the First Lebanon War broke out in 1982, the IDF called him up to complete a delicate assignment.

The Soviet Union supported the Arab world in their numerous wars against Israel, and the 1982 war was no exception. Placed in the corners of the courtyard of the Soviet Embassy in Beirut were Katyusha rocket batteries which could fire thirty-eight missiles a minute. They had caused significant casualties in the first days of the war. However, Prime Minister Menachem Begin ruled out an air or artillery strike out of fear of hitting the embassy. The Israeli military was at a loss of what to do.

The Chief of Staff of the IDF, General Rafael Eitan, decided to send in a Special Forces unit to neutralize the missile batteries. It was a suicidal mission, sending soldiers into a den of terrorists deep in the heart of west Beirut.

Brody was chosen as the second-in-command of the mission. So on the first Saturday afternoon of the war, Brody and eleven other soldiers infiltrated the area. As soon as they entered the streets they were spotted by snipers. Bullets rained down on them, followed by artillery fire and rockets. Pieces of concrete and shards of glass filled the air. The squad commander was cut in half by a rocket, and then just feet away from Brody, a piece of shrapnel sliced through the thigh of Raffi, the unit's radio man.

Brody hoisted Raffi onto his shoulder and dragged him behind a car where he applied a tourniquet. Sniper fire raked through the car and a piece of a glass cut across Brody's left eye. His eye filled with blood which coagulated very quickly. Brody could not see through his eye and assumed he had lost it forever.

Debris and black smoke filled the air, stinging the soldiers' eyes and clogging their lungs. Another soldier was killed. Brody, with Raffi on his shoulders, began darting from doorway to doorway to avoid the shooting.

"I can't believe that any purgatory is worse than that day in Beirut," Brody said. "I looked at my watch and I anticipated an expected life span of an additional sixty seconds."

Brody felt helpless, with no ability to get himself out of the situation. He suddenly did something he had never done before — he cried out to Hashem to save him.

"I looked up. All of a sudden it came out of my mouth: 'Hashem! G-d, get me out of here! Is this want you want from me? Is this it?"

Suddenly he heard a voice call out to him. "Eliezer Rafael," it called, using Rabbi Brody's Hebrew name. He had not heard his Hebrew name since his bar mitzvah. He realized that his prayers to Hashem were being answered.

"Don't worry my son. I'm going to take you out of there," the voice continued. "You need to change your life and I'm going to take you out of here. But you're going to change your life because this isn't your war."

Suddenly two hundred feet overhead, screaming out of the sky, came two fighter jets with Stars of David on their wings. The ground shook and the planes sprayed the snipers with bullets. Then everything suddenly quieted down.

Rabbi Brody looked up with tears streaming from his good right eye. The tears melted the coagulated blood in his left eye and he began to see through it again.

Just then an IDF halftrack vehicle appeared on the street and four medics jumped out. They took charge of Raffi and the other casualties. The medics told Brody that they had been in east Beirut, which was controlled by Israel's Christian allies, and had made a wrong turn. As they were trying to make their way back, somehow they had ended up on that street.

The medic vehicle departed and the soldiers regrouped under Brody's command. They continued the rest of the way to the embassy and destroyed the missile launchers, clearing the way for a full-scale IDF invasion of west Beirut.

After the war, questions filled Brody's head. Why did he live through the battle? And what life changes was Hashem asking for?

Brody found his way to yeshivah, first to a Karliner yeshivah and later to Aish HaTorah. There he joined the famous Israeli actor Uri Zohar and others who were beginning to find their way back to Judaism. Rabbi Brody spent eight years at Aish HaTorah and eventually became a Breslover Chassid.

After teaching at Aish HaTorah for one year, he was hired to become the rabbi of the Ramle prison, where he remained for four years. He said it was the most challenging job he has ever had — but also the most rewarding, as he saw the power of the Torah and *teshuvah* to help even hardened criminals return to a proper path.

"I studied the works of Rebbe Nachman and turned them into a *derech* for emotional health. It was the best training, because in prison you have more emotional problems concentrated under one roof than anywhere else, and people with the worst possible backgrounds. Hashem helped me to save umpteen marriages and suicides."

The prisoners respected Rabbi Brody's background as a hardened special-forces soldier. He began giving classes to the prisoners and learning one-on-one with them, and introduced many of them — for the first time — to a G-d Who loves them.

"I was doing rehabilitation through *teshuvah*. That got really recognized.

"The great thing about *teshuvah* rehabilitation is that they won't come back. The commander of a prison wants two things — industrial quiet and a low return rate. When he gives the government those two things he gets promoted. I was his show-boy. I was giving him both by making *teshuvah*."

Rabbi Brody is now the Mashgiach of the Chut Shel Chessed

Yeshivah and frequently speaks to Israeli military units. He is also a widely published author both in print and online (at his Lazer Beams website).

"My life isn't my own. It belongs to the Jewish people and the Ribbono shel Olam. I don't deserve a moment to live. That's why I dedicate myself to Him."

As an IDF soldier, Brody's goals were clear: obey your commanding officer's orders and fulfill your mission perfectly. He has the same goals now, but his officer and mission are from a much higher source.

AN UNTOLD MIRACLE FROM THE 2006 WAR IN LEBANON

IN MID-OCTOBER 2006, Rabbi Brody was sitting on a train in Tel Aviv on the way to Haifa. A young Israeli naval sergeant entered the car and sat down in a nearby seat. Rabbi Brody smiled at him. Moshe* sighed deeply and sheepishly asked, "Can I talk to you, Rav?"

"Of course," Rabbi Brody said and asked him how he knew that he was a rabbi. Moshe replied that he had heard Rabbi Brody eulogize a fallen friend during the Lebanon war that summer.

Moshe had the clear look of a fresh *ba'al teshuvah* — a new beard was growing on his face, and the knitted *kippah* on his head was still stiff from being worn only a short time. After a few moments, he began sharing the miraculous story which happened to him during the war.

Moshe had been onboard the Israeli missile ship Hanit on Friday night, July 14, 2006, when it was anchored off the coast of Beirut. The evening began as a typical quiet Friday night, but quickly turned into a rollercoaster as the sailors saw the miracles of Hashem's Hand again and again.

"Usually, the crew would eat Friday night dinner in two shifts," Moshe told Rabbi Brody. "But this time, since we were in a war zone, our three religious crewmen went to Lieutenant Colonel A., the skipper, and begged that we all need Hashem's help. The first miracle is that the skipper agreed to leave only four sailors on the bridge, and allowed the rest of the crew to pray together, to participate in a proper Sabbath meal. The rest of us piled into the synagogue and prayed a lengthy Minchah and *Kabbalas Shabbos*.

"I was bored and wanted to eat quickly and then catch a few hours of sleep because I had the midnight watch. But I stayed with the rest of the crew. Then all of us had a Shabbos meal together: fifteen different sailors said Kiddush, each in the custom of his fathers. I'm talking about guys who aren't even religious! The meal was drawn out. I had a headache and was dying to go to sleep."

Just as the sailors began to *bentch* after the meal, a missile fired by a Hezbollah unit on shore slammed into the rear of the boat. Flames shot skyward as the entire end of the boat burned. The ship should have sunk from the missile strike or the fire that immediately spread, but miraculously it stayed afloat. The missile had missed every critical piece of the ship, and instead hit a crane above the chopper landing pad which absorbed the impact. In another astonishing miracle, the nearby helicopter-refueling tank, which was full of fuel, did not explode.

Much of the crew should have been on the deck or around the ship when the missile hit. Instead, the fifteen sailors were down below in the galley and were saved due to their drawn-out Shabbos dinner.

Moshe had beads of sweat on his forehead and tears filled his eyes as he continued with his story.

"The newspapers don't write about the miracles that we all saw. I ran to my bunk on the deck right below the landing pad. It was charcoal; my metal bunk was completely melted down and all my possessions were ashes. If I hadn't been detained in the chapel and in the dining hall for the Shabbos meal, I would have been charcoal too. I haven't stopped thanking Hashem since then. I've changed my life."

Moshe reported that even more miracles happened aboard the ship that night. The engine room was burned to a crisp, but a pair of tefillin in perfect condition was found nearby. And in the middle of the destruction the sailors found a Book of *Tehillim*, also unscathed. It was discovered open to *Tehillim* 124, which acknowledges the unceasing protection Hashem gives us. Among its words are these (124:2–4):

> "Had not Hashem been with us when men rose up against us, then they would have swallowed us alive, when their anger was kindled against us. Then the waters would have inundated us; the current would have surged across our soul."

Moshe saw Hashem's Hand repeatedly that night. He should have lost his life, but Hashem sent him miracle after miracle to save him.

The Israeli military never expected the Hanit to be hit. It assumed the boat was far enough offshore to be safe, and didn't know that Hezbollah had missiles of the range to hit it. Within a few seconds, those security misconceptions were shattered. And within those few seconds, Moshe's many misconceptions about life and Judaism were shattered as well.

The many miracles Moshe experienced opened his eyes to Hashem's constant involvement in his life. Hashem is always with us, usually below the surface, but sometimes He sends a miracle to remind us of His constant watchful presence. Sometimes it takes a whole series of miracles to bring someone to recognize Him.

As Rabbi Brody described it, the Hanit took a direct hit from a

Hezbollah missile, but Moshe turned the navy's military setback into a personal spiritual victory.

Three times a day in the blessing of *Modim* in the Shemoneh Esreh, we thank Hashem: "*ve'al nisecha sheb'chol yom imanu* — and for Your miracles that are with us every day."

Our lives are full of miracles, from the small daily life-sustaining events to major salvations. However, the Gemara (*Niddah* 31a) cautions us that even the recipient of a miracle often does not recognize it as such. A person can explain away miracles as "coincidences" or "twists of fate." Sometimes a miracle only comes through a difficult situation or a personal setback. People will usually lament the difficult event that occurred, without realizing that it contained a tremendous hidden kindness or a miracle from Hashem.

Hashem constantly creates miracles in our lives. It's up to us to notice them and take the appropriate messages from them.

---

8 The Fire within Us

TORAH STUDY IS THE LIFEBLOOD OF THE JEWISH PEOPLE. It is compared to both fire and water, for it lights a spark inside a Jew's soul and waters the seeds of his commitment to his religion.

Torah study is the heart of our service of Hashem. A Jew's ongoing learning of its words connects him to Hashem and gives him knowledge of how to properly observe the mitzvos.

It is also the core of a Jew's soul, and sometimes just hearing its sweet words can bring a person back to his roots.

Climbing Down from the Ivory Tower

RABBI AARON GRUMAN is the director of Torah Links, an outreach organization based in Lakewood, New Jersey, and which has branches throughout the state. Once for Shabbos he hosted Steven Kraft, a young man who had attended Harvard University and was exploring his religious roots. In the afternoon Rabbi Gruman gave him a tour of the nearby Beth Medrash Govoha, one of the largest yeshivahs in the world.

After walking through the buildings of the yeshivah, Steven asked if they could visit the library again. Rabbi Gruman was surprised — the yeshivah's library was the least organized room. Volumes of Gemara were spread out on its tables, their pages bent and many of their bindings falling apart. He asked Steven to explain his interest.

"He told me that when he was at Harvard, the library was sacrosanct. No one talked there, no one really read the books. But here were books being loved, pored over, lived. That impressed him."

For Steven Kraft, even after having attended the pinnacle of the American educational system, nothing moved him as much as seeing those volumes on the tables. In the yeshivah library he saw sincere learning, with an excitement and vibrancy. This wasn't the staid ivory towers he had encountered in Harvard Yard — here were authentic studies that came to life in the hands and mouths of the yeshivah's students.

When a newcomer enters a Jewish hall of learning, it is easy to be overwhelmed and even intimidated by its intensity. Sometimes the roar of the learning can be heard a block away. People learn with emotion and intensity, driven by an internal fire to try to pursue the truth and connect to Hashem through their learning. The Torah is alive and Jews learn it with excitement.

In the library and in the students of the yeshivah, Steven saw intellectual discourse that was genuine and that truly mattered. He saw students who loved their learning and were truly committed to it. The students he witnessed saw their studies not as a way to further their careers or to create a strong financial base for their lives, but to arrive at an understanding of what truly matters in life.

Those worn pages of the Gemara that Steven saw also represented a lifelong commitment to learning that doesn't end when a person graduates. Steven saw in them something real and authentic and he decided then to dive into the sweet waters of the Torah with full energy.

The Gemara (*Shabbos* 105a) asks: when Hashem gave us the Torah, why did He begin the wording of the Ten Commandments by referring to Himself as "*Anochi*" instead of the usual word "*Ani*"?

The Gemara answers: *Anochi* is an acronym for the words "*Amirah neimah ketivah yehivah* — a pleasant statement was written [and] given."

That is the essence of the Torah. It is unfathomably sweet and beautiful. Just a few drops of it, or simply just seeing the purity and sincerity through which people pursue it, are enough to send a Jew's soul soaring.

A TRUE, LASTING HERITAGE

NOSSON (MARK) SACHS became *frum* while attending college in the 1970s. With no structure at his university with which to further his Jewish growth, he decided to transfer to a religious university. There he finished his degree, learned the ropes of being observant, and eventually received *semichah*.

Like honey on his tongue, Rabbi Sachs said his desire to become a rabbi was driven by the utter sweetness of the Torah he was studying.

"I believed that my wife and children deserved a *talmid chacham* [for a father]. For my kids, I wanted Torah to be the center of their lives. I had a passion for it. It was such an important part of my relationship with Hashem.

"I joined the *semichah* program not to be a rabbi, but just for the Torah knowledge."

After receiving *semichah*, Rabbi Sachs looked for a way to continue applying his passion for learning and teaching, and so decided to become a chaplain in the U.S. Army. Over his three decades in the service, he has traveled the world, both in and out of war zones, giving strength to soldiers and civilians, teaching them, and helping them to connect to their Judaism.

Returning stateside, Rabbi Sachs spent most of his days in Pittsburgh, Pennsylvania, as a chaplain at UPMC Shadyside Hospital, in addition to serving in the army for reserve chaplain duty. He has since made *aliyah*.

When he initially joined the army, he was assigned to be the Jewish chaplain for the U.S. military community stationed in and around Frankfurt, Germany. During his three-and-a-half-year assignment, Rabbi Sachs hosted weekly Shabbos services on the base as well as monthly communal meals. He also drove to outlying bases and Jewish communities to provide religious services, and to teach and help soldiers and lay people.

In Frankfurt, he met an American named Ed who was working for a branch of a U.S. bank. He asked him if he would be interested in learning Gemara together. Ed demurred, saying he didn't know how, so Rabbi Sachs offered to teach him.

As they learned together they developed a deep rapport. Ed revealed that he had attended a Jewish day school while growing up and had loved it. His parents worried that he was getting too religious for them so they pulled him out in the fourth grade.

Ed soaked up every page of Gemara that he studied with Rabbi Sachs. They once learned in the Gemara (*Berachos* 8b) that a person must show honor to a *talmid chacham* who has lost his learning, just like the broken tablets still maintained some of their holiness. When they read the words, Ed started to cry.

"This is truth, this is beautiful. I want to own this!" Ed said.

"It's already yours," Rabbi Sachs replied.

Hashem placed the *Eitz Chaim*, the Tree of Life representing the Torah, in the very middle of the Garden of Eden. The Chafetz Chaim explained that this shows that the Torah is available to every Jew. No matter what his background, level of observance, or intellectual capabilities, he has his own unique portion in Torah. The Torah is the birthright of the Jewish people.

Indeed, outreach workers say one of the most effective tools to inspire their students is to simply learn Gemara with them. Though they cannot explain how it works, but they see it again and again.

The Gemara unlocks a Jew's heart and penetrates him like nothing else. By the time Rabbi Sachs and Ed reached the twentieth page of Gemara, Ed had decided to *kasher* his kitchen and had begun to keep Shabbos.

Ed and his wife later moved back to America and enrolled their two children in Jewish day schools. They continue to maintain a *shomer Shabbos* home, all growing out of the Gemara pages that Ed learned with Rabbi Sachs.

Rabbi Aharon Feldman, the Rosh Yeshivah of Ner Israel in Baltimore, spent fourteen years as a Rosh Yeshivah at Ohr Somayach in Yerushalayim before taking up that position. Speaking at the Association of Jewish Outreach Programs conference in 2008, he revealed the secret of his work at the yeshivah:

"I never had a theological discussion with students. It's *talmud Torah* which brings them back."

⇨ ⇦

The world today offers instant fulfillment of a person's desires and physical pleasures, but the pleasures vanish as quickly as they come. However, when Jews come into contact with eternal, immutable words of Torah, they often immediately recognize the Torah's lasting, true sweetness. The Torah is like water on their parched souls.

I was once in Tzefas for Shabbos and spent lunch with a sincere, deeply religious man. His long wispy beard and the piercing look in his eyes were signs of his long journey of discovering and returning to his roots. When I asked him what he did for a living, he described that he was learning in yeshivah with the words, "I'm learning how to be a Jew."

His words stuck with me. He had already been observant for several years, and knew how important it was to catch up on the Torah study he had missed as a child. Despite his outside appearance of living an established, observant lifestyle, he was still working on his insides, immersing himself to try to learn the ins and outs of Judaism.

There is much to learn when a person returns to his roots. It is necessary to spend time in a yeshivah or seminary, or to seriously attend classes. This time is essential for his continued growth and grounding as an observant Jew.

Learning is not just an intellectual pursuit. Torah study gives a structure and foundation for Jewish life. It is a roadmap for *ba'alei teshuvah*, helping them to grow both in the short-term and in their future lives. Time spent learning helps people create foundations for their future life and observances, and even the upbringing of their children.

⇨ ⇦

Success in Torah study requires hard work. This rule is even more true for *ba'alei teshuvah*. Growing up attending schools based on a western educational model, they enter the sea of Torah to find vastly different goals and methodologies. They have many years of catching up to do. Thankfully there are plenty of tools available today, from yeshivos and seminaries geared for *ba'alei teshuvah*, and a plethora of books and online resources in English. Many communities also offer classes to help adults to gain the necessary skills and knowledge.

Even with these resources, much work is still required from the individual to gain proficiency in the language, style, and content of the Torah.

Ba'alei teshuvah today can gain strength from the great Rabbi Akiva. Before he decided to become religious at age forty, he was not even able to read the letters of the *alef-beis*! Furthermore, he even had a loathing of rabbinic leaders.

However, at age forty, he committed himself to learning Torah, literally entering a school at the most basic level, and slowly building himself up to becoming one of the greatest rabbis of all time. By the time he passed away at age 120, his knowledge and Torah leadership were unprecedented in his generation. He was labeled as the definition of *kavod haTorah* (*Sotah* 9:15).

Fred Sugarman*, a Harvard University-educated investment analyst who became *frum*, is one of these *ba'alei teshuvah* living a page from the life of Rabbi Akiva. The first Gemara *shiur* he ever attended was not a slow-paced, comfortable class for newcomers. He entered a high-school level Gemara *shiur* at Yeshivah University for young men who had grown up religious. Despite his strong secular educational background and gifted intellectual skills, it took him only a few moments to realize just how much catch-up work he had to do.

"Never mind the need simply to learn Torah. There was a lot of information I didn't have. I didn't have vast experience in Mishnah, Gemara, and halachah. I had to learn data. Most of first semester was spent simply trying to learn yeshivish!

"When I entered my first Talmud class, I had no idea what was going on. The premise of all other classes I had been with [before becoming *frum*] was: the teacher stands at the front and presents his well-thought out ideas of the material. The students then go home and apply it to the readings.

"The presentation of the Talmud is completely different — there's a give-and-take between the *talmidim* and the rabbi. I was hard at work just trying to take notes. I utterly had no idea what was going on. Students were not sitting in neat rows. They were shoving forward to be near the rabbi. The rabbi was at a desk in a sitting position with a book in front of him. I couldn't see him all the time. There was no clear curriculum.

"Plus, I simply didn't share many of the assumptions of the *shiur* and yeshivah — basic assertions and assumptions that the Gemara will make of human behavior.

"There I was, a thirty-year-old man in the presence of twenty-year-olds. I was a thirty-year-old man with an Ivy League education in a high-school class. It felt absurd."

Despite the challenges, Fred stuck with it. He worked hard, and slowly mastered the terminology and the structure of the Gemara and yeshivah system. Over time he moved up in his learning. He has since become the rabbi of a synagogue in New York.

⇨ ⇦

Another *ba'al teshuvah* who faced similar difficulties during his first few years of learning in yeshivah also refused to give up. He describes the beauty and excitement that he now feels for Torah study:

"Stick with the Gemara. It's the most amazing ocean of knowledge I've ever come across. I had learned in yeshivah for four years, but couldn't break in. It was very frustrating. But once you break into the Gemara, it's the most amazing landscape ever. It's the most intricate, beautiful world; one that is directly related to our world, a legal system of how to enact justice in our world."

In *Mesillas Yesharim*, Rabbi Moshe Chaim Luzzatto describes a two-step process to becoming holy:

"The beginning is hard work [but] the end is a gift."

He explains that Hashem expects us to do the initial work to become holy and to work hard to prevail in the struggles that cross our paths. When we push ourselves, Hashem aids us and helps us to accomplish our goals (Chapter 26).

This is true in every area of life, but primarily in Torah study. These words are an important guide for *ba'alei teshuvah* trying to learn the ropes of the Torah system, or anyone struggling to learn particular Torah concepts. Learning takes hard work, but Hashem showers His assistance when He sees our sincere effort.

FILLING IN THE PUZZLE

SOMETIMES, IT TAKES only a single word of Torah to send a Jew heading in a new direction.

Beverly Singer* grew up in a Conservative Jewish home on Long Island, New York. She attended Cornell University, and took classes there through Jewish outreach organizations. She was intrigued by the intellectual stimulation of the classes, but could not foresee herself becoming observant.

After graduating college in 2011, she kept in touch with one of the outreach rabbis. He invited her to attend a trip to Israel in the summer of 2013. During that trip she first experienced life as an observant Jew, as she kept Shabbos and kosher the whole time.

"All of my previous learning had primed me to be more open to it. It didn't come out of nowhere. That was the first time I entertained observing anything."

Upon returning to New York, she tried to maintain the excitement and spirit she had felt during the trip and tried to continuing observing Shabbos. However, she felt like she had not created a sufficient base to do so, and unfortunately her interest petered out over the next few months.

In December of that year she joined another two-week-long trip to Israel sponsored by the same outreach organization, and spent time learning at Neve Yerushalayim. There her interest was fully piqued.

"I was always interested in learning intellectually. I was blessed with a strong passion for learning Torah. I really connected to learning on that trip."

Beverly moved back home after the trip and was now able to fully embrace a religious lifestyle. She committed herself to keeping kosher and Shabbos, and started to dress more modestly.

She also began learning every day, both at home by herself, and attended a weekly class in Manhattan. Inside, her heart was tugging at her to return to Israel to learn in seminary for a longer period of time; there were still many holes in her knowledge of Judaism and mitzvah observance that she needed to fill in. Yet she felt like she needed to settle down and begin a career.

One day she was sitting on the subway on her way to her Torah class when she began feeling some inner tension, and even some creeping doubts about her life.

"At that moment, it really sunk in. This is real. But I asked myself, am I really doing this, am I going all the way? How is this possible? Am I serious?"

She began to feel forces inside of her pulling her in different directions. One side was trying to drag her away from her newfound commitments, while the other part of her was trying to pull her back up and remind her of her interest in returning to seminary.

Beverly glanced at the woman in the seat next to her. She was calmly filling out a New York Times crossword puzzle, blithely ignorant to the major spiritual wars being waged beside her inside Beverly's heart.

As Beverly peeked over the woman's shoulder to look at the puzzle, she saw her fill in a five-letter word: "T-O-R-A-H."

"It was the craziest thing ever!"

Beverly took that as a clear sign to silence her inner doubts and remind herself of her commitment to return to seminary. Soon after that experience on the subway, she packed up her life in America and boarded a plane to return to learn in Yerushalayim, where she began to learn at the seminary Midreshes Rachel V'Chaya.

"I was always searching, looking to figure out what my real way of thinking should be, always questioning what to believe — always looking for something but never able to find what it was. Now I found it. Looking back, I can tell I was seeking a way of life. I don't have questions of my beliefs that I used to have. Now I feel settled; I have a path in life."

In several places the Torah describes some of the physical rewards that we will receive for observing mitzvos, and the punishment for failing to observe them, G-d forbid. In the beginning of *Parashas Bechukosai* the Torah tells us, "If you will go in My statutes and observe My commandments and perform them, then I will provide your rains in their times, and the land will give its produce and the tree of the field will give its fruit" (*Vayikra* 26:3–4).

Rashi asks: What does it mean to "go in My statutes?" He answers: "You should be *ameil*, labor, in Torah." And how do we fulfill the following words, "Observe My commandments"? He tells us: "Through laboring in Torah in order to observe and to fulfill."

Torah study requires serious, sustained work. We need to immerse ourselves in it. Rashi here teaches us that one of the primary goals of Torah study is to know how to properly observe the mitzvos. Without learning the rules and specifics of the commandments, it is impossible to fulfill them properly.

The contemporary teacher and leader Rabbi Gamliel Rabinowitz once told a lawyer: Just as members of the legal profession need to learn the rules and proper etiquette of a judicial court, the same applies to us as Jews. If a lawyer spoke or acted out of order during a trial, he could be found to be in contempt of court. Any claim that he had not learned a particular law would not exempt him from the consequences of his actions. So too, a Jew cannot claim ignorance of the particulars of Hashem's rules if he fails to properly learn halachah.

It is especially imperative for *ba'alei teshuvah* to engage in serious Torah study to "learn the ropes" of the mitzvos and to know how to fit into the religious world. Both men and women need to learn how to properly observe the rules that are incumbent upon them.

A Question of Priorities

HARRY SILVER* HAD the adventure role of a lifetime. During the first Persian Gulf War, he was a member of a U.S. Air Force unit tasked with saving injured soldiers from the battlefield. Often under enemy fire, he and his teammates flew out in helicopters to extricate soldiers and transport them to MASH units behind the frontlines. In the chaos of war he began to discover an even more electrifying journey, as he discovered his route back to Judaism.

Harry was raised in a classic Conservative Jewish background in New York, which included trips to synagogue to celebrate each holiday, and Kiddush and *HaMotzi* every Friday night.

"My parents were very focused on instilling in us Jewish values as they saw it. Like many other people, being Jewish was only one part of you — you were American, a lawyer, a football player, and you're Jewish. That's how I experienced it — very compartmentalized," Harry said.

In 1987 Harry was working as a lawyer in the federal government in Washington, D.C. when he volunteered for the Air Force Reserves. He joined out of patriotism and a desire to be involved in public service. He also thought it would be beneficial to his career, as many of his superiors had also served in the military. And since he joined during peace times, he never expected to be mobilized for actual combat service.

Harry became a medical service corps officer in an air evacuation unit. Two years later when the U.S.-led international coalition declared war on Iraq during Desert Storm, Harry was activated for service.

Harry had the typical Jewish mother, who decided that war was no place for her son. Against his protests she called the head of his squadron to get him out of serving.

Her attempts were unsuccessful, but they earned him notoriety in his unit.

"When I got back to my unit, just as I feared, word got around that my mother tried to get me out. People had a ball with it. It was embarrassing, but it was my mom."

Harry traveled with his unit to the Persian Gulf at the start of the war. There, as the military forces geared up for battle, he began to face questions about his religious observance as his Jewish identity stood out for the first time in his life.

The first issue was his dog tags. A dog tag typically lists a soldier's religion, so a body can be given the correct religious ceremony after death. The military recommended that Jewish personnel write "none" for their religion, because if a Jewish soldier was captured, his religion could become a liability for him and his unit. This was an affront to Harry.

While in the service Harry kept a minimum degree of *kashrus* and refused to eat any of the meat served. One of his commanders was a gentile from Texas, with a big, thick moustache as wide as that state. At breakfast every morning, he picked up a sausage and biscuit in the mess tent and tried to tempt Harry to eat them.

"At first it was funny, but it became pernicious after awhile. Even though he wasn't serious about eating it, he was serious about making a point about why I wasn't eating it."

During the war Harry also had a recurring thought, which became clear many years later due to a lesson he heard from Rabbi Noach Weinberg.

"Rabbi Weinberg said, 'To know what you want to live for, you have to know what you're willing to die for.' I said, 'This is crazy. What am I doing here? I'm risking my life to liberate an Arab country that doesn't even let Jews in.' Before I was all gung-ho, [saying] let's go forward, but later I said this is crazy!"

Harry had a lot of free time on his hands during the war, so these thoughts often percolated in his brain. He resolved that immediately after the war he would travel to Israel to try to find the answers.

A few months later, he toured the country as part of an Israel Bonds trip. The trip was overall uneventful, but toward the end he met up with a friend who was learning at Yeshivas Aish HaTorah. Harry spent time with him and his friends from the yeshivah. He was struck by their seriousness and values and began to think that their world held the answers to his questions.

At times, however, he felt that the guys seemed a bit too perfect for him, leading him to suspect that some of it was feigned. That feeling evaporated on Erev Shabbos.

"I remember thinking, 'It's very nice, but these guys are a little over the top.' Friday came, and they had a basketball game. You could see they were working on their *middos*, trying to speak in a holy way. But on Friday when I got on the basketball court, the elbows were flying. I said: these guys are regular guys."

For Harry, meeting students who were growing in their Judaism and yet were still normal American twenty-year-olds made him think that this was a world he could fit into.

Following the trip, Harry began studying with a rabbi near his home in New York City and started to find answers to his questions. The observant Jews he met in New York in synagogue and at Shabbos tables showed the same sincere religious fervor he had seen in Yerushalayim.

"The people I was meeting seemed like the type of people I wanted to be. They had clarity in terms of what was important in life. They were steady, grounded, and just focused on giving to others and being kind. This provided a great framework for it, like a cookbook to get to the place I want to be."

One of his early Shabbos meals was with a family on the Upper West Side. Before the meal, the host went around the table and introduced each person and said something specific about him. When he got to Harry, he mentioned that he was triathlon athlete.

"I remember sitting there feeling so proud. It was nice to be recognized."

Harry became more observant and spent a short time in yeshivah in Israel. Sometime later he found himself at the same family for Shabbos and was even sitting in the same seat. Once again his host went around the table introducing the guests.

"He said that the first person had written *sefarim*. The second had just finished *Shas* for the third time. The third also had done something notable. Then he got to me and he said the exact same thing he said years earlier, that I ran triathlons. I remember being so embarrassed," Harry said. "The thing that had made me feel so good now wasn't worth so much. I said, 'I just came back from yeshivah, can't you say something else?'"

Harry realized at that moment how much he had changed in the few years since the first Shabbos meal. He had previously prided himself on his physical achievements, and now realized they were worth less than he had thought. Instead, his physical goals were beginning to be replaced by spiritual pursuits.

"Before becoming *frum*, I think my happiness came from self-absorption. I was happy, but a lot of it came from doing things to make myself happy — whether it was the military or sports," Harry said. "What I realized is that true happiness comes from going in to out, as opposed to going from out to in. It's about giving. I always had it in me, but what's great about Yiddishkeit is it gave me a perfect framework to give to others."

That experience at the Shabbos table planted a seed in him, a knowledge that he needed to return to Israel to spend a serious amount of time learning. However, he could not imagine how to do so.

Harry had worked as a lawyer for his entire career, and had spent most of his time in a federal government department in New York City. For years he had his eye on a coveted promotion, to become chief of the unit. Though he worked hard and was well liked, he was turned down repeatedly throughout his twelve years on the job.

In April 2001, he met his wife and they wed in November.

The two of them had both become *frum* later in life and never had the chance to spend significant time learning in Israel. They decided to try to take a year of absence from their jobs and go learn after their wedding.

"My office was so excited that I got married. I was already forty-two. I approached them for a year of leave and they approved it. They were just so happy that I had finally got married."

Though his department gave him the green light to go to Israel, they made it clear that this would end any hope for a promotion. A new administration in Washington was revamping the department and nothing was guaranteed other than that his position would remain open.

"I did the *cheshbon*, we talked it out, and we decided we wanted to go so much, so whatever happened, happened," Harry explained. "The opportunity to spend time learning in Eretz Yisrael overrode the risk, even though it would be a big risk. It was clear that my career would top out, but we decided it was better to build a marriage."

In February after their wedding, they packed up their house and their life and left for their year abroad. Looking back, Harry has no doubts that they made the correct choice. He said it was a formative year as they learned to depend on each other and grow in the ideal spiritual environment.

Upon his return to America, Harry found his job still open, despite the many changes taking place in his office. Three weeks after his return, the deputy chief of his department called Harry into his office to discuss some of the changes that were occurring. There was a very significant change he needed to hear about — he was offered the position of chief of his unit!

"It was a very powerful experience for me. You do the right thing, and all of a sudden miracles happen. There's no reason I should have been made chief at that moment. When you do what's right, you don't have to worry about these career issues."

For Harry the message was clear — he took a risk to pursue spiritual goals and Hashem rewarded him both in this world and the next. Like Nachshon ben Aminadav who jumped into the Red Sea causing the waters to split for the Jews, Harry jumped into the water of Torah and Hashem showed him miracles. His years of hard work certainly paved the way for his promotion, but it was his single year of demonstrating a clear commitment to Hashem that guaranteed it.

That was the biggest message for Harry — reach out to Hashem and He will do even more for you.

The Chafetz Chaim explains (based on an analogy of Shlomo HaMelech): Hashem planted in each person unlimited potential. Just as a field can produce tremendous amounts of fruits and vegetables if properly cared for, the human soul can reach incredible levels of productivity only when nurtured.

How does one maximize the potential of his soul? Just as a field requires dew and rain, the soul requires the light of the Torah. The more of the Torah's wisdom and sanctity given to the soul, the more it will shine.

And if a field is not properly weeded and nurtured, it will produce thorns and thistles. So too a Jew, even if he has begun to grow, can quickly slide back to his previous behaviors without the nourishment of the Torah. He could produce spiritual "thorns" that could detract from his natural holiness and wisdom and uproot the growth he has achieved.

The Chafetz Chaim cautions us: a *ba'al teshuvah* must erect "fences" for himself to prevent him from returning to the mistakes of his past. Through appropriate Torah study, *teshuvah*, and proper behavior, he will guarantee that his field will not be overgrown with thorns, but will produce the most beautiful fruits as he reaches his spiritual potential (*Ahavas Chesed*, Part II, Chapter 11).

9 Charting a Course through the Year

EVERY JEWISH HOLIDAY PROVIDES ITS OWN UNIQUE MOments of inspiration. Sometimes a Jew will be encouraged to become observant because of the excitement of the dancing on Simchas Torah, the beauty of a Pesach Seder, or a deep Torah lesson about the meaning of a holiday that enraptures him. Every Yom Tov offers its own peek into the beauty, truth, and eternal relevance of Judaism.

The Yamim Tovim also bring with them unexpected challenges of "learning the ropes," as *ba'alei teshuvah* are confronted with rules and practices that are foreign to them (and sometimes even seem bizarre!). In addition, Hashem often showers outreach professionals with extra Divine assistance to help them bring the splendor of the holidays to other Jews.

JUST ONE QUESTION BEFORE *NEILAH*

RABBI ARYEH GIBBER moved to Norfolk, Virginia, in the summer of 2001 to work in Jewish education and outreach. He was young, fresh out of yeshivah, and excited about the opportunity to teach others.

As soon as he and his family settled in and began exploring the area, their plans were thrown into the wind as Hurricane Isabel approached. They were forced to evacuate, and returned to Baltimore to wait out the storm. The storm tore through the city just days before Rosh Hashanah, leaving wrecked homes, downed power lines, and fallen trees.

"When we drove back into town, it literally took us fifteen minutes to drive six blocks (and Norfolk is a far cry from midtown Manhattan!), because so many roads were blocked off by fallen trees. The Shabbos following the storm, the shul davened *Kabbalas Shabbos* early so people could get home before dark since there was no power in the shul or homes or streetlights. There were trees, branches, and debris strewn around the neighborhood for a good few weeks."

On Yom Kippur night, the small community gathered in the synagogue. The typical emotions of the day — of lives hanging in the balance — were heightened by the recent events.

Rabbi Gibber took his seat against the *mechitzah*. It was a short *mechitzah*, and the women were elevated slightly above the men.

Rabbi Gibber stood somberly, his body wrapped in his *kittel* and his tallis draped over his head. All week a tumult of thoughts had circulated through his mind — the recent hurricane, his family's adjustments to the new community, and his wife's pregnancy and upcoming delivery (not to mention thoughts of *teshuvah* for Rosh Hashanah and Yom Kippur!). Finally now, at one of the most influential moments of the year, he was able to put all of these thoughts aside and gather his concentration for the prayers.

The chazzan recited the drawn-out Kaddish right before the Shemoneh Esreh of *Neilah* and everyone took their three steps back.

"Just as I was about to begin, I felt a tap on my shoulder. I looked around, looked up, and saw a woman around seventy-, seventy-five-years-old. She said, 'Excuse me, Rabbi, I have a question for you.'

"I said to myself, 'This is why HaKadosh Baruch Hu put me here — who knows what questions Hashem puts in a person's head right before Neilah — maybe she wants to make a change, maybe she wants to reconnect with her children.'

"I told myself, 'I have to set aside my Neilah for a few moments to help her.'"

The woman pointed to the Ner Tamid at the front and asked, "You think they had a generator to keep that running during the hurricane? Because if the eternal light went out during a power outage, that would be a shame!"

Rabbi Gibber said that was his first real taste of life in an out-of-town community. The question certainly wasn't what he expected (and gave him a great chuckle!), but it provided a glimpse into the lives and concerns of the people he would be meeting and helping in the community.

Ironically her question also foretold the role he himself would play in the community — as a *ner*, a light, trying to create sparks in the *neshamos* of Norfolk's Jews.

TESHUVAH IN TIKRIT

EVERY YEAR AS the High Holidays approach, Jews around the world consider the direction of their lives and contemplate changes they want to make. U.S. Army Chaplain Rabbi Nosson Sachs saw this process elevated to the highest degree when he was sent to Afghanistan in 2006 and Iraq in 2007 for Rosh Hashanah, Yom Kippur, and Sukkos.

Amidst the uncertainties of war, he helped Jewish soldiers grapple with the greatest questions of the purpose of their lives.

And in the most unlikely of scenarios, he learned his own lessons about *mesiras nefesh* and the nobility of the Jewish soul.

During his rotation in Iraq, Rabbi Sachs literally walked in the footsteps of our forefathers. He hosted Yom Tov davening and provided other religious services for Jewish soldiers in the most improbable and uplifting locations. And in the fullest sense of seeing the downfall of our enemies, one of the highlights of his tour was hosting an emotional Simchas Torah in Saddam Hussein's palace.

"I spent Rosh Hashanah in the International Zone. Saddam had a presidential palace there and a house that was used as the headquarters of the Republican Guard, his elite forces. There was a gorgeous, beautiful board room, which we decided would be the perfect place for a *shalosh seudos*," Rabbi Sachs said. "It was ironic — the place where Saddam Hussein had lorded around, we made it *kadosh*. A week later was Shemini Atzeres, Simchas Torah, and Shabbos. We made a *melaveh malkah* there. The place where he made his plans and ruled, we talked about escorting the Shabbos Queen and the meaning of Shabbos."

Tikrit is just 250 miles from the ruins of the ancient city of Nineveh. On Yom Kippur afternoon that year when he read the story of the prophet Yonah's mission toward Nineveh, it meant more to him than it had ever before.

On Yom Kippur he was joined by twenty-two soldiers and civilian contractors, many of whom did not attend synagogue back home, but who had risked their lives to come to the service.

"Some of them convoyed through dangerous areas, dodging snipers, risking their lives to go to davening. I asked myself, 'What do I usually risk coming to daven? Not much.' These people went out of their way and did something a little bit dangerous to go to shul."

One of the attendees, a lieutenant, told Rabbi Sachs that one of her soldiers also wanted to attend the Kol Nidrei service, but missed it because he was in a hospital with a serious intestinal illness.

A few days later, Rabbi Sachs went to visit the soldier. As he entered the hospital tent, the soldier tried to sit up in his bed out of respect for Rabbi Sachs' officer rank. Rabbi Sachs quickly sat down to not trouble the soldier.

"He took my hand in his, told me he had been in the army for six years and had never met a rabbi. He was so touched that I had come to see him. He had questions that a rabbi would dream a congregant would ask him — do we believe in Olam HaBa, *teshuvah*, doing what is right, asking forgiveness. The questions you ask when you really care."

"He kept me for about forty-five minutes. That interchange happens in a war zone, when you're much closer to your mortality."

While in Afghanistan in 2006, Rabbi Sachs visited a base on the Pakistan border which had been hit by rockets six times the previous day. On the following day, it was attacked again.

Upon arriving, Rabbi Sachs was told that a Jewish soldier wanted to meet him.

"I was introduced to an enormous man. His father was Irish. His mother was Jewish. O'Reilly, it's a great Jewish name.

"He was very troubled. He had been in Iraq on a previous deployment, in four vehicles that struck IEDs [improvised explosive devices]. The last time it jettisoned him thirty feet out of the vehicle. He was the only survivor.

"He had been a member of the Grateful Dead motorcycle group. Since the IEDs, he thought a lot about his life, mortality. He had done things that he regretted. This soldier's question to me was, 'Yom Kippur is coming. Can G-d forgive me? What do I have to do to be forgiven?'

"Yes," I said. "Hashem will forgive you. Here's what you have to do."

Rabbi Sachs says the interactions that he and other chaplains have in the field, with Jews asking sincere questions about their religion, could happen nowhere else.

"To be a rabbi in such an environment, with a person in a panicked state, is a big responsibility. He would never come to an Orthodox shul, so we have to come to him."

The Miraculous Sukkah of Afghanistan

For the holiday of Sukkos in 2006, Rabbi Nosson Sachs was stationed at the Bagram Air Base in Afghanistan. The Presbyterian chaplain at the base had assured him that the base had not just one, but two sukkahs available for the coming holiday. Rabbi Sachs was ecstatic — of the fifteen personnel who had attended his Yom Kippur services on the base, eleven said they would be interested in coming back for Sukkos, so there would be enough room to seat everyone.

Four days before the holiday began, Rabbi Sachs opened the boxes and immediately realized they didn't hold two sukkahs, but rather the broken parts of a single small pop-up sukkah.

With the holiday starting only days away on Friday afternoon, Rabbi Sachs had to quickly design and build a new sukkah. The process of building the sukkah against all odds and in the most unlikely of locations showed him Hashem's Hand more clearly than almost any other experience of his life. Over the next four days, a wildly diverse and completely unexpected array of characters arrived on scene to assist in the construction.

Rabbi Sachs first sketched plans of a sukkah and brought them to the sergeant major involved with the base's Engineering

Corps to see if they could build it. The sergeant major handed him a stack of papers which required several signatures.

"How long do you think it will take to build it?" Rabbi Sachs asked. "The holiday starts in four days."

"Maybe we could finish it by December," the sergeant major replied.

Rabbi Sachs gulped.

Rabbi Sachs decided to try to build the sukkah himself. He and the Presbyterian chaplain ran around the base for the next few hours getting all the necessary signatures.

Rabbi Sachs next went to the base's building supplies store. The two Bosnian Muslims manning the store had never heard of a sukkah before, but they were eager to help. They said all the supplies would be available by Thursday afternoon.

The only items they did not have were metal L brackets which were needed to connect the sukkah to one wall of the chapel. The valley surrounding the base is very windy, so Rabbi Sachs needed the brackets to provide stability to the sukkah. However, in a country of mostly mud huts, metal brackets were almost nonexistent. After spending an hour driving around the base looking for a source of brackets, Rabbi Sachs finally found a building in which aluminum air-conditioning ducts were manufactured.

Rabbi Sachs ran into the building and asked the man inside, this time an Afghani Muslim, if he could make L brackets. He was excited to make something other than air-conditioning ducts.

"How many you need?" the man asked. "I can make a lot. A thousand?"

"Actually, no. Twenty will be sufficient," Rabbi Sachs said.

Rabbi Sachs returned two hours later. The man had made sixty brackets.

Thursday afternoon came around and Rabbi Sachs picked up the rest of the materials from the supply store. He had requested wood beams to build the frame of the sukkah, but the only beams available were twelve feet long! So he borrowed a small saw and began the time-consuming process of cutting the wood.

At the same time on the base was a group of civilian comedians who had been brought from the States to entertain the troops. They were set to return to the U.S. but had been unable to arrange a transport out of the country. Soldiers and military supplies are given priority on aircraft in a theater of war; for civilians not essential to the war effort, finding a way out can be a challenge. Each day the comedians tried to arrange a flight back to America. It was especially pressing, as one member of the group was set to get married the following Monday.

The groom happened to walk by Rabbi Sachs as he was trying to cut the wood and asked what he was doing.

"I'm building a sukkah," Rabbi Sachs responded.

"What's a sukkah?"

Rabbi Sachs explained the fundamentals of the holiday, and noticed a sudden flash of insight on the comedian's face.

"Is everything okay?" Rabbi Sachs asked.

"You know what my full-time job is? I'm a carpenter by trade. A carpenter!" he yelled. "Don't you get it? Now I understand why I'm stuck here! If I help you, I'll get out of here."

"Hallelujah!" Rabbi Sachs shouted.

The carpenter began cutting the wood, and in three hours the entire frame was assembled. And just as the comedian hoped, he and his friends caught the next flight home.

Two pieces of the sukkah were still missing: Rabbi Sachs had not yet figured out what to put on the sides and top.

While he was finishing assembling the frame with the comedian/carpenter, an officer walked by and asked what they were doing. Rabbi Sachs described the fundamentals of the Sukkah.

"What are you going to use for the walls?" the officer asked.

"I'm not sure yet," Rabbi Sachs said.

"Come with me."

The officer brought Rabbi Sachs behind his quarters, where there was a large, unused bundle of camouflage netting. When they brought the netting back to the sukkah frame to see if it would work, it fit to the inch.

Next, he needed to try to find a source of *s'chach* to cover the top of the sukkah. Outside the base was a huge expanse of tall river reeds which would have been perfect, except that the entire area had been mined by Russians and was therefore off limits.

Within the fence of the base were several hundred thin, barren trees. On Friday, Rabbi Sachs began hacking branches from trees with the small saw that he had. A woman working for the Red Cross saw what he was doing and offered him a machete to make it easier.

After a short while, he had cut enough branches to cover the top of the sukkah, and the woman helped him bring them back. He laid them on top on the sukkah shortly before sunset.

Now the next problem arose: the valley surrounding Bagram experiences extremely strong wind storms every fall afternoon which threatened to blow the branches off the sukkah. The winds kick up dust and throw around anything that's not firmly secured down. However just as he finished the construction, the wind miraculously stopped blowing and didn't start again until after Sukkos.

Friday night came and eleven Jews joined Rabbi Sachs in the sukkah for a beautiful meal, full of singing and *divrei Torah*. It was the first time most of them had ever eaten in a sukkah. Rabbi Sachs also had a lulav and esrog with him in the sukkah, available for anyone to use during the week.

For most of the weeklong holiday, Rabbi Sachs sat in the sukkah learning Gemara. The occasional passerby, whether Jewish or non-Jewish, poked his head in out of curiosity. A few Jewish personnel recognized the sukkah from their youth and stopped in. Rabbi Sachs invited them to learn with him, and several accepted his offer.

The *Zohar* says that when a person sits in the sukkah, the Shechinah spreads Its wings over him from above. That sukkah in Bagram enveloped and protected the people inside it from their enemies waiting all around them. In the middle of a war zone, for a few days, they were able to felt the spiritual bliss of the miraculous sukkah of Afghanistan.

⇨ ⇦

One other experience during the holiday of Sukkos taught Rabbi Sachs that we can never underestimate the power of even seemingly small actions. One day he received a parcel from friends in Pittsburgh. They had sent him two packaged instant kosher meals to supplement the army rations.

"I opened up the package, and was so excited to have meatballs and spaghetti! I decided I was going to eat them for supper in the sukkah that night."

He hurried to the sukkah, ready to enjoy a memorable meal. He peeled back the foil cover, poured in hot water and savored the sweet smell of meatballs filling the sukkah.

Just as he was about to start eating, a lieutenant colonel with whom he was becoming friendly passed by the sukkah and stuck in his head. The man was Jewish but not observant. When he saw Rabbi Sachs, he entered and sat down next to him.

"Will you eat with me in the sukkah?" Rabbi Sachs asked.

"No thanks, I'll just go to the mess hall and get a meal."

(I thought, great, they serve completely *treif* food there!)

"C'mon, I have spaghetti and meatballs here. When was the last time you ate spaghetti and meatballs?"

The lieutenant colonel's eyes opened up larger than the meatballs and he accepted the offer.

"I thought to myself, it was *mitzvah goreres mitzvah*. My friends thought they were just sending it to me, but they created another mitzvah. A Jew who would have eaten *treif* that night didn't because they sent the meal. And maybe next time he would also avoid eating *treif*. You can never denigrate even a small mitzvah, because you never know where it's going to end.

"That little mitzvah, you should run for it, because you don't know what Hashem will do with it. You should run for it and you could end up with a pile of mitzvos."

A MODERN-DAY CHANUKAH MIRACLE

LEAT KUZNIAR GREW up in Toronto, Canada. As her parents were Israeli, she always played with a dreidel from Israel during Chanukah. On it were the letters *nun, gimmel, hei*, and *pei* representing the phrase *"Neis Gadol Hayah Poh* — a great miracle happened *here*." In contrast, all of her friends played with dreidels whose letters stood for: "a great miracle happened *there*." But as she later found out, great miracles happen everywhere, and it was exactly a modern Chanukah miracle that helped light the spark of her own religious journey.

During college, Leat attended the classes of a local Jewish outreach organization headed by Rabbi Benjie Jacoby. One Chanukah the organization arranged a trip to one of Canada's foremost ski resorts outside Montreal.

After a few hours of uneventful driving to the slopes, the charter bus stopped at a rest stop. A few minutes later the students re-boarded the bus and settled into their seats for the remainder of the trip. Some sat down to chat with friends while others closed their eyes, being lulled to sleep by the sound of the bus motor revving up to merge with the speeding traffic.

Suddenly the tranquility was shattered by the shriek of brakes. Screams filled the bus as students were thrown from their seats.

The driver had experienced a sudden seizure and had lost consciousness behind the wheel. One of the students, Shai, happened to be at the front of the bus throwing out a banana peel when he noticed the driver slumped over the wheel. Shai instinctively pulled on the emergency brake.

The bus came to a stop just inches from the rock wall on the side of the highway.

The students staggered to their feet and surveyed the damage. Amazingly there were no serious injuries and no other vehicles had been hit. The students exited the bus, squeezing out through the small space between the door and the wall. They called for emergency assistance and waited for an ambulance to arrive for the driver.

After the paramedics arrived, the students and staff members walked along the side of the road back to the service station to wait for new transportation. It was already getting close to nightfall. As darkness descended, Rabbi Jacoby gathered the students, all shaken from the accident, to light the Chanukah menorah in an empty area off to the side of the station.

"As our candles burned, I turned to a friend and remarked *"Neis gadol hayah poh*!" Leat said. She and the other members of the group knew that they owed their well-being only to the miracle that had occurred that day. Without the presence and quick thinking of Shai, the bus would have slammed forcefully into the rock wall and the trip could have ended quite differently.

For Leat there was another deep message to the adventures of the day. There in the parking lot they stood as the only Jews for miles, under the curious eyes of non-Jewish travelers. They proudly proclaimed their faith as they lit the menorah and sang Chanukah songs. They demonstrated to themselves and those around them their awareness of Hashem's constant attention to the needs of His children.

"Right there in 'Hicksville,' surrounded by truck drivers, mounds of Super-Sized McDonald's Fries and tacky Xmas decorations, we lit our candles and sang the traditional Hebrew songs, unencumbered by the many inquiring eyes staring our way," Leat recalled. "In that service station our small group made a statement — we allowed our inner light to shine, unhindered by the questioning glances from those around us."

As she became more observant, Leat gained a greater appreciation for the real message of Chanukah — during the holiday we recall not only the miracle of the oil and the military victories, but also the tenacity of a small group of Jews to fight for their religion.

"The true miracle of Chanukah is the fact that a group of Jews, no matter that they were small in number, allowed their inner light to shine outwardly and refused to be engulfed by the encroaching darkness of the surrounding culture. The light of these Jews inspired those who were unable to withstand the pleasure of the hedonistic world around them to return to their traditions.

"It is precisely the miracle of Chanukah that allows us to pronounce clearly that we are proud Jews — whether in Yerushalayim or 'Hicksville,' Ontario!"

It was that message, of being able to stand in a rest stop and thank Hashem and proudly sing Jewish songs, that helped Leat realize the essence of being an observant Jew. It's a message of Hashem's unceasing love and concern for us, and a reminder that He continues to make miracles for us everyday.

The Boyaner Rebbe, HaRav Mordechai Shlomo Friedman, *zt"l*, visited Israel in 1957 during Chanukah. After lighting the candles one night, he addressed his followers who had come to be with him.

He suggested a novel approach to Chanukah: He noted that the halachah requires the lighting of the candles to be "*taaseh v'lo min he'asui*," lit anew and not be previously lit. He said that just as we approach the mitzvah from the perspective of *taaseh*, a new action, we should pray to Hashem that He should perform new miracles for us each year.

Chanukah is a time of miracles, both old and new. And it took a shining new Chanukah miracle to help Leat Kuzniar come home. And that is why she continues to use a dreidel with the letters *nun*, *gimmel*, *hei*, and *pei*, for miracles continue to occur wherever a Jew happens to be.

One Last Piece of Chametz

SPRING IS THE time of rebirth, as trees and plants begin to flower and give forth new life. Pesach, the holiday of the springtime, is a sign of this rebirth. The Sfas Emes notes that the holidays of Pesach and Sukkos are on opposite ends of the spectrum — just as physical seeds that are planted in the fall will emerge during the spring, so too during Sukkos we plant seeds of spiritual growth inside ourselves that will burst forth during Pesach.

Akiva and Allyson Frankel* met during college, started to become religious together, and eventually married. They have been on a steady upward spiritual climb ever since.

During their first few years of marriage as they took their initial tottering steps to establishing a *frum* home, they frequently debated whether to hold on to their television set. They had each grown up in nonobservant homes, in which televisions were placed centrally both in their physical homes and family lives. But as they grew together in their religious observance, Akiva and Allyson felt increasingly dissatisfied with the role of television in their lives. They disliked the non-Jewish values and inappropriate content that it brought into their home.

Over time they worked to cut down their television usage. They had finally whittled it down to news programs alone. However, the presence of the TV was still a major source of temptation, and they hoped to eventually rid their home of it altogether.

Pesach arrived, and with it the mitzvah of searching for *chametz*. Akiva and Allyson hid the customary ten pieces of bread throughout their small apartment. Unfortunately as hard as they tried, when the evening ended they had only found nine pieces of *chametz*! One piece of bread was still missing! Akiva went to sleep that night in a mild panic, concerned that he would unwittingly violate the prohibition against possessing bread during Pesach.

The next morning Akiva awoke, and instinctively went to turn on the television for the morning news program. There, sitting on top of the TV, was the final piece of missing bread. Akiva decided then and there to throw out the *chametz*, and the television with it.

"I said, 'It's *chametz*, and now it's out the door.'"

The Gemara (*Berachos* 17a) records the practice of Rabi Alexandri, who at the end of his Shemoneh Esreh prayer, would add the following supplication: "It is revealed and known before You that our will is to perform Your will. And who prevents [us]? The yeast in the dough."

Rashi said the "yeast in the dough" is a reference to the evil inclination, which dwells in a person's heart and tries to ignite passions and desires in him to tempt him to sin. During Pesach we rid our homes and ourselves of yeast products, fighting against this enticement in our hearts.

For the Frankel family, television was that source of temptation. And so very appropriately, that year they threw out the television with all of their other *chametz*.

Despite All Good Preparations...

Rachel Wygoda* and her brother began becoming observant in high school through their NCSY youth group. For college they decided to concurrently attend Yeshivah University and its women's program, Stern College. There they were able to solidify their religious observance and knowledge of halachah.

During their first year in college, as Pesach approached, they decided together that it was important to spend the holiday with their parents. Their parents were not observant, and they did not want to offend them by staying in school for the holiday. They therefore decided to go home for Pesach, and to do everything in their power to make it a perfectly kosher Seder.

The two siblings had thought of everything — they brought meat and handmade *shmurah matzah* with them from New York City. They asked the local Chabad rabbi to *kasher* their parents' kitchen. They even bought a whole set of new dishes for their parents ("my mother actually enjoyed feeling like a young bride who picks out new things!"), and used paper and plastic where it was necessary.

They also meticulously planned all of the details of the Seder. They carefully measured out the correct amounts of all of the items ahead of time, and offered to graciously be the official wine pourers for the table.

Their preparations proceeded perfectly. Their parents repeatedly expressed their gratitude that their children had come home for the Seder and how respectfully they had planned all the details.

Even guests had been invited. An aunt and uncle who had not intended to attend a Pesach Seder that year were invited and appreciatively accepted.

Rachel and her brother surveyed the table shortly before the Seder began. The table was set with the evidence of all of their hard work. Their new set of dishes glowed as the white tablecloth and cloth napkins completed the aura of a royal feast. They smiled at each other, as they silently reflected on their amazement that they had been able to pull it off. They had thought of everything...

Just then came a knock on the door. Rachel ran to open it. Her aunt and uncle had arrived just in time! As they entered, Rachel's aunt gave her a big smile and handed her a foil-wrapped package. "This is for you!"

"A number of things happened in the next few seconds — although thinking back on it, it seemed to take much longer. My brain processed the information coming to me both from my nose and my hands, and I gradually realized to my horror that the hostess gift warming the palm of my hand was — a freshly baked loaf of bread!" Rachel said.

She stood in shock, unsure of what to do next.

"Long before I became an observant Jew, my parents taught me Jewish values — one of them being that you treat other people, especially older people, with respect no matter what. So although part of me wanted to shriek and throw the bread out of the window, my 'good breeding' kicked in and I smiled at my aunt and said, 'Thank you.'"

Rachel "casually" put the bread down on a coffee table, explaining that "there just isn't an inch of room left on the dining table." Everyone proceeded to sit down and start the Seder.

Rachel sat on eggshells for the rest of the meal. She felt like all of their hard work and preparations had gone to naught with the arrival of the *chametz*. And what would she say if her aunt asked her to serve the bread?

"I couldn't help being tense. I don't know what I thought, (that the bread would suddenly sprout legs and jump onto my newly kosher dishes?), but this gift seemed like the elephant in the room."

Rachel and her brother tried as hard as they could to maintain their composure and smiles as the Seder proceeded. Thankfully, the evening passed without any further excitement.

"As soon as my aunt and uncle were out of sight (we checked by peeking through the curtains) my brother grabbed the foil package and slam-dunked it into my neighbor's garbage can with a satisfying clang."

Looking back, the event became a humorous milestone (or pothole as Rachel describes it) in their religious growth. Though she was initially upset at the gift, she eventually was able to view it with the proper perspective and acknowledge that it had been a positive challenge. The arrival of the *chametz* did not undo all of their hard work as she had initially thought. Rather only because of their hard work, they found themselves able to deal with the gift with grace and composure.

"G-d is always forcing us to grow in one way or another. Our own personal problems are as individually designed as our fingerprints," Rachel reflected.

The *Mesillas Yesharim* says that when a Jew is faced with challenges, he needs to view them like a toughened general preparing for war. Just as an experienced warrior runs into battle to show off his strategic prowess, a true servant of Hashem is prepared for any trial that comes his way, eager to show that his faith in Hashem and his convictions are rock-solid.

For Rachel and her brother, the *chametz* incident was that test. Their careful preparations and eagerness to maintain an evening of respect and upright behavior allowed them to sail through the challenge they faced.

---

10 Returning Home from Far Away

HASHEM PUT IN EVERY JEW AN INNATE DESIRE AND NEED to look for spirituality and connect with larger truths. He hopes we'll use these feelings to find our place in Judaism, but sadly, many Jews from non-observant homes have instead turned to other belief systems, from Christianity to Eastern religions.

Out of these masses, however, some have found their way home.

This trend is predicted in the Torah. Before his death, Moshe reminded the Jews of the blessings and curses that would befall them based on their future behavior:

> And it will be that when all these things come to pass — the blessing and the curse, which I have placed before you — then you will return to your heart in the midst of all the nations where Hashem your G-d dispersed you (*Devarim* 30:1).

The sixteenth-century commentator Sforno provided a prescient explanation of these words:

> You are going to probe and research the destructive nature [of the lifestyle of those nations amongst whom you live], and you will reflect and be struck by the sharp contrast between truth and

> falsehood. And with this you will perceive how far you are from G-d and you will be lifted up [out] of the knowledge and practices that are not according to His Torah."

Rabbi Ezriel Tauber, in his book *Days Are Coming*, explains that the Sforno was predicting that Jews will join other nations and religions, and through them some will eventually find their way to Judaism.

When a Jew returns to his roots, the journey home can be difficult and emotional. This is even more true for Jews who have spent time in other religions. They often formed deep emotional bonds with other people, and have to turn their backs on friends and family as well as the people who helped them. Plus they have built new identities for themselves based on the teachings of the other religions. They need to now dismantle these and rebuild their entire lives from scratch.

A Born-Again Jew

If you would have traveled through Iowa in the late 1970s, you would have found Alex Schwartz* standing on street corners handing out Christian missionary leaflets. He was Jewish from birth, but had been sucked into born-again Christian circles in college. If you track him down today, you'll find an Orthodox rabbi with decades of experience in Jewish communal service, *kiruv* and anti-missionary work. His dramatic escape from his missionary life was aided by an unexpected group of people, including a Christian preacher who helped him run away and a Conservative rabbi who introduced him to Chassidus.

Alex grew up in a Conservative Jewish family in the tri-state area. Jewish culture was important to them, but mitzvah observance was not. His Hebrew school and Hebrew high school taught him only the value of Jewish service, Israel, and the Holocaust.

"The one thing that was lacking from my Jewish childhood was spirituality," Alex said. "The idea that G-d is real, personal, and wants a relationship with each of us — this was entirely lacking."

Twice a year, Alex's maternal great-grandparents visited. They were Orthodox, but to him they were relics from the past. He was entrenched in the wonders of science and evolution; they were fossils holding stubbornly onto the rituals of the Old Country.

When Alex's great-grandmother heard that he was dating a non-Jew, she told him that he was breaking her heart. Her pleas fell on deaf ears.

"I still went out with her. Judaism was a culture to me. You don't change your life for a culture."

Alex attended college at the University of Iowa hoping to become a veterinarian. His freshman year was spent at parties with illicit substances, and as a result his grades were mediocre. Halfway through the year he realized that he had destroyed any chance to go to veterinarian school. He began sinking into depression.

One night during the middle of his emotional descent, Alex went out with his Christian girlfriend to see a Christian movie being screened on campus by a local missionary group. It was about the end of days and the Christian view of the punishments that non-believers will receive. Counselors were on hand after the film to speak further about its concepts. The movie struck a chord with Alex, playing on the unease and uncertainties in his life. He approached one of the counselors.

The man began throwing quotes from the Tanach at Alex to support Christianity. They were all mistranslated or out of context, but Alex didn't know that. Without knowledge of their proper meaning and with nothing to counter them, he found them to be very convincing.

"Much of what he said made sense to me," Alex said. "In my emotional state, I was so lost I was just groping for answers. I went back to my dorm room. The ideas of the film just worked on me and worked on me."

That night in his dorm room, Alex decided to accept the Christian founder to be his savior just as the movie had encouraged. He remembers feeling that he might be doing something very wrong. But the ideas he had heard that night were so convincing that he quieted his doubts.

Alex's academic advisor in the university was a born-again Christian who actively tried to convert his students. On numerous occasions over the year, he had tried to convince Alex. So when Alex showed up at his door the next morning and told him about the events of the previous night, the advisor could not contain his excitement. He gave Christian literature to Alex for further reading and introduced him to a campus missionary organization.

Within a short time Alex joined a nondenominational church and began attending its weekly bible studies and retreats. A personal counselor was appointed to guide him. The church teachers showed him other mistranslated verses and concepts throughout Tanach that "proved" the validity of their beliefs.

Alex soaked up everything he heard. He felt like Christianity offered a religious lifestyle based on values and having a personal relationship with the Creator, both of which were lacking in the watered-down Judaism of his childhood.

Alex hid his new beliefs from his parents until summer vacation. By that point he had decided to become a Christian minister. When he finally told his parents, his father reacted with anger; his mother with feelings of pain and hurt.

"I knew she wouldn't like it, but I didn't realize, and I don't think she realized, just how much Judaism meant to her. Whatever little Judaism she had growing up, she had grandparents who were *frum*, and she had known them as younger people who were more vibrant. This stirred something in her."

The summer with his parents was turbulent. His father had no kind words for him, and while his mother was still trying to use a softer approach, nothing sunk in.

Questions Asked, Questions Answered

When he went back to school in August for his sophomore year, Alex continued his rapid plunge into Christianity. He began studying one-on-one with a missionary named Charlie. Charlie soon became his close friend and advisor.

As time passed, Alex started finding holes in the religious doctrines he was learning. Charlie could provide only incomplete answers to his questions. The lifestyle, however, still seemed so complete and spiritually rich that he was willing to swallow the contradictions and difficulties — at least for the time being.

As time passed, Alex collected more of these questions. They nagged at him.

Alex discovered a more intense born-again Christian bible study group on campus and found that it could provide answers to some of his questions. He broke away from his previous church and from Charlie and joined this new organization.

His beliefs became much more severe and harsh, and he rearranged his classes to be able to attend the group's bible study session every day at noon.

Over the next two years under the guidance of this group, Alex began missionizing on campus, going around with his bible and sharing the gospel.

He was a diamond catch for the organization. They felt that a Jew who had accepted Christianity was compelling proof of the truth of their faith. He became a frequent speaker for the organization. Alex was also a talented songwriter and guitar player, and he wrote missionary songs and performed at Christian events.

A Heartfelt Challenge

During the summer after his junior year Alex was home again. His father still had nothing to say to him other than the occasional few angry words. His mother was more diplomatic, and tried to get Alex to speak to the new rabbi of their Conservative synagogue, Rabbi Jason Weitz*. Alex met him several times, but every conversation ended in a shouting match.

During the year Alex's mother had taken classes with Rabbi Weitz, looking for ideas that she could use to challenge her son's beliefs. During summer vacation, she and Alex stayed up late nearly every night talking as she tried to challenge him with her newfound learning.

She pointed out verses in the Christian scriptures that clearly contradict the Torah. She also showed him verses in the Torah which declare the mitzvos to be eternally binding on Jews, even after Mashiach comes. How then could certain Christian verses declare the mitzvos and rules of the Torah to be null and void with the coming of the Christian messiah? Alex tried to rebuff her well-researched points, but her arguments began to penetrate into him and to reinforce the questions he been struggling with.

Right before he left home to return to Iowa, his mother made one final statement that would prove to be a turning point.

"If you believe this is true, that JC is the Mashiach, prove it to me from the Torah," his mother said. "Show me in the Torah that this is so. If it's true I'll become Christian too."

Looking back, Alex knows his mother's offer was not sincere, but she was baiting him to try to pull him back.

Alex accepted the challenge and threw himself into this quest once back in Iowa. He sat down with a translated Tanach from his parents' synagogue and a Christian Concordance and looked up basic words such as eternal, salvation, Mashiach, and Torah.

"Christianity claims that the Torah was only given to show

mankind that it is impossible to reach G-d's perfect standard. I tried to find that idea in the Torah, but it was not there! The more I studied, the more I realized that I had made a terrible mistake. It was the opposite of what I had intended to find. The more I traced the verses from Tanach which were quoted by the Christian scriptures, the more I saw that the verses were misquoted.

"It became a burden. I would lie in bed at night and weep. I couldn't let it rest. The fact that G-d gave us a Torah, and then gave us a messiah whose purpose was to annul it, didn't make sense."

The more he read, the more he saw the mistakes he had made. He was now torn between two lives. Externally he was still going to bible study and performing in churches. Internally he knew it was all wrong.

During winter vacation of his senior year Alex went home for a visit. He was in a fragile emotional state. One night he was sitting at the kitchen table when his mother walked in.

"You don't love me, because if you loved me you wouldn't do this," she told him.

Her words finally hit deep at his core.

"I don't know if she knew the power of it, but that pushed me over the edge, I began to cry. I stood up, went to the den, and dialed my mother's rabbi. I said, 'I need to talk you. I need to talk to you now.'"

Rabbi Weitz refused, expecting another confrontation, but Alex convinced him that he was sincere. They agreed to meet that day.

"He shared with me the things that he had shared before, but the veil had been lifted from my eyes. It became clear that my involvement was mostly emotional. Most Jews who get involved in missionary groups have very weak backgrounds and are in a time of emotional vulnerability. A Christian gives them loving support and friendship. The Jew is impressed with their spirituality and conviction. The verses seem compelling, but it's mostly emotional.

That is why intellectual arguments alone cannot save a Jew who has converted. He must be won back with love as well."

Alex saw his world suddenly come crashing down like a house of cards. But unlike his pleasant entry into the Christian world, he knew his exit would be much harder. He had crafted an identity and beliefs over the last three years, and he did not know how to leave them behind.

"I was rejecting the faith I had followed for three years. I had stood on street corners, handed out tracts, gone to bible studies, and was now throwing it all away. It was an incredibly painful experience."

A Difficult Confrontation

After his meeting with Rabbi Weitz, Alex told his parents that he was finished with the Christian world. However because of his love and respect for his Christian friends and teachers, he felt an obligation to go back to Iowa for just one week to bid farewell. That decision almost proved to be his undoing.

He flew back to Iowa and asked his roommate, a fellow born-again Christian, to pick him up from the airport. When his roommate heard the news, he immediately called one of the Church elders. The elder met Alex the next night to pressure him to stay.

"I was a fairly major player in this organization. I wasn't an elder, but because of my music and personality, and because I was so committed, I wasn't someone they would just let go. It wasn't just for myself but for the impact it would have on other people. They had made tapes of my music to play for other people. It would be a powerful statement if I left."

Following the meeting Alex maintained his decision to leave but felt like he would have nowhere to turn once he did so. Over the week as he said goodbye to the rest of his friends, he felt as if he was abandoning them. He realized how hard it was going to be to leave this life.

The week culminated with a meeting with the entire group of Church elders on Friday afternoon, just one day before his scheduled flight home. They spoke for hours. They used every technique they knew, from guilt to pressure to emotional games. By the end of the afternoon, Alex had agreed to cancel his ticket and to stay for just one more week to continue the conversation.

Alex's older brother called him that afternoon, excited that he was coming home. Alex dropped the bombshell that he wasn't coming home yet.

"How can you do this? You've given these people three years of your life! It's time for you to come home and find out about Judaism. Give your religion the same chance you gave this other religion," his brother said.

Alex was shocked to hear the words from his brother's mouth.

"Looking back, it was a big deal for him," Alex said. "He's not a *frum* Jew, but maybe he had more faith than me. He told me if I didn't come home the next day, he would fly to Iowa on Sunday to drag me home.

"I began an emotional meltdown. I wasn't thinking. I was beyond anxious. I think I was on my way to a nervous breakdown."

In a raging sea of emotions, Alex felt the need to swim to solid ground to stabilize himself. He called his old friend Charlie. He opened up to him and told him everything he was feeling, how he was torn on one side by his family and roots back home, and on the other side by his friendships and the Christian lifestyle in Iowa. He even mentioned that he now wanted to go to a yeshivah to learn more about Judaism. Charlie invited him to come to dinner that night so they could speak further.

In the middle of a frozen Iowa winter, Alex collapsed on Charlie's couch in a raging sweat.

"What is wrong with you?" Charlie asked. Alex began to cry.

"I've sold my tickets home, I'm not going," Alex said.

"What do you mean? You've quit!"

"No, I've decided to stay another week to talk to the elders some more."

"This is wrong; you need to go home."

"I can't go home. I don't have tickets and I'm afraid that if I go back to my apartment the elders will try to keep me here."

"I'll help you. You can always buy tickets."

Alex knew that Charlie didn't like the elders of the other church and their doctrines, but he was still shocked by Charlie's reaction. This was the man who had been his first Christian mentor. That night Alex called the airline and secured a seat on the next day's flight.

Sneaking out of Iowa would not be easy either. Charlie invited Alex to sleep over that night and said he would drive him to the airport the next day, but Alex was unsure how he would be able to evade his roommates and the elders.

Charlie drove Alex back to his apartment so he could pack up his stuff. His roommates were there, on their way out to the weekly Friday night bible study group and Christian coffee house. Alex told them that he had decided to stay for another week in Iowa, but wanted to stay home that night to study and pray on his own.

As soon as his roommates left he began to frantically pack. Charlie picked him up a little while later and brought him to his house to hide out.

"When my roommates got home, they saw everything was gone. They started looking frantically all over town. They looked in the airport, the Greyhound bus station. They didn't think to look at Charlie's house because they knew he was a missionary also, so he probably wouldn't have helped me."

That night Alex still felt anxious but he knew he was doing the right thing. Before going to bed he opened a bible, looking for a sign from G-d. He opened to the beginning of the book of *Yehoshua* and his eyes alighted on the following words:

> Only be very strong and courageous, to observe, to do, according to the entire Torah that Moshe My servant commanded you. Do not deviate from it to the right or to the left, in order that you may succeed wherever you will go. ... Do not fear and do not lose resolve, because Hashem your G-d is with you wherever you will go" (*Yehoshua* 1:7, 9).

"I read that, said, 'Thank You, G-d,' and fell asleep."

The next morning Charlie drove him to the airport and waited with him for the plane. There he revealed why he had encouraged Alex to leave.

"You know I'm only doing this because I know you'll come back a stronger Christian. You'll go to yeshivah and learn. G-d is with you."

The time to board arrived and the two men bid goodbye. Alex stepped onto the plane feeling both free and miserable.

"I felt a void, a terrible emptiness. I just didn't know what I would do. I didn't think I would find anything in Judaism. The Judaism that I knew wasn't fulfilling, but I was willing to at least give it a try."

Alex arrived home. After a few days of rest and reconnecting with his parents, he asked Rabbi Weitz to recommend the next steps for him. Rabbi Weitz brought him to the Chabad-Lubavitch Yeshivah in Morristown, New Jersey. Alex spent three months there and was blown away by everything he heard.

"To talk about G-d with so much love, connection and intensity, it was better than anything I had ever seen. I was culture-shocked, to say the least, by my own culture. I experienced Shabbos for the first time. It was beautiful."

Alex later asked Rabbi Weitz why he didn't take him to the Jewish Theological Seminary, the flagship Conservative university.

"You never would have accepted what they would teach you. You're too much of a believer in G-d. You would not have accepted their critical method of teaching."

Alex went next to Yeshivah University and then to Ohr

Somayach. He couldn't believe the depth and clarity of everything he was learning. He knew this was the truth.

Alex met his wife while at Yeshivah University. He continued to learn for many more years, and eventually received *semichah*.

Extending a Hand to Others

Over the years, Alex has been able to use his experiences to help other Jews escape from missionaries as well.

"I understand the hunger, what it is to be searching, how seductive the missionaries are," Alex said. "I have an insight into the minds of those who are truly seeking and have gotten on to the wrong side."

While studying at YU, Alex worked with an Orthodox rabbi in Manhattan named Rabbi Yehudah Fine who had a novel program: parents would approach him about their teenage or college-age children who were involved in missionary groups. He would make a deal with the children and parents. The child would agree to spend three weeks living at his house, including spending two Shabbosos with the Fine family. At the end they could choose to further explore Judaism or return to the church. In exchange, their parents would agree to stop nagging them about giving up their Christian beliefs. The rabbi was able to save many people with this arrangement.

Alex sometimes came for *melaveh malkah*s at the Fine house. He would bring his guitar, sing a few Jewish songs (some of which he wrote himself) and then would speak to the students.

Once, the family was hosting a young woman from the midwest. It was already the end of her second week in New York, and Rabbi Fine was making no progress with her. He asked Alex if he could speak to her and maybe play some music. It was the last chance they had — she was leaving the next morning to fly back home.

The drive from Brooklyn took a long time that night and Alex unfortunately arrived late to the *melaveh malkah*. He had time for only one song. He chose a composition called "Nor-Eastern" that he had written upon his return to Judaism. It was full of emotional energy, and it encapsulated his feelings and fears about returning to Judaism.

Among the words of the song were these poignant lines:

Who am I fooling if I live a lie?
Can I hide what I believe from myself?
And will I avoid me? What would I say?
If I confront me with me?

So breathe in Nor-Eastern
And blow me away,
Fill up my sails as I have prayed,
And shepherd Your servant today.
L-rd, shepherd your servant, I pray!

Following the song, Alex spoke with the woman for over an hour. The conversation was heated and her raw emotions came to the surface. She accused Alex and another person present of playing a good-cop/bad-cop mind game. She refused to budge or even consider their arguments.

At the end of the evening, Alex got into his car to drive home and immediately broke down and cried. He felt demoralized and broken, and disappointed in himself that he had been unable to save the woman.

"I took responsibility for it. I felt like I had mismanaged it. I knew that I had failed a Jewish soul and she would remain lost."

He slept poorly that night. He was woken the next morning by a phone call. It was Rabbi Fine.

"*Yasher koach*!" Rabbi Fine said.

"Please don't be sarcastic with me. I'm sorry, I really tried."

"No really, it worked! Everything you said made sense to her."

Alex couldn't believe the news.

"Yehudah, you have to tell me what was the magic pill! What did she say? Which argument swayed her? I want to know what to use for next time."

"No, it wasn't anything you said. It was the song. This morning she told me that she laid down in her bed after you left and just stared at the ceiling. She could tell that the words of the song came from truth. She said the idea that kept popping into her mind was how could a person who wrote that song be lying to me? She said that idea opened her heart to all the discussions you gave."

From that day, the woman made a clean break from the church and threw herself into learning about her Jewish roots. She eventually married Rabbi Fine's *chavrusa* and they eventually moved to Yerushalayim.

Alex said the power of songs is that they reach deep into a person's heart to strike at their emotions.

"For someone struggling, music is very powerful. There is no question that the Jewish arguments against Christianity are overwhelming, but a person's emotional bonding and their psychological ties to the Christian community are often stronger.

"But if a person experiences something on the emotional level, not the intellectual level, it counteracts their emotional feelings. That's why showing love to other Jews makes the most difference. Arguments are secondary."

While studying at YU, Alex was once invited by a *frum* man in Toronto to spend part of Pesach with him and his family. Sadly, the man had a nephew who lived nearby and who had also gotten involved in a Christian group. Alex promised to visit the nephew before Pesach and try to speak to him.

Alex drove to his house and introduced himself. For over three hours the two men sat and spoke. They talked about their parallel experiences growing up in unfulfilled Jewish upbringings and their similar lives in the church. Alex shared his experiences of escaping from that life.

"He was literally sweating bullets the whole time, but I encouraged him. I asked him to please come with me to his uncle's house. We'll spend the last days of Pesach there. I told him I wouldn't push him, and he could ask me any questions he had."

The man turned down the offer. After Pesach ended, Alex called him. No one answered. He even stopped by his house on the way out of town. The young man was gone. He had packed up and left the city.

"I blamed myself. If he wouldn't have come I should have stayed in his house."

Month passed. Alex graduated college and then went to learn in Israel.

One day Alex was visiting Ohr Somayach to interview for one of their study programs. While walking around campus, a familiar face ran up to him. It was the young man from Toronto!

"He looked at me and burst out with exclamation. He hugged me, and said, 'Thank you, thank you!' I couldn't believe it.

"I said, 'What are you doing here?'

"He said 'I'm learning Torah!'"

The man said that he had indeed left Toronto for a few days, fearing that Alex might return. However once he came back, his uncle brought in a rabbi from New York who was known for his anti-missionary work. He was able to get through to the man.

"One person starts, another person finishes," Alex recalled. "You can't let yourself be discouraged."

Rabbi Yaakov Rosenberg, *zt"l*, a pioneer of Jewish outreach, established a summer learning program for Jews exploring their roots. It was officially called the Sinai Retreats but became fondly known as Moodus, after the Connecticut town in which it was originally based. During the program, students were paired with *frum*-from-birth tutors who learned with them, teaching them fundamental Jewish learning skills.

His father-in-law Rabbi Shimon Schwab, *zt"l*, spent thirteen summers in Moodus and often addressed the tutors. He once cautioned them not to underestimate the incredible *mesiras nefesh* of the students in overcoming the hurdles in their religious journeys. He said it would be more appropriate to call them "*ba'alei gevurah* — people of strength."

This is true of all *ba'alei teshuvah*, but especially of those who come back from other religions. After building a self image and a basic reality of their lives based on the teachings of the other religions, they need to tear apart everything in order to build their lives from scratch. That is true *gevurah*.

The Silver Lining

Few people have had as dramatic an impact on Jewish outreach and education as Rabbi Yehudah Silver. For five decades he has inspired thousands of Jews throughout America, Israel, and Europe. He has also been a driving force behind many of the most recognized international outreach ventures, including the Aish HaTorah Discovery program, the Seed program in England, and Gateways in the United States.

His story began just as dramatically, in a showdown with Christian missionaries in the early days of the State of Israel.

Rabbi Silver grew up after World War II in Chicago, where his father and grandfather were both rabbis in the Skokie Yeshivah. After graduating high school in 1961 he traveled to Israel to study in yeshivah. It was not yet common to do so, and consequently he was one of the only American yeshivah students in Israel at the time.

Christian missionaries were a pressing problem in Israel. In 1963, the anti-missionary and Jewish outreach organization P'eylim/Lev

L'Achim organized a major demonstration against missionaries throughout the country. The organization recruited more than one hundred yeshivah students and planned simultaneous protests in Haifa, Tel Aviv and Yerushalayim.

The organizers approached young Yehudah Silver and asked him to translate their protest signs into English. Their target was a Christian group in Haifa headed by a missionary named Samuel Birnbaum. The missionaries were preying on poor, uneducated Jewish youngsters from Iraq, Tunisia, Iran, and other Sephardic countries. Most of them were recent immigrants who had little knowledge of Judaism and the missionaries attracted them by offering free shoes and other gifts to their parents.

"Once I started getting involved and went along to the [protest] and heard what we were supposed to be doing, to go and get the names and address of kids they were targeting, it became very important to me."

Rabbi Silver's group traveled to Haifa, but the missionaries had gotten wind of the demonstration and had hidden the children in an adjacent apartment. The group broke into the home where they were gathered and stormed into the room. On benches around the sides of the room sat the young Jews under Birnbaum's watchful eye.

"The kids were sitting around the room absolutely frightened. The missionaries had told them that we would cut off their tongues and ears," Rabbi Silver said. "We said the Shema Yisrael with them. When we said the words '*Hashem Echad*,' Birnbaum jumped up and said, "No, Hashem is three!"

The missionaries called the police, who immediately came and arrested Silver and the other students. They were charged with trespassing, hosting an unlawful assembly, and resisting arrest. The government initially threatened to expel all of the foreign students.

They were put on trial and were found guilty. They were offered a sentence of either a stiff fine or time in prison.

The group asked the Steipler Gaon what they should do. He ruled that they should not pay the high fine and should instead go to jail. Rabbi Silver and eight other students from the Haifa group were sentenced to two months in prison, which was later reduced to one month. They served their time in the now-defunct Tel Monde prison near Netanya, while students from the other groups were sent to other institutions. For their month stay the students opened a yeshivah inside the jail, and many leading rabbis came to speak to them.

The episode had a dramatic impact. The group succeeded in its goals — to publicize the activities of missionaries in Israel. Media outlets in the country and throughout the world carried the story. The group was able to get the names and phone numbers of many of the young Jews in the missionary's group, and they reached out to them and their parents to try to bring them back to Judaism.

But perhaps the biggest impact was on the young Yehudah Silver. The events lit a spark in him of the urgent need to save Jews. The spark caught in him and has fueled his life until today.

When the students were released from prison, they each received a copy of a *sefer* written by the Steipler Gaon, with a personal message of blessing and success.

"Any accomplishment I have had in my life has come from that *berachah*," Rabbi Silver said.

His Brother's Keeper

When two non-observant brothers visited the concentration camps of Poland during high school, the experience launched them each on spiritual journeys of discovery. However, it took them in completely different directions — one was inspired to become *frum*, while the other became so disenchanted that he left Judaism and became Christian. Their incredible story is one of passion, profound family love, and the deep commitment of two brothers to help each other throughout it all.

David and Jonny Linn grew up in a Conservative Jewish home in the Forest Hills section of Queens, New York. In the mid-1980s when he was in high school, David heard about a six-week trip through Poland and Israel under the auspices of the Conservative Judaism youth group United Synagogue Youth. The trip would spend one week touring the death camps of Poland and five weeks in Israel.

The Holocaust had always been a significant topic in the Linn house and in David's conscience. Their mother had survived the Holocaust in hiding, and had experienced many near-death experiences. Her grandparents, great aunts, and great uncles had all been killed.

When David first heard about the Holocaust trip, he jumped at the chance to attend and see first-hand the milieu of his mother's childhood.

One day, during a tour of a concentration camp, David and the other teenagers were given time by themselves in a bunk house to contemplate and absorb their experiences thus far. David used the time to think about his own religious life in comparison to the experiences of Jews in Europe before and during the Holocaust. The stark contrast was nearly as sobering as the sights in the concentration camp.

"I started thinking about the extent people went to during the Holocaust in order to cling to a mitzvah or to their Yiddishkeit," David said. "To me, it was a bit of an epiphany in my thought process — that maybe there was something more there. I felt that, at the very least, there was something I was missing out on in what I considered my Judaism. My Judaism was cultural; it was important — but not that important."

During the trip and upon his return to America, David reflected further on how Jews in the death camps had risked their lives to perform mitzvos, and he wondered why the Jews he knew in America lacked the same enthusiasm.

"I realized that Judaism is something that should be very serious, and if so, you don't just play with it and decide when you're in and when you're out," David said. It bothered David immensely to see Jews casually breaking Shabbos or being lax with the laws of *kashrus*.

David began buying or borrowing all the books he could find on Judaism and began growing in his observance. However his eagerness to learn and grow was constrained by his involvement in his synagogue and USY — he had served as president of the New York City division of USY and eventually became one of its international chairmen.

While in high school David met Sandy, who would eventually become his wife. She and her entire family had begun becoming *frum* a few years earlier. While David and Sandy were dating, he attended Shabbos dinner in their home each week. Having a traditional Friday night experience left a big impression on him. David grew more in his Yiddishkeit and soon began attending local Jewish classes. By the time he graduated high school he had become *shomer Shabbos*.

David attended college, followed by yeshivah in Eretz Yisrael. He then returned to America to attend law school. But before starting, he and Sandy got married.

Divergent Paths

One year after David's trip, Jonny attended the same program. The experience also launched him on a spiritual journey, but in directly the opposite direction.

As a child, Jonny yearned for a direct relationship with G-d, but he did not know how to achieve it. He could not find the answers in his Conservative synagogue.

"I considered G-d to be real. I desired to talk to G-d at crucial moments in my life and childhood, but people around me were squeamish and embarrassed to do so," Jonny remembers. "I wanted to talk to G-d, but I was angry that I had to go to Hebrew school. It didn't seem authentic, just a very academic venture. There were no values instilled about loving G-d, loving the Torah, doing mitzvos, or learning. It wasn't there."

Like his older brother, Jonny had high hopes for his trip to Poland but the experience left him feeling empty.

"I had always been led to believe that I had to marry a Jew because of what Hitler did. The Nazis were such a focus for the Conservative world. I was always getting the message that we have to be Jewish because of Hitler. I said maybe we have to be Jewish because of something else, maybe G-d, and the Torah," Jonny said.

Jonny was also disillusioned by the way the trip was run and by the response of the leaders to the sights they were seeing. The trip presented the Holocaust as a horrific event which had befallen the Jews, but without any religious or spiritual messages. Jonny was filled with questions and craved spiritual answers, but the trip did not provide them.

Disappointed by his teachers' inability to provide a religious response to the questions of the Holocaust, he decided to abandon the few mitzvos he was keeping.

During college Jonny further eschewed all connections to Judaism. He didn't even attend Yom Kippur services. He still felt spiritually empty and wanted answers, but had nowhere to turn. The questions and issues he had encountered in the concentration camps were still at the front of his mind, and he blindly grasped for any direction he could find.

"I was shaken up. I didn't have answers to the Holocaust," Jonny said. "I said, 'It's not a question I will find answers to in the circles I'm in now.' It was scary, but I was willing to walk away from Judaism. I was walking away from it to find the truth that resonated with me. What was my identity? It came from being in the camps, being freaked out by the camps."

Jonny felt in his heart that Judaism was true but he couldn't find the answers to his questions, so in college he began exploring other belief systems, from New Age to Eastern religions. He also formed a five-piece rock band in college called On Air, and following graduation he and the other musicians moved to Boulder, Colorado, in pursuit of a music career. But despite the excitement and minor fame it brought him, he did not feel fulfilled by the rock 'n' roll lifestyle and was still thirsty for truth.

It was there that he met a young non-Jewish woman named Lin, who was also on a quest for answers and the truth. Jonny and Lin shared the ideas they were learning and embarked together on a journey of discovery. Jonny was still searching for a religion that would give him a personal relationship with G-d. He had long ago rejected Conservative Judaism. He and Lin initially turned to New Age beliefs, but he flatly rejected them due to their denial of a single deity.

Instead, he and Lin turned to Christianity. In it Jonny found many of the answers he was pursuing and found it fulfilled his need for a direct relationship with G-d. Jonny converted to Christianity, and he and Lin got married. He became deeply involved in Christianity, and at one point he mailed a letter to his family members telling them of his newfound religious beliefs and encouraging them to convert as well. David showed the letter to his rabbi, who encouraged him to stay in touch with Jonny and to try to maintain a bond of love with him.

On Becoming an Uncle

Over the years David and Jonny were able to maintain a close connection despite their increasingly diverging religious beliefs. Jonny still looked up to his older brother David and admired his personality. Jonny recalled noticing positive changes in his brother ever since he became *frum* in high school.

"Something about him was settled. He was gaining a lot of

strength from whatever he was doing. I noticed that the kind of person he was really outshined most people I knew, and I really attributed that to him being religious," Jonny said.

Jonny's admiration for his older brother was enhanced when David became a father at age twenty-four. In Jonny's mind, the birth of David's first child solidified his spiritual growth and represented much of what he admired in his brother.

"I saw this person who didn't have any money, put himself through law school, married and had a child. I said this stuff is not easy. He's sincere that he's doing it because of the will of G-d. He really believes in what he's doing," Jonny said. "I saw there's nothing stronger than that."

Jonny put his music skills to use by becoming the choir director of his church. His band was still performing and was growing in popularity. When David's daughter was born, Jonny decided to put to music the feelings of admiration he had for his brother. He wrote a song called "Davey Pray," in which he implored his older brother to pray for him:

> *"Well, I don't understand, but I want you to know / If there's something you know that the rest of us don't / Davey pray for me, pray for me..."*

Jonny's band had been invited to perform live during a show on a local radio station, KBOL in Boulder, Colorado. The show's host asked the band to play the song "Davey Pray" and to explain its origins. In his introduction Jonny said he wrote the song to demonstrate that no matter the spiritual differences between him and his brother, their love for each other was unbreakable.

Jonny later described the song as one of the best he had ever written.

"It was not just a song I wrote for my brother, but my heart was in it. It pulled people in. The song had a magnetism to it," Jonny said.

Responding to the Call

David was also deeply touched by the song, and clearly saw in it his brother's Jewish spark trying to get out. He realized that through the song, Jonny was subconsciously begging for a lifeline and was asking David to help him out of his situation. David's rabbi put him in contact with Rabbi Tovia Singer, an expert in anti-missionary work who has helped thousands of estranged Jews escape from Christianity and other religions.

At the time, David and Rabbi Singer were both living in New York and Jonny was in Colorado. Due to the distance Rabbi Singer ruled out a face-to-face meeting, but suggested that David send Jonny some of his tapes which show the truths about Judaism and how missionaries intentionally misinterpret verses in Tanach to support their beliefs.

David called Jonny and asked if he would mind receiving an assortment of Rabbi Singer's tapes, and whether he would listen to them with an open mind. At first Jonny bristled at the idea, but seeing that David's intentions were pure and out of sincere love, he accepted.

"My brother said, 'You're not educated in the Jewish side of story, you never investigated the *frum* side of Torah. It's not what you grew up with,'" Jonny recalled. "He called me on my integrity and said you have to investigate this if you want to take it seriously."

Jonny accepted his brother's challenge and began listening to the tapes. At first he listened to the tapes together with his wife, but the ideas didn't sit well with her. So Jonny began taking long trips in his car, listening to the tapes and memorizing every word.

"The wisdom in the tapes overshadowed and obliterated every non-Jewish concept I had ever heard like a total eclipse. It blew everything away," Jonny said. "If this is true, it is my calling to find out more."

One day Jonny called David and sounded in distress.

"He sounded really shaken up. I thought he was in trouble," David said. "He said, 'Oh my gosh, I didn't know that Christianity had mistranslated a lot of this stuff.'"

Jonny realized he needed authentic knowledge of the Tanach so he asked David to send him a copy with the original Hebrew and an English translation. David sent him an ArtScroll Tanach which had recently been published for the first time. Jonny began pouring over it and compared it to the Christian teachings he had been hearing.

One day David received a phone call of a very different spirit from Jonny. This time Jonny sounded angry and accused the Jewish sources of lying.

David related this to Rabbi Singer, who said that Jonny's pastor or other people in his church or family had probably given him resistance to his new questions. Faced with this pressure, Jonny pushed back not at them, but at David.

"I thought that was the end. It was worth the shot, but it failed," David said.

Despite the news, David continued to keep the lines of communication open. Their father was observing from the sidelines and actually took Jonny's response as a positive message. He realized that at least Jonny had begun to internalize the ideas on the tapes.

The relationship between the two brothers became chilly for a while. A few months later, Jonny told David that he and his wife might be coming to New York for Thanksgiving. David asked him if he would be interested in meeting Rabbi Singer face-to-face, since he would be in the New York area. Jonny reluctantly agreed.

The Value of a Bag of Rugelach

Jonny and Lin arrived in New York for Thanksgiving, planning on returning to Colorado on Thursday night. At the time Rabbi Singer was traveling and would not be available to meet them during their short visit. David scrambled to find another way to make the best of the situation, and got in touch with a friend who had previously been involved in a Messianic Congregation and had exposed their techniques. Jonny met David's friend and heard about his experiences, but left unchanged.

Meanwhile, David was still valiantly trying to reach Rabbi Singer in the hopes that he would arrive back in New York before Jonny left. Their father convinced Jonny to stay for the weekend, but his wife returned to Colorado.

Finally, at 10:30 P.M. on Thursday night, David reached Rabbi Singer, who had just returned to New York. He said he would be willing to meet with Jonny that night. Jonny and David drove over an hour to Monsey directly to Rabbi Singer's office.

Rabbi Singer walked in to the meeting holding a bag of fresh pastries from a bakery.

"Jonathan," he said. "I have rugelach in this bag that alone are worth being Jewish for."

Jonny was shocked by Rabbi Singer's demeanor and knowledge. He told David that he had expected a hunched-back, aloof old rabbi, but Rabbi Singer was far from that. He was clean-shaven, funny, and approachable.

Rabbi Singer and Jonny spoke that night for two and a half hours. Jonny had already listened to all of Rabbi Singer's tapes so he was familiar with many of the sources. In their meeting Rabbi Singer got directly to the personal issues in Jonny's life, from the two brothers' childhood, Jonny's journey, and the Christian ideas he had been taught. Jonny was most affected by Rabbi Singer's debunking of the supposed miracles and other so-called evidence that Christianity used as proof of its validity.

"He showed me that there are miracles in all religions but it doesn't make them true. People are always claiming miracles, but G-d put them here as a test," Johnny said. "That was powerful to me. It was the last thing I was holding on to."

Rabbi Singer said of the thousands of Jews he has helped, Jonny stood out as someone truly driven by an intellectual quest for honesty.

"He is a very special young man. He wanted to know the truth. When he saw the *emes*, the emotional element would not sway him," Rabbi Singer said.

As the meeting came to a close, Rabbi Singer told Jonny a lesson from the life of Eliyahu HaNavi about the importance of taking decisive action immediately.

"Tonight you saw things that were true. It has changed your thinking. Tomorrow you have to make sure to hold on, not to go back to your old ways of thinking."

The Light of Shabbos

Jonny spent that Shabbos with David and his family. He was on a spiritual high from his meeting with Rabbi Singer. He tried to absorb each element of Shabbos, asking questions on every topic from challah to mikveh.

After Shabbos, Jonny returned to Colorado. Rabbi Singer had suggested two particular tapes he should listen to on the flight to solidify the growth he had achieved during the weekend. Rabbi Singer also cautioned David about the influences Jonny would face back at home from his church and family, who would be working on overdrive to reel Jonny back in.

Rabbi Singer suggested getting Jonny and his wife to attend an upcoming Gateways Seminar weekend. At the time, Rabbi Singer was a speaker at every Gateways event and he said the weekend would be a perfect way for Jonny to continue his growth. It would also provide a forum for his wife to be exposed to Judaism and to be able to ask Rabbi Singer any questions she had.

Though he suggested the idea, Rabbi Singer did not expect it to be accepted because the next Gateways Seminar was over the Xmas weekend. He doubted whether Lin would want to miss the holiday with her family. David decided to mention it just in case. Jonny jumped at the idea.

"I told my wife, 'I'm going to Gateways. I'm going to start studying this. I can't accept belief in Mr. J. any longer.' She said, 'Okay, I'm going to come with you,'" Jonny recalled. "She inspired me to get involved in searching for more wisdom in life."

David raised money from some friends to pay for the tickets for Jonny and Lin to fly in for the weekend. The Gateway classes opened their eyes to a world of truth and real spirituality that they had never imagined.

"We were floored. What we were stumbling on was not just information. This was a whole different way of thinking. A whole different way to live," Jonny said. "We're very intellectual, very intense people. ... Once we saw the wisdom of the Torah on many levels, it was infinitely greater than anything we had ever seen before. Everything else was laughable, a joke."

David and his wife went to meet Jonny and Lin in the hotel for an event held after Shabbos. They could already see the changes occurring inside them.

"My brother came out of his room and was beaming," David said. "When we saw his wife, she was happier than I had ever seen her."

A New Life

Jonny and Lin returned home from the weekend committed to their new Jewish lifestyle. Even before flying back to Colorado, they made the critical decision that they could no longer stay there. They needed to move to an established Jewish community where they could learn more and grow together.

The church leaders redoubled their efforts to convince the couple to stay, but Jonny and Lin rebuffed their attempts.

Jonny and Lin quickly packed up their life in Colorado and moved to Passaic, in part to be closer to David's family. They attended more Gateways events. Lin eventually converted and the couple remarried in a proper Jewish ceremony. They now go by the names Chaim and Chaya Nechama.

Chaim and David's father passed away in 2000. After his passing, David revealed that their father had helped to fund the Gateways events as a way to bring Chaim back to Judaism. Their mother has since become *shomer Shabbos* as well.

"They wanted to build me up because they saw I would take the ball and run with it," Chaim said. "I saw dramatic, drastic life changes happen as I began to learn Torah. My life was never that good."

Chaim looks back now on the events that brought him to where he and his family are today, and the challenges of incorporating the new messages into his life.

"G-d's purpose wasn't just for me to find the truth and move on, but to live with it. To seek G-d out when He can be found," Chaim said. "The real challenge is dealing with my life now and bringing it under the auspices of the Torah."

Rabbi Singer says he meets with fifteen to twenty Jews a month like Chaim, either in person or over the phone. He said Chaim's story is typical. Many Jews enter Christianity because they're looking for meaning. They often have a desire to identify with Judaism and so are attracted to Christianity specifically because of its Jewish roots.

When they join the church, they often become steadfast followers of Christianity. Ironically, Rabbi Singer says it's easier to reach out to Jews such as these and bring them back to Judaism than those who have weaker attachments to Christianity.

"The vast majority of Jews who convert become religious fundamentalists because they believe in the Torah. It's easier to get them out because once they see how the church has manipulated the words of Tanach, it's like a theological crime scene. It just shatters them," Rabbi Singer said. "The more firm their beliefs are, it's like an eggshell. The whole thing falls apart."

Chaim still reflects on the irony that his journey back to Yiddishkeit was launched by the song "Davey Pray."

"There was no logical explanation to ask him to pray for me when I was sure one hundred percent that I didn't accept any of this stuff," Chaim said. "The song was thematic, that he should pray for me because he's religious; but it was really just a cry for help to somebody that I saw as a solid, shining example."

Though Chaim didn't know the real message of his song at the time — that he was looking for help — the words were clear to David. Thankfully David heard his brother's cries for help and helped to pull him out.

Taking Action

Rabbi Yitzchok Lowenbraun is the national director of the Association of Jewish Outreach Programs and has been involved in outreach and anti-missionary work for many years.

Once in the late 1970s, the local newspaper, *The Baltimore Sun*, carried an article about how a major Christian missionary group was planning a gigantic campaign to target Jews in the city that summer. At the time, Rabbi Lowenbraun was the Regional Director of NCSY. When he read the article, he immediately took action — he got the Baltimore Jewish Federation involved and organized a community-wide protest and call-to-action program.

Over four hundred people turned out for the event, which he ran with Rabbi Motty Berger, an expert in anti-missionary work.

As soon as the two rabbis began speaking, they detected that there were "plants" in the audience, two couples who had been sent by the Christian missionary group to challenge the event and stir up trouble. From their questions, it was clear that these couples knew too much to be regular event attendees.

"One of the tactics, if you have someone who is a plant, is you want to engage them as much as possible so they don't talk to anyone else. Motty went over and engaged them."

The end of the story? The two couples became *frum* and have since become involved with anti-missionary work themselves. Once they saw the truth of Judaism and the falsehoods that they had been hearing, they quickly realized the proper path for their own lives.

Following the rally, Rabbi Lowenbraun was able to receive funding from the Federation to start an anti-missionary organization called Yedid. One of the organization's goals was to train Jews in anti-missionary work.

To prepare materials for the program, Rabbi Lowenbraun needed copies of the New Testament, but he did not know where to find them. However, near his office was the Lederer Foundation, a missionary organization that translated Christian works into Yiddish.

"I knocked on the door and said, "I need some New Testaments." The old woman who answered was so very happy to give them to me!"

On another occasion, Rabbi Lowenbraun received a call from a Jewish man from York, Pennsylvania whose daughter Beth Simpson* had fallen into a Christian group. She was engaged to a Christian man attending the Messiah College, a local missionary university.

Rabbi Lowenbraun called Beth and invited her to come for Shabbos. She even brought along her fiancé.

Over Shabbos the couple spent one meal with the Lowenbrauns and the other with the Bergers. Rabbi Berger spoke for hours with them, trying to show them the light of Judaism and the mistakes they were making.

"Motty is much smarter than these guys. He really got through to them."

On Sunday morning, Rabbi Lowenbraun spoke to the couple again. He asked the fiancé a pointed question about Christianity and Judaism. The young man's answer revealed what he really felt about Jews — that all Jews are doomed for eternal damnation due to their beliefs.

Beth could not believe his words. She decided on the spot to break up with him.

"It's a pretty amazing story. It usually takes longer. But once she realized what they believe about Jews, it helped her to get out," Rabbi Lowenbraun said.

Before heading home to Pennsylvania, Beth came to bid farewell to the two rabbis in their office. She could not stop thanking them enough for having saved her.

As she was leaving, she stuck out her hand to shake Rabbi Lowenbraun's hand. Rabbi Berger jumped in and explained that they do not shake women's hands because of the rules of proper touching between the genders.

She said "Okay," thought for a second, and then proceeded to give Rabbi Lowenbraun a hug.

"It teaches you a lesson. You never know what to expect."

Trying Every Ism but Judaism

Enid Langbert is the model of hard work and success that America values: despite being divorced at a young age and having to raise her three young children on her own, she became a successful lawyer and rose through the system to eventually become a judge in New York City. However, discovering and returning to her Jewish roots was a more arduous journey.

Enid did not come from an observant background, but she always felt a longing for spirituality. She bought into the hippie movement of the 1960s and moved to a commune in upstate New York. It was based on the teachings of a guru named Gurdjiesf who tried to synthesize Eastern mythic traditions and make them accessible for Westerners.

She lived on the commune for twelve years. Already a lawyer, she was working on a messy divorce case during that time. One of the assets at issue was a metaphysics bookstore. Neither party wanted it so she bought it.

In the store, Enid discovered a set of tapes on Kabbalah by an Orthodox Rabbi. She listened to it and could not believe what she was hearing.

"I said, 'Oh my G-d, Gurdjiesf stole the whole thing from Kabbalah!'"

The tapes led her to question the beliefs of the commune and she eventually left it. She moved to Woodstock, New York where she joined a Reconstructionist synagogue that used many Eastern teachings. She felt at home. But after several years, she moved to New York City as her career progressed. She became an administrative law judge for the Taxi and Limousine Commission of the city of New York. Then, in her mid-fifties, she felt an empty hole of spirituality larger than she had ever felt before, and looked for something to fill it.

In Manhattan, someone recommended that perhaps she would find her spiritual connection in an Orthodox synagogue and suggested the Lincoln Square Synagogue. She went the following Shabbos morning. However, sitting in her seat, holding a prayer book half in a language she did not understand, she decided this was exactly what she was not looking for.

"It was my first venture into Orthodoxy and it was just impossible. You just sit there, and there was nothing. It was completely baffling, not an enjoyable experience at all," Enid said. "I had never been to a synagogue where they didn't pray in English, and where they did not pray the entire service aloud together."

However, while walking down the staircase on the way out of the synagogue, she happened to meet Rabbi Ephraim Buchwald, the director of the National Jewish Outreach Program. He introduced himself and said he ran a Jewish education program in the synagogue. She immediately sensed in him a fountain of truth and a possible source of answers to the spiritual questions she pursued. That chance meeting would change the rest of her life.

"It was one of those moments you remember. I looked in his eyes, someone introduced us, and I immediately said to myself, 'He is my teacher.' That's how my bond formed. He is just such an extraordinary person."

Enid joined Rabbi Buchwald's classes and began learning with him one-on-one. In particular they focused on learning the meaning and beauty of the mitzvos.

"Before that, essentially I thought ritual was meaningless. To me, once something became ritual it became lifeless," Enid said. "To turn that around, and see how beautiful ritual is and how embracing mitzvos are, was incredible!"

Enid recalls that the Eastern-based quasi-mystical teachings she had learned in her younger years were based on an egocentric doctrine, of nurturing the selfish needs of each individual. The desires of each person become their spiritual pursuit. Rabbi Buchwald showed her the fallacy of that perspective, and that true happiness in life is based on the selfless pursuit of higher goals. In short, Judaism was the exact opposite of what she had previously believed, and she embraced it.

"If I had to categorize the single key of what he gave me, it would be to realize that it's not about my will but His, and to really realize what that means."

Since her first encounter with Rabbi Buchwald on the steps, Enid has been on an express train to teach herself and her family about Torah-true Judaism.

"I didn't give religion to my children. Neither of my sons was bar-mitzvahed. It didn't have a role in my life then. ... It would be very terrible if my great-grandchildren were not Jewish. That's my job for the rest of my life, to bring it back to my children's and grandchildren's lives because I didn't give it to them earlier.

"For so many years nobody told me about it. It's so thrilling for me now. I'm just a junkie for Jewish learning. Give me a class and I'll go to it!"

Enid now realizes that her original attraction to the Eastern teachings had actually been fueled by the Jewish spark within her.

"It's like a 500-pound gorilla in the room. Judaism was the gorilla in my life. I kept bumping into it but I didn't know it was there. I remember when I studied philosophy, there was one group of Greek philosophers who read only one of Plato's dialogues over and over again. I was so struck by that concept of reading something over and over again. Fifty years later I realized that's what Jews do.

"Lots of things struck me, and later I realized they were Jewish. Always being the other, feeling that you're the stranger, never belonging exactly to the land. Different things that you feel, only later I realized I felt that way because I'm Jewish."

The verse cited earlier from *Devarim* said that during the time when we are exiled amongst the nations, "You will take it to your heart." The following verse then joyfully predicts, "And you will return unto Hashem, your G-d, and listen to His voice, according to everything that I command you today, you and your children, with all your heart and all your soul" (30:2).

The Abarbanel explains that a wave of *teshuvah* will precede the coming of the Mashiach. He explains that people will feel the *teshuvah* in their hearts, even though they will be unable to express it with their mouths. Then they and their children will begin to observe the mitzvos again and will respond to Hashem's call. They will feel a longing for the Torah.

That is the longing being felt today by so many of our Jewish brethren. They hear the call and they feel the need to return spiritually, but some of them stumble onto the wrong paths. Thankfully, with assistance from Hashem above and the work of many dedicated professionals and volunteers, they are able to eventually find their path home and respond correctly to Hashem's beckoning.

11 Calling Out to Hashem from the Depths

THE BA'AL SHEM TOV TAUGHT THAT A VOICE CRIES OUT from Har Sinai everyday, calling people to return to Hashem's Torah. Many people don't hear it at all. But everyday there are scores of Jews who do hear the call, and they follow it to return to Hashem and become observant.

Sometimes the impetuses are challenges, or even tragedies. At other times they are disasters which are averted at the last minute. The events can shake a person awake and inspire him to change immediately, or they can lead to transformation only years later. But once people see the Hand of Hashem even within the darkness, they realize just how much Hashem loves them. This awareness inspires them to return to Him.

Counting His Blessings

AKIVA FRANKEL* GREW up in a marginally observant home in New York but was always fascinated by Jewish ritual. He attended Camp Ramah as a teenager. There, for the first time, he kept Shabbos and put on *tefillin* everyday. His soul felt alive. After the summer he tried to bring home some of the Jewish rituals he had observed, but found it difficult to do so.

He attended college in upstate New York and finally had the chance to explore more of his religion. He ate his meals in the university's kosher kitchen and sometimes attended events at the Chabad House. He was drawn by the Jewish cultural aspect, from matzah-ball soup to *zemiros*, but still resisted accepting Orthodoxy as a complete way of life.

As college progressed he worked his way toward his lifetime dream of becoming a doctor. Then, in his senior year as he was applying to medical schools, he suddenly found himself in the reverse position: he became a patient as he was diagnosed with cancer.

His entire life suddenly turned upside down. His carefully planned life goals were thrown off course by the news.

Akiva went for a lymph-node biopsy. When he awoke from anesthesia after the procedure, he was told there had been a mistake. The biopsy had found no sign of disease.

The proximity to his mortality shook him up to the core. Akiva immediately decided that he needed to do something different with his life.

"I had to change. I didn't know what to change, but I decided I had to do more. I just woke up saying there's more to life. Life is very short."

Akiva began growing religiously. By the time he had graduated college and headed off to medical school, he had given up eating non-kosher meat and had begun to wear tzitzis under his medical scrubs.

He was steadily growing in his religious observances. However, one additional event during his first year of medical school clinched his growth.

That day he was in the neuroanatomy lab, holding a human brain in his hands. Examining and contemplating the incredible capabilities that Hashem placed into the seemingly simple organ, he finalized his commitment to becoming observant.

"It was during Shevat, and very possibly on Tu B'Shevat, the time of awakening. I was holding this brain. I had been a biology and anthropology major in college and had been a big believer in evolution," Akiva said. "If you look at a brain quickly in passing, it's very non-descript and plain. It looks like a Jello mold. But in fact it is exceptionally complex. How anyone could logically say that it came out through random processes, I don't understand.

"All of a sudden, it clicked that it could not be random. It had to be something greater than human thought. I had already made major steps, but holding that brain pushed me over the edge."

Akiva's near-miss with his mistaken diagnosis, followed by his epiphany in the anatomy lab, led him to becoming a true servant of Hashem. Today as he works as a pediatrician dispensing medicine and wisdom, he knows Who the True Healer is.

The *Mishnah Berurah* 576:1 (1) says when a tragedy befalls a person, he should not view it casually, like it was a random coincidence. Rather he needs to know it was a message for him particularly, for him to analyze his actions and do *teshuvah*.

When Akiva woke up after the procedure, it was also a spiritual awakening, and he was able to use the event to begin to return to Hashem.

THE FIRE WITHIN HER

MY WIFE SHOSHANA'S religious journey began rather uneventfully, with several subtle experiences, until a single traumatic event flipped her entire life around. Through it she also learned the tremendous power of prayer and *emunah*.

Shoshana grew up in Queens, New York in a traditional Jewish household which had its own Jewish "traditions." Every Shabbos morning she and her father went to the local Conservative synagogue, and then to a Chinese restaurant to eat a pork lo mein lunch. Growing up she never saw the irony of her Saturday morning activities.

But with the mixed messages of the life she was living, something was already stirring inside Shoshana. The principal of her Conservative Hebrew school was *frum*, as were several teachers in the school. They often shared stories of their religious observance, though they did not openly advocate a particular doctrine. Shoshana loved hearing about their experiences.

When she was thirteen and a religious teacher in the Hebrew School invited the class to her house for Shabbos, Shoshana jumped at the chance. She was astonished when she arrived and saw that she alone had taken the teacher up on her offer. It turned out to be a memorable experience.

"It was me with this single twenty-year-old teacher and her parents. It was beautiful, the food was delicious," Shoshana said. "It looked like a Thanksgiving day meal."

Shoshana's own parents worked long hours, so eating meals together was a rarity. But this first Shabbos showed Shoshana that she could have the same type of home.

"I yearned to sit down with a family," Shoshana said. "I always had a fascination with people who observed mitzvos."

With these positive experiences, a desire began burning inside Shoshana to connect to religious people and to become part of their universe. Growing up she lived near the religious community of Kew Gardens Hills. Whenever her parents needed a bar mitzvah present or other piece of Judaica, they would go to Main Street, the primary shopping district of the community. Shoshana always tagged along.

"Whenever I went to Main Street, I would dress up. I'd put

on a long skirt, sweater, long sleeves. It would be August and I'd be wearing a turtleneck! People were probably looking at me thinking this girl is absolutely crazy. I was trying to fit in and to be as modest as possible but I didn't know you could be cool and modest."

Then came the accident.

One rainy Sunday, Shoshana and her parents were driving home from their weekend house in Vermont. They stopped at a roadside restaurant so her mother Elaine could make a call on a payphone. As Elaine was about to cross the street to get back into the car, a drunk driver took a curve too fast, jumped the curb and slammed directly into her. Elaine's lifeless, broken body was thrown fifteen feet.

Shoshana and her father ran from the car to Elaine's mangled frame. When Shoshana saw her mother's distorted, inert body, she said the only prayer she remembered from Hebrew school — the Shema. She also made a promise to G-d.

"I made a deal with G-d that if He saved her life, I would become more observant," Shoshana said.

G-d heard her prayers. Inside the restaurant at that very moment was a group of paramedics eating lunch. They immediately ran out and started treating Elaine before the ambulance arrived.

Elaine suffered twelve broken bones and brain trauma, and was in a coma for several days. She spent months in the hospital. It was a long, multi-year uphill battle to a full recovery.

For Shoshana, the commitment she made with G-d solidified her desire to grow in her observance, but where would she start? She didn't know how to be *frum*. So for the next few years, during high school, she started making whatever small changes she knew about, such as using two sets of dishes at home.

Things picked up in college. As the rabbis teach, "In the way a man wants to go, Heaven helps him" (*Chullin* 7b). On her first day at the University of Michigan, Shoshana met a girl who would take the spark inside her and set her shooting off in the right direction.

Naomi Brenner lived across the hall from Shoshana. She was Orthodox and had grown up in Ann Arbor, a town surrounding the University. On Shoshana's first Shabbos in college, Naomi invited Shoshana to go with her to the local Orthodox services on campus, and to her family's house for Shabbos lunch.

From then on, Shoshana spent every Shabbos and holiday either at Naomi's house or at one of the other Orthodox families near campus. "I always cherished how families would take time to sit down and spend time with each other. The food was always delicious no matter where I went. It always had a special taste on Shabbos."

Shoshana began devouring Jewish books and taking religious courses, and after four years was solidly on the path to becoming an observant Jew.

Her mother's accident from years earlier had left another mark on Shoshana. Watching as the paramedics worked on her mother's lifeless body, she vowed to find a way to help other people in similar situations, and decided to become a doctor.

Throughout college she worked hard to achieve that dream. She had a perfect record: a grade point average of 3.9 from a top ranked university, phenomenal grades in her premed studies, strong performance on her MCATs, as well as research and relevant work experience. She applied to thirty-eight medical schools, confident that she would have a wide selection of choices.

Shoshana was rejected from every school.

At the last minute she applied to a couple of overseas programs, and in the end was accepted into three programs, all of which happened to be in Israel. She figured that G-d wanted her to be there, and it proved to be the ideal place to cement her religious commitment.

A few weeks before she left, Shoshana and I met and we

immediately knew that we each had found our *bashert*. I had also become observant during college and wanted to go to learn in yeshivah in Israel after graduation. Shoshana's imminent departure was a perfect excuse to go.

G-d sent one more messenger for Shoshana after she arrived in Israel. During orientation, Shoshana met Michelle Weissman, from New York, who was *frum* from birth and would eventually become her roommate and inseparable friend and guide. Until that point, almost everything Shoshana knew about living a Jewish life she had learned from books. Living with Michelle brought it down to the practical, everyday level.

When they first moved into their apartment and Michelle made the counters kosher, Shoshana was blown away.

"I remember her taking a pot of boiling water and throwing it on the counters. I thought she was crazy. But I soon learned that's what you need to do," Shoshana said. "After a year of living with her it didn't seem like playing a role anymore. It seemed natural; it was very comfortable."

After we got married and Shoshana finished medical school, we moved back to Queens. Both of our sets of parents have continued to show support during our journey. Michelle invited us to go to her parents' home with her for our first Rosh Hashanah in America. From then on, we spent many of the Jewish holidays with the Weissman family.

Since the majority of our *teshuvah* journeys had been spent in college and Israel, we did not have connections with *frum* families or experience in the *frum* world of New York. Spending time with the Weissmans was thus a critical component of our becoming established in the *frum* world as a young family. It also gave us the chance to learn up-close about the running of a *frum* home and the practical halachos of Shabbos and Yom Tov.

The impact of such kindness on a *ba'al teshuvah* cannot be overstated. When a *ba'al teshuvah* is welcomed as part of a *frum* family, the experience gives them practical grounding in the life of the *frum* world.

The Torah portion of *Vayikra* begins with the words, "And He [G-d] called to Moshe." In the word "*Vayikra* — And He called," the last letter, *aleph*, is written untypically small. The eighteenth-century Chassidic leader Rabbi Menachem Nachum Twersky of Chernobyl in his *sefer Meor Einayim* writes that this is a hint to the heavenly spark that exists inside every Jew.

He says that this tiny spark calls to us to do *teshuvah* and to return to Hashem. The call starts out quiet, almost inaudible. But if someone hears it and responds, G-d embraces him with open arms, just as the second half of the verse says: "and Hashem spoke to him from the tent of meeting."

Shoshana's mother's accident, and the other early exposure that she had to Orthodoxy, planted that spark inside of her. As she followed her commitment to becoming religious, she fanned that spark, and it eventually grew into a brilliant light that is still guiding her forward on her life's journey.

Putting the Pieces Back Together

LIFE DOES NOT always turn out how we would like. Yet we know that even events that are difficult to handle and impossible to understand still come from Hashem.

And sometimes it is those very events which can inspire individuals, and even entire communities, to grow.

Norfolk, Virginia, was never known to be a bastion of Orthodox Judaism, but its port and the local U.S. Navy base have attracted scores of Jews to settle in the area over the years. However, even as Jews have come and gone over the years, there has always been a small Orthodox presence in the city.

Jeff (Efraim) Brooke grew up in Norfolk and was raised Conservative. He married Amy, who had grown up in a Jewish home in New York that was traditional but not observant. When she was nine years old, she and her family moved to Norfolk. After the couple wed, they decided to settle there.

One day after their children had grown up and moved out, Amy's parents were sitting at home flipping through channels on their television. They stumbled upon a televised class given by Rebbetzin Esther Jungreis *a"h*. They were mesmerized by her persona, her passion, and the stimulating content of the class she was teaching. They immediately called her New York-based Jewish outreach organization Hineni and ordered many of her tapes and books. Over the next few years, Jeff and Amy watched in disbelief as her parents became observant, literally before their eyes.

"We thought they were acting a little bit odd," Jeff said. "We were observing them in an interested but confused way."

During this time, Amy became pregnant with their first child. Jeff realized that they needed a more spiritual direction in their life to help guide them in properly raising their child.

Simultaneously Jeff's twenty-five-year-old brother experienced a relapse of the leukemia which had afflicted him during childhood. Every procedure was attempted, including a bone-marrow donation from their mother. Sadly, all of the efforts were to no avail. He passed away just a few months after his relapse.

"Putting the two together — having any kind of loss makes one think about his place in the cosmos, and having a child, makes you think about where you are and where you're going. It was a time of spiritual searching," Jeff said.

For the week following his brother's death, Jeff sat *shivah* with his parents in their house. He was grappling for answers that no one had, and the atmosphere of the *shivah* house did not help.

"*Shivah* in a non-observant Jewish home can be disconcerting. People don't know what to say or how to behave," Jeff noted. "It's bad enough when an older person dies, but it's horrendous when it's a young person."

At the back of his parents' house was a den, and Jeff would steal away there during *shivah* to escape the cacophony of visitors in the front sitting area. On one of the early nights of *shivah*, he was joined by Rabbi Shlomo Goder, a twenty-three-year-old rabbi who had recently arrived from Monsey, New York.

Rabbi Goder moved to Norfolk to officially become the Rabbi of the small local Orthodox shul, the B'nai Israel Congregation, but his main goal was to create a turnaround in the Jewish community. He had brought with him three other *frum* families, who together were planning to learn with local residents, and would be offering Jewish classes, Shabbatons, and NCSY events.

On nearly every night of *shivah*, Jeff was joined in the back room by Rabbi Goder and at least one of the other men who had arrived with him. They spoke to him about the Jewish perspective of death and also gave him an opportunity to share his feelings.

Jeff was incredibly impressed — the group had just moved to town and Jeff had barely met them, and yet here they were going out of their way to show their care and concern to a Jewish family simply because they were fellow Jews. For Jeff, the presence of the religious Jews in the *shivah* house also provided a much-needed grounding and perspective.

"They were not working me over, but were sincerely concerned about our family. We spent a lot of time talking about life and death," Jeff said. "In retrospect I couldn't tell you one [specific] thing we talked about. But it was just the fact that someone would care enough to come and be there."

Following *shivah*, one of the men invited Jeff and Amy to their house for Shabbos. They loved the experience. They began to see the religious lifestyle as something truly beautiful and meaningful.

They soon got involved in the local Orthodox synagogue, which just happened to be located near their house. They received many more Shabbos invitations and made friends in the community.

Jeff began learning one-on-one with one of the men and loved it. Through their new experiences with Rabbi Goder and other religious families, Jeff and Amy began to understand and appreciate what had attracted her parents to become observant over the previous few years.

Jeff's learning also helped him to realize something else that he had sorely misunderstood about Judaism. He had always felt that there had to be a spiritual side to life. He just didn't know how to find it and never thought that Judaism had the answers.

"I always had sort of a feeling, of being very spiritually unsatisfied. But I was never able to pinpoint it. I thought Orthodox Judaism was not for me. I never explored other religions, but I just thought it was a gap in my life and that's what it was meant to be," Jeff explained. "But when I came in contact with something authentic, to know that my own religion is the source of something so true and spiritual, it was an awakening."

Over time Jeff, Amy and their three children (a daughter and twin boys) became observant. Jeff's brother and sister-in-law also became *frum*, in great part because of the sincere warmth of Rabbi Goder.

"[Rabbi Goder] was a brilliant guy, very charismatic. A great tennis player, a big *talmid chacham*. He was about as black hat as they come, but without being in your face and offensive. He didn't yield on anything, but would go out and play a set of tennis with you or talk in a nice conversational way," Jeff said.

The Brookes were not the only people affected by Rabbi Goder. In a short time he caused a sea change in the community, as people began connecting to their Judaism. His down-to-earth nature and ability to relate to everyone he met made people feel comfortable to embrace Judaism.

A leading member of the community said the one thing that most inspired him to become observant: he told him that Rabbi Goder was the best short stop he had had ever seen. To meet a rabbi who was learned, approachable, and fun to be around shattered all of his preconceptions of Orthodox Judaism.

Unfortunately, the community was about to face a tragedy of its own. Just as suddenly as he had arrived, Rabbi Goder was taken from the community. Three years after moving to Norfolk, Rabbi Goder became tragically ill and passed away at age twenty-six from the same disease that had taken Jeff's brother.

Upon visiting the *shivah* house, Jeff received a first-hand tutorial in proper Jewish mourning traditions.

"His *shivah* was one of the first *frum shivah*s I had been to. I saw how it was supposed to be."

Rabbi Goder's death came at such a critical stage of growth for the community and for many local families. He had inspired many people, but they were still only taking their first tottering steps toward *frumkeit*.

One would have expected that his death would lead people to question religion and would therefore stunt the nascent development of the community; but in reality, however, it had exactly the opposite impact.

"It was a huge tragedy in the community. It's hard to say what the loss of a *tzaddik* is," Brooke said. "Thank G-d things rebounded quickly. It was tough, but it had a profound impact on everyone."

Seeing how Rabbi Goder and his family responded to his illness taught people deep lessons about emunah. They saw how the family never stopped thanking Hashem and never questioned the decree. Even after his death, the composure showed by Rebbetzin Goder gave other people strength.

"Talk about G-d working in mysterious ways. I think that this was one of the turning points in the growth of the *frum* community here," said Rabbi Aryeh Gibber, who arrived in 2001 to work in Jewish outreach and education. He arrived several years after Rabbi Goder had passed away, but heard countless times about the incredible influence that Rabbi Goder's life and death had on people.

"We can't even begin to try to understand why something happens, but sometimes we see the results of something. That whole period of time had a tremendous impact on people here — the way he handled the situation, the way his family dealt with it. It brought a number of people closer to him and to Yiddishkeit.

"I understand he had a very magnetic personality. He was young, enthusiastic, and engaging. His wife was also very talented. People still talk about him as if it was three years ago, not twenty. I've heard people talk about how they were inspired by him, how he gave *chizuk* to others instead of taking it, how his wife was a pillar of strength. A number of people said they were taken by how well the couple dealt with something very difficult," Rabbi Gibber said.

Rabbi Moshe Feinstein *zt"l* said that sometimes Hashem takes a *tzaddik* away from this world because it is only then that people take proper stock of their lives. In Norfolk, Rabbi Goder's death had an impact on the entire town, forcing everyone to examine their lives and decide where they wanted to be going.

Since those events, the entire Jewish community of Norfolk has been growing. Another engaging rabbi took over the shul and was able to keep up the momentum and draw people to further growth.

Sometimes a fire will spread swiftly through a forest, burning thousands of trees into nothing but ash and char. But from the fire, new seedlings will sprout to produce a gigantic new forest. The inexperienced eye marvels at the miracles involved — how a tiny seed can produce a new tree hundreds of feet tall, and how the seeming destructive strength of the fire was the very power necessary to release the inner delicate seed from its hard outer core.

So too, the passing of Jeff's brother and Rabbi Goder caused tremendous grief and sorrow to those who knew them, but their deaths succeeded in lighting flames in countless Jewish souls.

Looking for His Lost Smile

For former Saturday Night Live cast member and stand-up comic Marc Weiner, becoming observant gave new meaning to his act and helped him find his smile when tragedy struck.

Marc describes his childhood as, "a weak Jewish upbringing. I had a surprise bar mitzvah."

After dropping out of college, Marc worked on a sailboat, where he found his voice and a captive audience entertaining the kids on board with a medley of juggling and comedy. Later he became a street performer on the streets of New York City. In 1980, he auditioned for Saturday Night Live alongside his homemade puppet Rocko Weineretto. He was hired in February for the season, and got the chance to work with well-known actors such as Joe Piscopo and Eddie Murphy.

Though he was a member of the SNL cast for only that season and one show during the following year, he was able to use the experience as a springboard into a successful comedy club routine. He crisscrossed the country on his newfound name recognition.

He was at the height of his career and his life. One would think he would feel like his life was perfect, but he felt like something was missing.

"Life seemed kind of empty. I had no spirituality. I realized that if I was the last Jew alive and someone asked me about Judaism, I couldn't tell them anything," Marc said. "While I was on the plane traveling to one of my shows I remember thinking, 'Is this what I am meant to do with my life? Comedy and puppetry? That's all?'"

So Marc began learning about Judaism. He began reading books and attending classes.

Next he began looking for a synagogue to attend whenever he was home in Manhattan. He stumbled upon the Lincoln Square Synagogue, known for its Beginner's Minyan led by Rabbi

Ephraim Buchwald. He began attending every week and went to local families for Shabbos and Yom Tov meals. Even though many of the prayers and practices were foreign to him, he soon felt at home. He felt the nagging emptiness inside of him becoming filled up. He found a community of people similar to him, looking for answers and trying to grow spiritually.

The experience also provided a plethora of new material for his stand-up comedy performances. He even developed a new routine, which he still performs for Jewish groups, based on his first time attending synagogue. A segment of that routine:

This guy said to me at shul, "Do you want to come to me for Shabbos dinner?" I said, "Great, what night would be good?"

...Later that night sitting around the table, Mr. Schwartz picked up a glass of wine and began reciting Hebrew words. I have no idea of what's going on here, I just see it's Hebrew. He finishes, and then the next guy picks up his glass and said more Hebrew words. I'm getting scared, what Hebrew words do I know?

Finally it came to me. I didn't know what to say. The only Hebrew words I remembered were those I learned for my bar mitzvah, so I started reciting my haftarah!"

But of much greater importance than just gaining new fodder for his routine, he realized that he was experiencing true, authentic Judaism that held the answers to his questions.

"It hit me that this is what I had been missing — this connection to G-d," Marc said. "I was getting the feeling of a sense of community. I was not alone anymore."

Marc began taking his new observances with him on the road. At first he continued his Friday night performances, but would walk back from the club to his hotel afterward. After one performance, the owner of the club was concerned about him walking back through a dangerous neighborhood, so he drove his car alongside him as he walked.

As Marc grew in his observance, he eventually gave up performing on Shabbos altogether. Because he saw the truth of Judaism and the degree to which it enhanced his life, it was easy to give up on his Friday night gigs.

"In *Bereishis* after G-d finished the creation on the sixth day, He called it '*Tov Me'od,*' very good. That's Shabbos. It doesn't get better than that. ... Shabbos is about total connection with G-d. We rest, eat — all of our needs are taken care of.

"I wanted to observe the Sabbath and I didn't care about any of the professional repercussions."

A typical night at a comedy club would see him performing for only twenty or thirty minutes, with plenty of time backstage to hang out with other comedians. Many of them were Jewish, and several had the same questions about their purpose in life. Marc would tell them about his journey and share with them some of the ideas he was learning.

One of his fellow comedians followed Marc's lead and also became *frum*. When he did so, the friend began asking his employers for a unique item in his contract. For every show, he asked that his payment include three specific volumes of Gemara, so that each of his three sons would have a complete set!

Marc committed to observing Shabbos in 1984 and married shortly thereafter.

Then tragedy struck. His wife gave birth to a son named Avi Shalom who was born with severe medical problems. Their life became one of unending hospital visits, consultations with specialists and plenty of prayers.

Sadly, Avi Shalom passed away before his fifth birthday.

Marc felt like the beauty and order of his life had crumbled. He grappled blindly for answers but felt like there were only questions. He had changed his whole life and given up on so much for Hashem, and could not understand how a loving G-d could have done this to him. His son's passing, coupled with employment problems, led him to have severe doubts about his observance.

"During those difficult times, my relationship with G-d was really strained. I was just trying to survive, both emotionally and financially. I didn't have a career. Here I was *shomer Shabbos* and no one was hiring me. I lost a son. I had a family to support. I was very angry at G-d."

With no money coming in and trying to start a new comedy show, Marc made the drastic decision to begin working on Shabbos again. He continued to keep kosher, but dropped virtually all of his other mitzvos and religious observances.

He and his wife began having marital strains as well and eventually divorced. He now felt even more empty and alone. He felt like he had truly hit rock-bottom.

"I couldn't stop blaming G-d," Marc said. "I was so confused about why these horrific things happen to innocent children."

Life continued this way. He could not comprehend why these events were happening. He was down — very down — and saw no way back up.

And yet after several years in the depths, something inside of him began to crave a new connection to Hashem. He started to put on tefillin again. Inside of him his emotions were a boiling turmoil, but at least externally he was trying to reach out to Hashem.

One night he sat down to recite the Shema. He had an epiphany that night — for the first time instead of blaming Hashem, he simply cried out to Him for help.

Marc's tears flowed. They were not tears of blame and anger. Instead they flowed from an inner desire to return to Hashem.

"I really went right back to G-d in the deepest, most profound cry for help, and G-d answered. He said, 'Open your heart to Me.'

"I restarted the process of opening my heart. I felt like G-d was asking me, 'Where is all that anger?' I went searching my heart for that anger, but I couldn't find it. It was gone.

"I said the Shema and cried. In the Shema, Hashem says: 'Love Me with all your heart, all your soul and all your resources.' As I was saying it, I felt like there was no more anger, just love at the deepest level."

That night reciting the Shema was a true turning point for Marc. He realized, despite all that he had endured, that Hashem still loved him. He knew that Hashem still desired a warm, close relationship with him.

"The Shema was my new connection with G-d, at my deepest moments of pain and suffering."

Marc slowly began rebuilding his life. He began observing Shabbos again and gradually returned to mitzvos observance.

Over time he learned new techniques on how to relate to sorrow and tragedies. Through them he was able to fully return to Hashem and eventually become completely *frum* again. He realized that he did not need to view the events as barriers to his relationship with Hashem, but could choose to have a positive connection with G-d despite them.

This change in perspective also helped him to find new ways to understand himself and those around him.

"I had always been stuck in my old paradigm of thinking that bad happens to good people as a form of punishment. Only once I found a new consciousness of life-affirming, new forms of communication, could I begin to reconnect fully," Marc explained. "Like Adam he had a choice. G-d said: You can connect to Me by not eating the fruit and then I'll take care of everything. When we connect with G-d, we're okay.

"By this paradigm shift, I could go back even to my Judaism. The way I see G-d, the Torah, and the mitzvos now are all about connecting, how to connect with G-d. By doing mitzvos and acts of kindness, it's all about choosing life.

"During the High Holidays, being inscribed in the Book of Life, means choosing life-affirming thoughts, language, and forms of communication. Then we can connect. Whether we're using them for G-d or toward yourself or others, it's the same."

Since rediscovering his connection with Hashem, Marc has tried to use his new awareness to help others. He developed a counseling and teaching tool called the Empathy Labyrinth which is based in part on Jewish teachings. He presents it to Jewish and non-Jewish groups to help other people deal with challenges and tragedies in their own lives.

"I dedicated my life once again and refined it, to how can I inspire and support people in connecting to G-d. That's what I was doing years ago as a comedian through humor," Marc explained. "But now I'm doing it by helping them grow and deal with challenges. The spiritual work is just so satisfying, to connect someone up to their Divine source, it's what it's all about."

Marc found a concrete way to turn the pain he had felt into a positive method to help others. In doing so, he has also been able to use his skills as an entertainer for a higher good.

"When people are stuck in judging, evaluating, and diagnosing others, it cuts off the connection between them," Marc said. "The Torah is all about life-affirming thoughts and actions. G-d is telling us how we can connect with Him. It's all about connections and about choosing life."

Since his early days long ago as a traveling comedian, Marc has been on a journey not only of discovering Hashem but of figuring out ways to connect to Him. And when setbacks and hurdles arose that could have thrown him off course, he was able to eventually get back on to his journey and to help others to do so as well.

In the fifth blessing of the Shemoneh Esreh prayer, entitled *Hashiveinu*, we ask Hashem to help us to do *teshuvah* and return to Him.

The *sefer Olas Tamid* said that when a person tries to change his previous actions and desires to return to his Creator, Hashem initially bestows on him a spirit of purity. However Hashem then hides His face in order to test the person, to measure his sincerity.

At this point it's up to the person to find his own path home and continue the process of getting closer to Him, even in the face of difficulties. In the words of the blessing, we beseech Hashem to cause us to return to Him. Even when difficulties arise to throw us off course, we beg Hashem to help us overcome them and return to Him out of love.

12 A Call Heard in the Most Unlikely Places

EVERY DAY, HASHEM'S VOICE CALLS OUT TO JEWS TO RE-turn to Him. The voice travels even to the most unlikely of locations, from the ends of the earth to deep under the ground.

OUT OF AFRICA

JULIE KAMINSKY'S JOURNEY to becoming observant was launched in one of the most improbable locations — and from a surprising cause. In the country of Guinea in West Africa, a group of religious Muslims inspired Julie to discover her own religion.

Julie grew up in a Conservative Jewish home. After college she wanted to find a unique experience that would allow her to help mankind in a foreign country, so she joined the Peace Corps.

She was supposed to be assigned to a program in Eastern Europe, but one month before graduation she received a phone call telling her that the assignment had fallen through. Would she instead consider going to Guinea? Julie's fluency in French would serve her well in Guinea, and she was offered the opportunity to teach English in a high school there. She agreed, and ten days after graduation she left for Africa. Among the items she took with her was an ArtScroll siddur, which she had received from her brother, who himself had become a bit more observant in college.

Julie's small village in Guinea was populated with devout Muslims. Julie was very open about her religion and wore a Jewish star around her neck. The town's residents treated her well, and actually looked up to her because they knew that many of their own religious beliefs had originated in Judaism.

"They thought I was amazing; Judaism — that's the basis of their religion. Everything comes from our religion. All they wanted to do was show off their knowledge. They told me, 'We know about Abraham and Moshe.' They loved it when they first saw my ArtScroll siddur — they would see the Hebrew and compare it to their knowledge of Arabic," Julie said.

The townspeople peppered Julie with many questions about Judaism and wanted to know how it compared to Islam. For example, they recited blessings after meals and prayed five times per day, ritually washing their hands, legs, and back each time. They wanted to know how Julie prayed, but she was at a loss to answer.

"There were all these parallels to stuff that I knew. It was so much part of their life that I felt left out since Judaism wasn't so much part of my life," Julie explained. "They related to me by the fact that I had a religion — they asked me, 'When do you pray? What do you say?' but I had trouble answering their questions."

Within the first week, Julie burned through all ten romance novels that she had brought with her. She then dove into her ArtScroll siddur, pouring over each page and every footnote to try to find answers to the questions she was receiving. The ideas she was reading began to penetrate her soul as well. In her ample free time, she began to compare her own upbringing of loose religious commitments to the fervent Muslim practices she was seeing around her and the genuine Jewish observances she was reading about in her siddur.

Julie also learned more about Shabbos from her ArtScroll siddur. She didn't know many of the rules, but tried to apply the few that she knew. She actually found it very easy to observe Shabbos in Africa, because there was no electricity and few distractions. However she was unable to observe the mitzvah of lighting Shabbos candles, because they melted almost as soon as she lit them due to the intense heat!

Julie's mother had sent her a Jewish calendar to help her keep track of the holidays. She had a friend who was also serving in Guinea for the Peace Corps. Her friend had become religious in college and though they lived one hundred miles apart (a six day's journey!), the two women tried to get together for most of the holidays. Julie's friend had built an *eruv* around her house to connect it to her outhouse. The two women even made makeshift Pesach Seders together with whatever items they could scrounge up. Watching her friend trying to observe Shabbos and the holidays in Africa gave Julie the strength to try to do the same.

After her year-and-a-half assignment ended, Julie packed up her few belongings and her newfound religious observance and moved back to America. She had left an impression on the people of the village, but their impact on her was far greater.

"Africa was the beginning, a start, an opening, a chance to look at something in a different way. I realized I could look at something unbiased and not judge people. It had the same effect on my Judaism. I could view it with an open mind, not how I was fed it in Hebrew school. I knew there was value in this for me and my life."

Living in Africa and seeing how people helped each other despite their abject poverty taught her about the importance of being part of a community. When she returned to the States, she moved to Atlanta, Georgia, and immediately searched for a Jewish community to join. A friend told her about a class given by a local Jewish educational organization, the Atlanta Scholars Kollel. Through the class she found her way to the Orthodox synagogue Congregation Beth Jacob.

The first time Julie walked into the local Orthodox neighborhood she was intimidated, but again her experiences in Africa helped ease her in. She told herself to imagine being in Africa again and to try to find common ground with the people she was meeting. In only a short time she felt at home as everyone wished her "Good Shabbos!" and welcomed her, embracing her in ways very much like she had felt in Guinea.

Julie learned one additional lesson from her time in Africa. While there, she had become sick with an illness that debilitated her at times. No one there could identify it or offer a remedy. Upon returning to America, she was diagnosed with lupus.

Being diagnosed with the disease taught her critical lessons about her absolute reliance on the kindness and support of Hashem, as well as the power of *tefillah*.

"Later when I learned *Modeh Ani* and the morning blessings, I thought back to that. I was seriously thankful that I could get out of bed and straighten up. After a year of being totally in pain physically, I could focus on not just feeling bad, but little things — today it didn't hurt to open my hand as much as yesterday, so thank G-d for that.

"When I started thinking that I needed to get sick with this horrible disease to appreciate feeling well and healthy, I realized that I need to appreciate what G-d gives me so He doesn't take it away. Sometimes you have to lose something to appreciate it."

Hakaras hatov means not only thanking Hashem for what He gives us, but the phrase literally means acknowledging the gifts that we have. Julie's experience in Africa and her battle with lupus have given her plenty to be thankful for.

"When I'm adding thank-yous at the end of Shemoneh Esreh,

I add thank-yous for letting me have enough to eat. I never appreciated that until in Africa and saw people without food. Even having a hospital to go to, a car that works," Julie said. "Life can really be a struggle every day for a lot of people in this world. To not have to struggle like that, you feel incredibly lucky. When you start bringing luck into an equation, that's a G-d thing. It's not something you have control over, but you can still be thankful."

Julie eventually wed and is currently raising her family in Atlanta. While the community is home to many people with stories of other dramatic returns to Judaism, Julie had one of the longest journeys, going the furthest both physically and spiritually to find her way back.

Finding G-d, Seventy-Five Feet Underground

DEEP IN THE bowels of the earth under the plains of North Dakota, Mike Bram soared to the spiritual heights of Judaism. He was discovering a brilliant new world, filled with life, beauty and a happiness that he had never known before. But he had to balance that excitement with the stark realization of his job — as a nuclear missile launch officer for the U.S. Air Force, he was sitting at the controls of fifty nuclear missiles that in an instant could bring unprecedented death and destruction to the world.

Mike served in that control room for twenty-four hour shifts, with little to do other than wait for launch orders that thankfully never came. In the back of his mind he was always aware of his potential to cause mass genocide, but he tried not to think about it. Instead he used his time to consider his own life, where it was heading, and what really mattered to him.

"A nuclear missile launch officer has the lowest retention rate in the Air Force. It's a high-stress job, with severe consequences for mistakes. There's no such thing as a good day. Either nothing happens or you make big mistakes — 'Hey, I killed eight million people today.'

"There was definitely an awareness of life and death, but most of us tried not to think about it. The Air Force actually didn't want us thinking about it.

"Things happen very fast. They want you to remain busy, not thinking about what you're doing when turning that key. They do make you see an air-force psychiatrist, but they don't ask you about morality or what you think about killing everyone in the world. Instead, they speak to you about claustrophobia."

Mike grew up in Reform Jewish home. He drove to synagogue every Friday night with his father ("I was the curly-haired kid who always slept in shul"), attended Pesach Seders, Jewish youth groups and Hebrew school. He attended the University of Minnesota, where he majored in astrophysics in the hopes of becoming an astronaut. It was there that his religious observance was first challenged, ironically by his evangelical Christian roommate.

"He and I became friends, and his friends became my friends. His friends were all evangelical Christians. I became their project. They thought G-d sent me to them, but really G-d sent them to me.

"They would ask me questions: How come it says [in the Old Testament]; 'Don't eat pork,' and you do? Why does it say: "Don't work on Shabbos,' and you do?" They were trying to show me that the Old Testament was no longer relevant, but it got me thinking that maybe I should do something. After a year and a half of almost constant badgering, I exploded. They stopped, but the ideas still festered in my head."

After Mike's junior year of college, he attended a friend's Labor Day Pig Roast. He looked at the whole pig skewered on a stick over the fire and thought it was the most unclean, most unkosher food he had ever seen in his life.

The next day Mike vowed to never again eat pork or any other forbidden foods.

Shortly afterward, Mike was in a sandwich shop on campus and ordered a sandwich piled high with bacon. Watching the worker preparing his meal, Mike suddenly remembered that he had stopped eating bacon!

"I had to walk up to counter like a schlemiel and say, 'I just remembered I don't eat bacon.'"

"You just remembered?" the server asked him.

"Yes."

After graduation in 1999, Mike joined the Air Force. His first assignment was at Vanenberg Air Force Base in California for training. He wanted to get in touch with his Jewish heritage, so he began wearing a *kippah* off and on, even though he still knew little about actual Jewish practice.

In November he received orders to go to Minot Air Force Base in North Dakota. Mike craved a Jewish community, but the closest was five hundred miles away. The Air Force at the time had only ten Jewish chaplains and none were stationed near Minot. However, Mike found out the Air Force had volunteer Jewish lay leader positions which allowed non-chaplains to perform religious services. Mike volunteered for the position and began arranging weekly Friday night services for the few Jews on the base and nearby town.

The following fall, the MacGuire Air Force Base in New Jersey hosted a conference for all the Air Force Jewish lay leaders. One day of the conference was spent in nearby Lakewood. Mike visited a Jewish book store and bought his first ArtScroll siddur and a translated *Kitzur Shulchan Aruch*.

He also met a Jewish chaplain who was stationed in New Jersey. Mike implored him to come to North Dakota where he could serve the local community, but the rabbi demurred, saying that for his family's needs, he had to stay in a more populated area. When Mike left New Jersey, the rabbi gave him a pile of books to take back with him. The two men kept in touch, and every week the chaplain sent him a list of new books to read.

During Mike's twenty-four hour shifts in the control room, he had only six hours of required work and so was left with plenty of time to devour the books. He slowly began taking on mitzvos. Hundreds of miles from any Jewish community, seventy-five feet underground, he tried to figure out on his own how to live as an observant Jew.

Whenever Mike was not assigned to work on Saturday, he tried to keep Shabbos as much as he had learned from his books. He tried taking on other mitzvos, but found it difficult to do so on his own.

Mike also began putting more of his free time into his lay leader role until it became more important than his official duties. He rewrote the siddur used at the local services and taught a Hebrew course. Despite the important work he knew he was doing for the few Jews in Minot, he longed to move away. He wanted to move to a *frum* community, try to find a wife, and go to yeshivah to really learn how to be *frum*.

One Friday night in synagogue, someone told Mike that he should become a chaplain.

"I totally blew it off," Mike said. "I thought, 'I'm not a Rabbi,' but the idea germinated in my head."

The more he thought about it, the idea of becoming a chaplain appealed to him. It seemed like a way to combine his two interests, of serving his country and helping other Jews.

Mike also began to realize that there was only so much he could learn from reading books on his own. If he truly wanted to learn how to live as an observant Jew, and explore the possibility of becoming a rabbi, he needed to spend time in yeshivah.

Mike decided to leave the Air Force early to attend yeshivah. He separated from the military in February 2003 at age twenty-six and arrived in Monsey thirteen days later to begin learning at Yeshivas Ohr Somayach.

The night he arrived in Monsey, the whole yeshivah had gone out to attend the *sheva berachos* of one of the rabbis. Mike went along. It was an eye-opening experience to what he thought life was like in a religious community.

"Everyone was eating like kings, the food was fantastic, and everyone was dressed up. It was my first impression — I thought [in Judaism] we eat like kings all the time and everyone gets dressed up every day!

"That first night in the yeshivah certainly beat any day in the mess hall back at the air-force base!"

Mike dove into his studies at Ohr Somayach and quickly progressed in the yeshivah. After nine months in Monsey he began working on his second goal and started to date. However, no one would even consider dating him. Every potential girl was scared away by the stress and travel that would be required as a chaplain's wife.

After six months without success, he finally realized that he had to give up his dream of the chaplaincy and find another occupation. With that, he continued to date but began considering professions outside the military chaplaincy world.

That week, he met his wife-to-be, Sara.

Sara was not scared away by Mike's previous military service — in fact she was enraptured by it. She was a military brat — she had grown up in the military as her own father had served in the U.S. Air Force for thirty-seven years. She had been raised in a home which was not religiously committed and had became *frum* in college.

At the time, Sara was living in Passaic. Friends of hers took her to Monsey for Shabbos to meet *shadchanim* and rabbis. Following

Shabbos, at a private *melaveh malkah* she met Rabbi Bookstein, an Ohr Somayach student living in Monsey.

Upon hearing that Sara's father had served in the Air Force, a light bulb went off in his head. He shouted to everyone in the room: "Does anyone have Mike Bram's phone number?"

No one had it, so Rabbi Bookstein drove over to the yeshivah and ran to Mike's dorm room.

"Mike, you want to get married?" he said.

"Sure, but why are you asking?"

Rabbi Bookstein told Mike about the woman he had just met, and called her from the room to set up the first date.

They first went out that Tuesday night, and by the sixth date they decided to wed.

"Rabbi Bookstein and his wife Rachel were very involved — they spoke to her throughout the process and were instrumental in helping us get married," Mike said. "We got engaged after six weeks. The Booksteins moved to California the next day. Their mission [of staying] in Monsey was to set us up and then leave."

Mike finished his studies at Ohr Somayach, both in Monsey and Yerushalayim. He was still planning on finding a career outside of the military, but one day he changed his mind. However, he had some trepidation about how to break the news to Sara.

"One day we were visiting my parents and I put on my uniform for fun just to show her. It struck me how much I missed wearing it."

He said to her, "We have to talk. I think I'm gonna want to go back [to the military]."

He assumed it would be a major battle, but without batting an eyelash, Sara said, "Okay."

In 2006, Mike entered the Air Force Reserve as a chaplain candidate. He received *semichah* from Ohr Somayach in 2008 and returned to active duty in the Air Force as a chaplain in June of that year. During his initial training, he even worked as an intern for the chaplain from New Jersey who had sent him his first reading material while he was in North Dakota.

"I enjoyed being in the Air Force, wearing a uniform, and serving my country. I'm a *yekke* so it fit my personality — the military is all about rules and regulations," Mike explained. "I didn't want to leave the Air Force. This was a way to combine these two aspects of my personality — being *frum* and being in the Air Force — by becoming a chaplain."

Chaplain Captain Michael D. Bram's military service has since taken him and his family around the world. He trained and served in Ohio and Washington. He had tours in Iraq and Afghanistan, and has been stationed, among other places, in Germany, Bahrain, Alaska, and in San Antonio, Texas with the 502nd Air Base Wing.

Rabbi Lord Immanuel Jakobovits, *zt"l*, the Chief Rabbi of the British Empire, would often meet with new couples before their weddings. He would quote the Torah's rule that a man in his first year of marriage is exempt from military service.

He would explain to them the Torah's rule is not just a personal obligation, but a national one: "By consolidating your marriage, this law teaches, you perform a greater service to your nation, to the survival of your people by having a stable home, than by joining the army and defending the people in a military battle. The ultimate security of our people lies in our homes. ...

"Happy homes come before powerful armies. Jewish homes are our principal fortifications, our first line of national defense."

Chaplain Bram is living that mantra — he knew that in order to properly serve the Jewish people (and his country), he needed to first go to yeshivah, learn to live as a Jew, and then build a strong home front. Only after doing all that could he go out and return to the military.

The Holy Potato

When Chabad rabbi Mendel Lifshitz and his wife Esther moved to Boise, Idaho, with the goal to build up the local Jewish community, they were greeted by fields upon fields of potatoes, but little else. But with plenty of help from Hashem, they were able to locate Jews hiding among the potato fields.

Idaho is not known as a hub of Jewish life. When the Lifshitzes arrived, the state had only a single synagogue, a Reform congregation, and virtually no other organized Jewish community resources. But that was exactly the environment that the Lifshitzes were looking for.

"I was working as a rabbi in Bal Harbour, Florida, when we got married. Esther and I decided we wanted to do something special and help other Yidden," Rabbi Lifshitz said. "I was doing *kiruv* work out there and helping them — I was very involved — but I realized as much as we were doing, we wanted to be in a place where we were really needed.

"In Florida or New York, rabbis are a dime a dozen. There are plenty of Jews that need to be reached out to, but we wanted to be in place where there's not much going on and our presence would be crucial. We started looking into different options through Chabad. The name Idaho came up. The first time it came up, we didn't know what to make of it. People hear Idaho and think potatoes, not Jews."

The Lifshitzes took an exploratory trip to Idaho to gauge whether they could make it work. They traveled the state, met with the few Jews they could find, and scoped out the Jewish resources. The low cost of living has attracted newcomers — and even major corporations — to the state over the last several years, and handfuls of Jews have been moving in. The Lifshitzes decided that Idaho was exactly what they were looking for. So immediately after Pesach, they packed up their bags and moved out west.

Soon after they arrived, Esther gave birth to a baby boy. Now they were faced with a brand-new challenge: they needed to invite ten Jews to the *bris milah* to make a minyan, but how could they go about finding them?

Their challenge was solved just in time, literally by a knock on the door. One morning shortly after the birth, Rabbi Lifshitz opened the door, to find the local mailman hand-delivering his mail. The Lifshitz's house had a mailbox by the street, but the mailman decided to bring the mail to the door to welcome the new family to Idaho.

The mailman stuck out his hand and introduced himself.

"I'm Hershel the mailman."

Rabbi Lifshitz was too shocked to answer.

"What? Your name is Hershel?" Rabbi Lifshitz finally stammered. "I'm Mendel. I wasn't expecting to find a Hershel in Idaho."

The mailman explained that he was originally from Long Island, New York. Other than knowing that his first name was Jewish, he had little connection to Judaism. He had grown up in a mixed-marriage home, and when he was eleven and his parents got divorced, he moved with his non-Jewish father to Idaho. After that he had no other Jewish connections until Rabbi Lifshitz arrived.

Rabbi Lifshitz points out the clear Hand of G-d present in the story. This wasn't Hershel's normal route; he was just filling in for another mail carrier who was on vacation that week. He happened to know of other Jews in the area, and he helped the Lifshitzes gather a minyan together.

The morning of the *bris milah* arrived, and the Lifshitzes were surrounded by an unexpected group of new Jewish friends. That group has grown significantly in the few years since then, and many people have taken on new mitzvos and other observances.

Other Jews have come across their paths in similarly unexpected ways. Rabbi Lifshitz was once shopping in a supermarket in Boise with his son. The two were speaking to each other in

Yiddish when a man approached them. He had grown up in a Jewish neighborhood in California and had moved to Idaho three years earlier. Having not heard Yiddish in years, his ears perked up when he heard them speaking.

Rabbi Lifshitz spoke with him and invited him for Shabbos dinner. The man took him up on his offer several weeks later.

"You never know what type of Yid a person is and what will inspire him," Rabbi Lifshitz said. "He was looking for chicken soup and *kneidlach*, but his *neshamah* was looking for a connection to Yiddishkeit."

One day, Rabbi Lifshitz walked into a local office to meet a Jewish man whom he had heard worked there. He gave his name to the receptionist and sat down in a chair to wait.

Suddenly the man burst out of his office with a look of horror on his face. When he heard that a rabbi had come to see him, he immediately assumed that there had been a death in his family. Why else would a rabbi be visiting him?

When Hashem promised Avraham that his children would become a great people, He told him first to count the stars in the sky (*Bereishis* 15:5). Once Avraham began counting, Hashem blessed him.

Rabbi Meir Shapiro explains that Avraham accepted upon himself an impossible mission. No person can possibly count all of the stars in the sky. But it was only when he accepted this task upon himself and began counting that Hashem blessed him.

Hashem waits to see if we have the strength and courage to do the near-impossible. Once he sees that we are prepared to do so, He steps in and gives us heavenly assistance to make it possible.

The Lifshitzes have seen that Divine guidance nearly every day in Idaho, repeatedly witnessing how Hashem has guided their work and has helped them to make contact with other Jews. They have brought many new Jewish resources to the state, from kosher food to Jewish education. Now when people think of Idaho, they don't just think of potatoes, but they think of Jews too!

A VERY UNLIKELY MESSENGER, IN A VERY UNLIKELY PLACE, WITH A VERY POWERFUL MESSAGE

ON AN ISLAND in northern Japan, at the foot of a low mountain chain, sits the tiny village of Yobito, Hokkaido. It's home to several hundred people who eke out a living as fishermen and farmers, and is centered around a small Buddhist temple. It's not the most common place for a Jew to find Hashem, but for Jason Katz*, the words of the local Buddhist priest sent him on a mission to return to his roots.

Jason grew up in the Detroit area and was very involved in his Reform synagogue, but it was a religious experience that lacked religious practice.

"There was no G-d involved. The only mention of G-d was in prayers, but otherwise nobody spoke about G-d," Jason said. "You just lived your life without Him."

Jason went to Japan as an exchange student during high school and lived in Yobito. His host father was Mitsuo Kiyosu, a forty-ninth generation Buddhist priest whose family traces its lineage back to the 1400s. He was the spiritual leader of the village and a source of wisdom and guidance to many.

Jason developed a close rapport with him. During high school and in the years following, he often spoke to the priest, drinking in his wisdom and advice for his own life.

"He was a tremendous example to me of two sterling qualities that I've never seen before in my life — patience and *chesed*," Jason said. "He is the center of the community. His wife is like a rebbetzin, doing everything for the community, always serving other people. I did not understand the word *chesed* until I became *frum*. I just saw him as very kind, giving."

Despite Jason's open-minded curiosity about the world and

various religions, the priest never pushed him toward any particular religious observance.

Years before, when he had first trained to become a priest, Mitsuo Kiyosu had studied with a Christian minister and a rabbi and thus had some understanding of each religion.

After college Jason moved to Japan again. He spent seven years there and frequently visited the Kiyosu family. After seven years he felt like he had to finally return to America, but he was unsure of a career path for himself. Before leaving, he decided to visit Mitsuo Kiyosu one final time for some well-needed advice.

After dinner, Jason sat alone with his host father at his kitchen table, sipping green tea. He mentioned his upcoming return to America and his uncertainty about a career path for himself. The priest deftly pierced through Jason's words and directed the conversation to the real issues that plagued him.

"My host father realized that I was searching not only for a job, but for spirituality," Jason said. Mitsuo Kiyosu described to Jason what he believed would happen to himself after death.

"When I die, there will be such-and-such spirit in the next world who will save me. I live this life with confidence because I know I will be saved when I die. On the other hand, a Christian person has their leader, who is only a bridge to the Jewish G-d. That's how he will be saved when he dies.

"But you, you are a Jew. You have a direct connection to the Jewish G-d. What more are you searching for?"

That comment opened Jason's eyes. He grew up hearing about G-d as the Judeo-Christian G-d, but he had only heard Christians ever speak about G-d. Mitsuo Kiyosu refuted this idea. He opened Jason's eyes to understand that it is not Christianity that has a direct connection to G-d, and not even his own Buddhism. It is only the Jewish people who have a direct conduit to G-d.

"He woke me up to the fact that I have a unique place in this world as a Jew and an intrinsic relationship to G-d," Jason said.

"G-d had been just a philosophical concept to me and was the last thing I was searching for."

While Jason didn't initially recognize it, something changed inside him that day.

"At that time I still knew virtually nothing about G-d, nothing about Torah, but my heart was different, like a seed was planted inside," Jason said.

Jason moved back to the States, and settled in Florida. A few months later a family friend recommended a class given by a local Chabad Rabbi. He soon began going each week. The class focused on the weekly Torah portion, in particular, and the Jewish perspective on life, in general. Jason was stunned by what he heard.

"It was so profound, so deep," Jason said. "My whole life I had been searching around the world. I had been to missionary camps and spoken to Buddhist priests and Hare Krishnas. I had no idea that there were such depths in Judaism."

Over the next two years the rabbi spoke often about G-d and His relationship to the Jewish people. Hearing these messages gave new life to that seed inside Jason. The class helped Jason acknowledge his personal connection to G-d, which gave him the reason to begin keeping mitzvos and delving into Jewish learning.

Jason eventually chose a career path for himself and became a physician. But that is only a side result of the story. The real story is how his quest for professional and personal direction led him to the ends of the earth to gain wisdom and a life direction from a most unlikely of sources.

In the beginning of the Torah portion of *Kedoshim*, Hashem commanded Moshe to speak to "*Kol Adas Bnei Yisrael* — all of the Jewish people" and say to them, "You shall be holy" (*Vayikra* 19:2).

The Alshich explains: Hashem told Moshe to speak to all of the Jewish people, to teach them that each and every person can become holy. Hashem is the G-d equally to all of the Jewish people, and each person is equally prepared to get close to Hashem.

Unlike other religions in which only certain designated "holy people" can become close to their deity, a key tenet of Judaism is that every person can reach the same level of holiness and closeness with Hashem. Every person can attach himself to Hashem through careful performance of the mitzvos and Torah study. Each person has his own potential, based on his individual personality, nature, and capabilities. However, we all possess an ability to become holy, each in our own ways.

Ironically, it was a Buddhist priest who taught that message to Jason. Mitsuo Kiyosu was the "holy man" of his village, living a sacred lifestyle while residents of the village continued in their daily, mundane lives. It was he who led Jason to realize that Judaism teaches the exact opposite path, that each and every person can become holy.

How Do You Say *Teshuvah* in Polish?

One of the most unexpected and inspiring story stories of *teshuvah* today is occurring in Poland. The Jewish community there is witnessing an epic story of rebirth, born out of the ashes of the Holocaust. Throughout the country, countless Poles who were raised as gentiles, some who were even taught as children to hate Jews, are coming to the startling recognition that they are actually Jewish. And despite the anti-Semitism that is still present throughout the country, Jews are not only reclaiming their identities but are even beginning to return to the religious lives of their forebears.

Today, several rabbis and Jewish organizations throughout Poland are helping people find information on their roots. American-born Rabbi Michael Schudrich has been working with Jews in

Poland since 1990 and has been the country's Chief Rabbi since 2004. He has been the "address" for thousands of Poles who suspect that their families had been Jewish.

"We cannot bring back the *korbanos* of the war. We have to memorialize and remember them and learn from their sacrifices. But there were also Jews that were lost to the Jewish people, not *al Kiddush Hashem*, but through children being given away or through people afraid to say they were Jewish. Those people can be brought back," Rabbi Schudrich said.

Take, for example, a man from Warsaw who now goes by the name Binyamin. The man grew up without knowledge of his family's roots. His mother had been orphaned during the war and all of her extended family had been killed. Growing up he repeatedly asked her about her family, but she refused to tell him anything.

Binyamin thought that the reason his mother was hiding her family identity was because they had been Nazis. This led him to begin researching his roots, and one day he found himself in the archives of Warsaw's Jewish community. When he described his quest, the archivist Yechiel Rosner told him that his family's name indicated either Jewish or non-Jewish Polish origins. The archivist told him to wait, and he would check in the organization's vast archives for further data that might be helpful.

Two hours later, Mr. Rosner returned with startling news — the archive had in its possession a birth certificate belonging to Binyamin's mother! Binyamin was astounded to discover that his mother had been born during the war to Jewish parents living in a ghetto, so not only was his mother's family not Nazis, but they were Jews!

Binyamin returned home and questioned his mother once more about her origins. Again, she refused to answer. Only when Binyamin showed her the copy of her own birth certificate did she finally break down and admit that she was Jewish.

"This is the secret of my life," she said. "Even your father doesn't know I am a Jew," she said. She begged Binyamin not to divulge the news to him.

So for the next two years Binyamin and his mother shared the secret and struggled with how to live secretly as Jews. And then suddenly one day, Binyamin's father revealed that he was Jewish as well! Binyamin eventually found his way to Torah observance, and he is now living as an Orthodox Jew in London.

The Jewish Priest

Three-and-a-half million Jews lived in Poland before World War II, and ninety percent were murdered during the Holocaust. After the war, as Jews staggered out of the concentration camps and returned to their hometowns, another two thousand were killed in pogroms perpetrated not by the Nazis, but by their former neighbors.

Rampant anti-Semitism continued after the war. Along with the iron hand of a Communist government that was no friend to the Jews, the few remaining Jews left Poland or remained and hid their identities out of fear for their lives. But unlike the Marranos of Spain who lived outwardly as Christians while trying to maintain Jewish rituals at home, the Jews of Poland lived as atheists or Roman Catholics and shed all Jewish observances and rituals. In fact, they hid their religion from everyone, including their own children.

"After the war, after the trauma from the Holocaust, people were terrified," said Rabbi Symcha Keller, who was born to Holocaust survivors in Lodz after the war and currently leads the community there. "If you see all your family disappear, if you saw with your own eyes Germans kill people like insects, after you survive you don't want to be Jewish. You want to be Polish, or a gentile, but not Jewish."

Rabbi Keller himself is a representative of the return of Polish Jews to their roots. He was born Krzysztof Skowronski, into a home in Lodz that was not observant. During his childhood there were two rabbis in Lodz who had survived the war and tried to rebuild the Jewish community in the city but they were constantly hounded by the Polish Communist Police. Keller studied with them in secret, and became a leader of the Jewish anti-Communist underground movement in the city.

Keller eventually left Poland to study in yeshivos in America and Israel. He returned to Lodz in 1993 to breathe new life into the Jewish community there. And in a perfect model of return, he eventually adopted the customs of the Alexander Chassidic dynasty, which had thousands of adherents in Lodz before the Holocaust.

Rabbi Keller relates that several years ago, a local practicing Catholic priest found out that he was Jewish! He began attending synagogue while continuing to perform his Catholic duties, torn about which religion to follow.

From Skinhead to Shochet

One of the most remarkable stories of return is that of a man named Pawel. He was raised in an observant Catholic family and joined a skinhead gang during high school. Gang members greeted each other with the raised right-hand Nazi salute and attacked blacks, gypsies, and foreigners, verbally and sometimes even physically. Pawel and his friends once toured the Auschwitz concentration camp, making jokes that the job the Nazis had done there was not sufficient.

Pawel's family was very unhappy with his involvement in the gang and his beliefs. They were all strong, believing Catholics, so the intensity of their reaction surprised him. His grandfather, especially, reacted angrily when Pawel went out on his anti-Semitic forays. Plus, his devoutly Catholic father seemed to prefer quoting the Old Testament to the New.

At age eighteen, Pawel married his Catholic high-school girlfriend, a fellow skinhead, and they had two children. Four years later Pawel's wife decided to investigate some nagging questions that she had about her family's background. She eventually found her maternal grandparents listed on a register of Warsaw Jews. On the list she also found Pawel's maternal grandparents!

The news shook Pawel. The Jews that he had always reviled were actually his own people!

Pawel's wife began learning the elements of Judaism and started to introduce certain Shabbos rituals and other observances into their homes. Pawel confronted his parents and although they acknowledged the truth, they reacted with unease. They even pressured Pawel to urge his wife to sweep her Judaism back under the rug. They had hidden their Judaism from their own children out of fear of anti-Semitism, and the religious life that Pawel's wife was beginning to explore represented a profound threat to them.

Pawel refused his parents' pressure, but at the same time he was not prepared to take the Jewish leap himself. He struggled, unsure of whether he wanted to embrace Judaism or not. But eventually he and his wife decided to live as Orthodox Jews. They studied with Rabbi Schudrich. Pawel now goes by the name Pinchas and has become a *shochet*. Now in his black hat and proud of his newfound identity, he has become an unlikely model of Polish Jewry's rebirth.

He has also been a victim of his own previous anti-Semitic behavior. On many occasions, young Poles have taunted him about his style of dress, and old Polish women have muttered obscenities at him on the street.

Pawel has three brothers; one is his twin. One Friday night, Pawel's twin tried calling him on his cell phone but could not reach him. So he went to the Warsaw synagogue to try to find him, but Pawel was not present. On that Friday night the synagogue was just one man short of a minyan. When Pawel's brother walked in, Rabbi Schudrich asked him if he could stay to be the tenth man. Incredibly, he said yes.

A Sudden New Identity

Rabbi Schudrich was once visited by a fifty-two-year-old man from Bialystok named Zbiszek. His mother had passed away four months earlier. Following the funeral, his mother's neighbors approached him and told him astonishing news: the woman who had raised him, whom he had called "mother" all his life, was not biologically related to him.

Zbiszek had been born Jewish. In 1942, as Jews throughout Poland were being killed, Zbiszek's parents, fearing that they might face the same fate, gave up their son to this woman. She took care of Zbiszek during the war, and when his parents did not return, she adopted him and raised him as her own son.

Under Nazi rule, any Pole caught hiding a Jew was killed. This woman knew the risks, which did not diminish even after the Nazis fell from power. In fact, after the war, she would have faced extreme unpleasantness, if not danger, if her Polish neighbors knew that her "son" was Jewish, so she hid the truth. Only a few very close neighbors knew his real identity, but she swore them to secrecy and they had dutifully remained silent for five decades. But now that she had passed away, they decided it was time to reveal the secret.

Zbiszek trembled when he first heard the news, totally confused about what to do. He was tormented — should he continue living his comfortable life as a Christian, as he had been raised, or should he embrace his newfound religion, of which he knew nothing? Did he owe it to his adoptive mother to follow her religion, or to his biological parents whom he did not remember?

Finally Zbiszek decided that he wanted to embrace his true religion and live proudly as a Jew. Unfortunately, he did not know how. So he found his way to Rabbi Schudrich, who calmed his fears and taught him the basics of Judaism. Zbiszek spent the next few years studying together with Rabbi Schudrich and attending classes. Today, he goes by the name Zecharyah Asher, and is an active member of the Polish Jewish community.

Completing His Grandfather's Work

Once, a twenty-six-year-old woman named Lydia came from Lublin to meet with Rabbi Schudrich and discuss documents she had discovered three years earlier that listed the names and Jewish religion of her maternal family. Since that bombshell, she had wrestled with the shock of her new identity. Before contacting Rabbi Schudrich, she had decided that she wanted to live her life as a Jew. She was now looking for the best road back home.

In Warsaw she learned the basics of Judaism and the meaning of her Jewish identity from Rabbi Schudrich. She returned to Lublin committed to trying to keep kosher, Shabbos and the holidays. Her non-Jewish husband of six years, Mirek, was very supportive.

Several months later, Mirek came to Warsaw to meet with Rabbi Schudrich and told the rabbi that he was so touched by the Jewish traditions that he wanted to convert. He said he also had another reason to convert. His grandfather had grown up in Lublin, and during the Holocaust he had saved a Jew who had escaped from the Majdanek concentration camp. Unfortunately, the Nazis had discovered the Jew and killed them both.

Now Mirek felt a need to complete the work that his grandfather had begun in saving a Jewish life. He, himself, would become a Jew. Mirek converted soon after his meeting with Rabbi Schudrich. Eventually, he and Lydia settled in Israel. In doing so, they followed the path of many other Jews in Poland — after becoming *frum*, many Jews have moved out of the country to Israel, England, or America for more spiritual growth and religious opportunities.

When a Jew returns to his roots in Poland, it is vastly different than a Jew doing so in America. It means subjecting himself to the anti-Semitism present throughout the country and placing himself within the sights of people who openly hate Jews. Returning to his roots under these conditions requires a clear recognition of the truth of Judaism and having strong faith in Hashem.

"Like Moshe in Egypt, taking Israel out of Egypt wasn't so hard," Rabbi Keller explained. "But to change the mentality of the Jewish nation was quite hard. It's the same story here. Despite being three or four generations after the war, many families still have little connection to Judaism."

Shortly before Hashem took the Jewish nation out of Egypt, He told Moshe to command them to place blood from a lamb on the doorposts of their houses. He called this a sign of their allegiance to Him, and it was in the merit of this action that He passed over their houses when He killed the Egyptian firstborns (*Shemos* 12:13).

The lamb was a deity to the Egyptians, so the Jews had a justifiable reason to be frightened when they were given this command. The *Mechilta* says that it was in the dual merit of this mitzvah, along with the mitzvah of circumcision that all Jewish males had observed shortly before this event, that they were redeemed from Egypt. Both actions required incredible strength and *mesiras nefesh*, and together they gave the Jews sufficient merit to be released.

Jews in Poland and similar places know that they face high risks if they return to their roots and outwardly proclaim their religious observance. But scores of Jews are doing so. And just as Hashem took the Jews out of Egypt only after we displayed our commitment to Him, He today rains His blessings and assistance on these contemporary Jewish heroes when they display similar loyalty to Him.

WHEN IN ROME...

FEW PLACES ON earth represent the downfall of Jerusalem and the continued exile of the Jewish people as much as the city of Rome. Its monuments and Colloseum portray the greatness of the Roman Empire, and its Arch of Titus stands as a stark commemoration of the destruction of the Beis HaMikdash. And so it is with sweet irony that the exalted city of Rome was the impetus for a young Jew to return to Judaism.

Growing up in Atlanta, Georgia, Asher Siegelman was surrounded by the values and culture of America. But he felt that the society was empty and he was disappointed by the ideals around him. He was especially frustrated by the lack of genuine role models he could follow.

"In my senior year of high school, I realized that I had never really found people I could look up to in a really serious way," Asher said. "I had always been looking for people who were not only brilliant, but good people. Good men who treated their wives well and had good families. It's not a model that's very prevalent in Western civilization."

The role models that America swoons over — the sports stars, actors, and politicians — left Asher wanting. With the media filled with the daily scandals of these seemingly perfect people, Asher groped in the darkness for a true example he could follow.

"When I was secular, I saw many people whom others looked up to as mentors, people who mistreated their wives, who were dishonest in business, and who were crooked individuals. People need someone to look up to, need someone to follow, someone to help them out in life," Asher said.

Like many Jews searching for answers, Asher traveled to Israel and spent a year studying at Hebrew University. He felt that Judaism could answer some of his questions, and so he immersed himself in his religion. He spent the year learning Hebrew and experiencing Jewish culture, practices, and holidays. He also deliberately searched for Jewish mentors and teachers.

He began finding role models throughout Yerushalayim, from simple Jews eking out an existence in the Old City to leaders of communities and yeshivas in other neighborhoods. These were all people steeped in their religion and whose moral beliefs pervaded their daily lives. He was impressed by their sensitivity, intelligence, and the deep respect they showed to others. These were the role models he had always craved.

The more that Asher got to know such people, the more he realized that their values and convictions came from their religious beliefs. Judaism is centered on moral and ethical standards and directs us to be "a light unto the nations." As the Talmud writes, "Any Torah sage whose interior is not like his exterior is not a Torah sage" (*Yoma* 72b). It's not enough to look pure and upright, but one must have these values at the core of his being.

Asher later began learning at Yeshivas Machon Shlomo in Yerushalayim. In the yeshivah and community he met many more brilliant, upstanding Jews.

One of the rabbis at Machon Shlomo left a particularly deep impression on him. Rabbi Meir Triebitz had attended the prestigious Juilliard School of Music before receiving a PhD in mathematical physics from Princeton University at a young age. He eventually found his way to Israel where he became a rabbi.

"A person like that, with that kind of brain, wouldn't be falling for nonsense," Asher said. "I met amazing people. People who had come from the secular world and were at the top in terms of brain power and were religious people, who became religious via free choice. I recognized that this was the best way to live."

Meeting brilliant, intellectually honest, and observant people such as Rabbi Triebitz helped Asher appreciate the beauty and eternal relevance of Judaism.

"I'm very fortunate to be Jewish and to have been able to access these individuals I have come to know. Many Jews never have the chance to meet these kinds of people," Asher explained. "It also ingrained in me a desire to hold myself to a higher standard. Hanging out with great people makes you better. You grow, you progress and you can mentor others when the time is right."

Asher decided he wanted to follow the religious lifestyle of these refined individuals. He began taking on mitzvos, but he felt himself unable to accept one particular mitzvah: tzitzis.

"It's one thing to put on a *kippah* and tefillin in the morning, or to keep Shabbos. But tzitzis, you're adding it to your clothing to wear it all the time. It makes you hotter, it's something you notice, it's always on you. That was something — it declared me as a very religious person. I felt like I wasn't ready for that move."

Asher has always prided himself on his intellectual honesty and the consistency of his ideals and actions. That is one of the reasons he was so strongly drawn to the religious role models he was meeting in Yerushalayim. And yet when he noticed a disconnect between his prayers and his actions regarding tzitzis, he was bothered by this inconsistency. Still, he felt like he was not yet prepared to take this on.

"I heard myself every morning and eventually every night reading the Krias Shema [which has a paragraph] about tzitzis. And yet I wasn't wearing them! I was giving myself a hard time — I called myself hypocritical because I didn't want to put them on, but I didn't want to give up praying.

"There's no way to do it slowly. A *kippah* or Shabbos, you can do it slowly. But tzitzis, you can't put on one corner at a time. For some reason I looked at it as a big deal."

During Hebrew University's spring break, Asher decided to go to Italy for three weeks. It was only there that he began noticing certain changes occurring in himself and particular religious issues that had begun to bother him. While in Israel he was surrounded by other Jews and had gotten used to eating primarily kosher food. Now in Italy he was on his own. He missed the company of fellow Jews. He also wasn't particular about eating kosher food there, and this fact bothered him.

In the heartland of the Catholic church, Asher spent much of his time visiting churches, cathedrals, and other religious sites. In those places, he felt even more alone.

"I thought, what am I doing? They were beautiful sights, but very much the antithesis of Judaism. I wanted to be there having a good time, but I also wanted to do the right thing."

Arriving back in Israel, Asher made two major changes. He decided he could no longer maintain his inconsistency, and so decided to identify himself as a religious Jew by beginning to wear tzitzis. Second, although much of the food he ate on campus was kosher, before his trip he had sometimes eaten non-kosher food prepared by his non-religious roommate. Upon returning to Israel, he decided to give that up as well.

"I really identify that moment as the turning point that really helped me identify myself as a religious person. Yes, I keep kosher. Yes, I'm a religious person."

With these experiences, Asher in time became fully observant. His parents and brother had separately become religious, and his brother even moved to Israel for awhile and studied with him at Machon Shlomo.

The Gemara (*Shabbos* 56b) documents the founding of the city of Rome, and said it was created specifically due to the sins of the Jewish people, and came into existence in order to eventually oppress them.

What a beautiful turnabout that the very city of Rome helped Asher return home.

---

13 Polishing Diamonds

SOMETIMES IT TAKES A JOURNEY HOME FOR A WOMAN TO realize just how special and liberating it is to be a *frum* female.

Unfortunately many people grow up with skewed messages and stereotypes of the role of women in the Jewish world. They are much like the person who could never appreciate the value of a diamond ring, thinking it was a mere rock, until one day a jeweler teaches him how to appraise it.

And yet when the people become exposed to the truly beautiful role of women in Judaism, those stereotypes are quickly shattered. They see the great respect showered on women in marriage and in Jewish history. They hear about the *shalom bayis* classes that men take before marriage to ingrain in them how to treat their wives as queens. They also learn about the sincere respect that Jewish women have for themselves, due to their G-d-given gifts and talents, and not based on their looks.

Real Women's Lib

ALLYSON KRAMER* WAS the definition of a liberated, flag-waving feminist. She was an accomplished, driven career-woman who felt like she had to prove her worth. Yet on the way she discovered a far more beautiful world that completely changed her view of herself and the universe.

Allyson grew up in a Reform household in Staten Island, New York. On the subway one day she met Bobby Hakim*, a handsome young Jewish man. They met briefly, and parted ways just as quickly.

Months later they happened to meet again at a party and hit it off. Bobby had grown up in a traditional Sephardic-Israeli background on Great Neck, Long Island. He had always attended an Orthodox synagogue and kept some practices at home but was overall non-observant. She smiled when she heard he was in dental school in the city, for she was also considering a career as a dentist.

She decided to apply to the same school, and was accepted! Allyson and Bobby met again soon after she began her studies there, dated for three months, and became engaged.

Bobby had already watched his siblings become observant — his sister had become a Lubavitcher and his brother had returned to the family's religious Sephardi roots. However he and Allyson were not drawn to any particular Jewish religious observances. They searched for a synagogue where they both felt comfortable but came up empty.

"For a time, at the beginning of our marriage, we would look for places to go. For him my synagogue was like a church. If I went to his dad's synagogue, I felt like I was in a Chinese temple — they all spoke Hebrew and I didn't understand it."

A friend suggested they try out the Aish HaTorah synagogue in Midtown, the local branch of the global outreach network. The synagogue turned out to be the perfect match for both of them. Bobby didn't know the particular laws or reasons for the mitzvos his family observed, so for him the educational component was captivating. For Allyson the shul provided an entirely different religious experience than she had ever experienced.

The Hakims went first for the High Holidays and then an occasional Shabbos. Families from the synagogue invited them for lunch and they loved it. They began attending more often and felt at home. Allyson later also went to Israel as part of an Aish HaTorah women's mission.

During this time, Allyson began feeling a discord between many of the goals and ideals emphasized in the larger world and those that she was seeing in the Torah world. In particular, Allyson had always felt caught up in the secular world's focus on a person's earning potential as the end-all-and-be-all. But she then found an alternative in the *frum* world's values and found them to be liberating.

"All of a sudden you have an epiphany. You're caught up in a certain world that's not meaningful for you. You look around and see people who are driven non-stop in terms of work," Allyson said.

In the *frum* world, where the emphasis is on family ties and on each individual having a responsibility to others, Allyson found a different direction for her own life.

"Could I work more, make more money? I could, but what's the price I would pay? It's a sense of maturity, not being part of the rat race, just focusing on what's important. I value relationships more than I value things. It's changed the way I practice dentistry. I have a relationship-based practice. I see fewer patients and spend more time with each. That's not typical."

Before becoming religious, Allyson also subscribed to the secular world's belief that a person's job defines his or her complete self-worth. She had always prided herself on her strength as an empowered woman to have a profitable career. However, in the *frum* world she saw other more substantial and nurturing roles for herself as an empowered Jewish woman.

"I'm about as feminist as can be — I'm a dentist. People are impressed, but so what? What does it mean? It's not an emphasis of the character of person. I found that in terms of feminism, the thing that doesn't fit well with me is the need for women to feel like they have to be like men to be equal. When I see women wear a tallis or female *kippahs*, or the need to read from the Torah… people feel like they have to make a statement or prove themselves. I don't have that need. I feel secure in who I am, that doesn't define me."

Allyson also realized that she had always misunderstood the differing roles of the genders in prayer and synagogue.

"In synagogue, women want to sit with their husbands. Why? If you go infrequently to shul, you think of it as theater — you have the cantor singing, you're not praying, you're observing. But if you're truly going to pray to G-d, why does it matter who you're sitting with?"

The more Allyson saw of Torah Judaism, the more she understood the true, lasting value of her life and her priorities. From a world of chasing the dollar and seeing each person only on a surface level, she instead found a world of true values of family, character development, and self-worth.

For Allyson, her journey into the *frum* world has been truly liberating.

A Message from a Mikveh on Masada

As an empowered young liberal woman in the 1970s, Yocheved (Eileen) Hande was driven to set her own path in life. But later as she learned about the beautiful roles of women in Judaism and the rules that apply to them, she found a higher calling and a significantly more refined direction for her life.

Eileen's earliest religious exposure came from her maternal

grandparents, the Beckensteins. When they immigrated to America in the early 1900's, they shed most of their religious beliefs but continued to perform select mitzvos. Eileen has fond memories of her grandmother lighting Shabbos candles. She also spent the major holidays with them, savoring the tastes of the Old World, which included homemade borscht and potato kugel.

She also worked for many years in the family's Lower East Side fabric store, "Samuel Beckenstein's." It was there for the first time that she met Chassidim who worked at the store or who patronized it, so she was exposed in a small way to their religious lifestyle. She recalls one day asking her father, who himself came from a non-observant background, why some of the salesmen left early each Friday afternoon. He said that they had to leave to prepare for Shabbos. It was the first time she had heard that a person could have such a high level of religious commitment that it could affect his professional life as well.

In her own life and career path, Eileen took pride in her physical accomplishments. She was a sportswoman and threw herself into jogging, yoga, and other physical pursuits. In college and graduate school she studied Physical Education and conducted research in motor learning psychology.

She also turned to meditation as away to find religious fulfillment. Through meditation she discovered a more spiritual space inside her, and she began to listen to the quiet voice of her soul. One day she felt that voice telling her to learn Torah and keep kosher, so she purchased a Hertz Chumash and began studying from it. She also embarked then on a year-long journey to becoming fully kosher.

In the late 1970s, she and her husband Bruce took a three-week trip to Israel. They joined a tour group and hit every tourist trap in the country, though they heard little of the religious side of Israel. One day, during a tour of Masada, Eileen noticed a series of steps that led into a cut-out area several feet below the level of the floor. She asked the tour guide what it was. He brusquely identified it as a mikveh.

"What's a mikveh?"

"A ritual bath where Jews can cleanse themselves spiritually."

"You can do that? That's so beautiful!"

A few days later Eileen and her husband were shopping in Meah Shearim, buying some Judaica items to bring home. An English-speaking Chassidic man walked over to them and started speaking to them. He asked where they were from, and asked them if they would be interested in seeing what a religious home looked like.

From her experience years earlier interacting with Chassidim, and always looking for new experiences to expand her knowledge of the world, Eileen said they would love to come.

"My husband didn't want to, but I thought, 'Wow! We're going to get inside a *frum* couple's home. I was so drawn to it. Even then I had a feeling of *kedushah*. I didn't know the word for it, but I so excited to go inside and see a *frum* family up-close. It wasn't just any couple, but a real, *frum* Meah Shearim family!"

Inside the apartment the man helped Bruce put on tefillin, one of the first times he had done so. His wife taught Eileen some of the rudiments of family purity, including the use of the mikveh.

"Can you imagine? It was straight from Hashem!"

From that experience, Eileen began observing the rules of family purity. She felt they were a way to connect to G-d.

"Until then I always knew that I was missing something, but I didn't know what it was."

Upon returning to America, Eileen continued meditating and learning Torah on her own, praying to Hashem to send her the teachers that could guide her growth.

A real turning point in her life came when she and Bruce were invited to a meal on the last day of Pesach at the home of a rabbi who had been close to her grandparents. In that house she saw a model of the home she wanted to create for herself.

"I recall walking into their home and seeing a sea of Yom Tov candle lights. They probably had forty candles! They had a long dining-room table with the finest linen, crystal and silver. I looked at it and felt at peace in their home."

At the end of the evening she turned to her husband and said, "I want 'this' for our family!"

Years later as she thought back to that Pesach meal, Eileen finally realized what the "this" was. She said she had felt the presence of Hashem, and the peace and holiness of the home. She desired the same for their family as well.

Sometime later the Handes moved to Roslyn, Long Island. Still on a quest for spirituality, Eileen stumbled upon the local Center for Jewish Meditation. It had been established and sanctioned by the Chabad Rebbe. He had realized that many Jews were searching for spirituality but were being led to incorrect sources, so he encouraged the creation of such centers to provide a proper direction. The center taught the fundamentals of Jewish Meditation and the importance of living a more relaxed spiritual life.

The center was run by a local couple, and two Chabad rabbis came frequently to teach classes. They taught about Judaism and the spiritual relevancy of the upcoming holidays. With her previous attraction to meditation, Eileen was deeply affected by the classes and was overjoyed that she had found a Jewish approach.

She also joined another weekly Torah class and eventually brought in a rabbi to help her *kasher* her home.

After several years Eileen and her husband joined a group that was forming a new Orthodox synagogue on the North Shore of Long Island. She continued to race into observance like the runner that she had always been, while her husband preferred to remain as a spectator standing on the side. He never stood in the way of her mitzvos observance and did not object when she decided to send their children, two daughters and one son, to seminary and yeshivah.

The highlight of her week was Shabbos.

"The Shabbos table — this is where it begins. The life, the love. It's about bringing people back to who they really are. It's about creating a relationship of love between people and G-d. When they feel the love and acceptance, and see the peace and joy in your life, they begin to search to get it for their own lives."

Eileen's newfound love of Shabbos made her reflect on her initial exposure to Shabbos years earlier, when she saw the Chassidic salesmen of her family's store leaving early for Shabbos.

"Looking back, now, it's hard to believe that I had absolutely no idea what Shabbos was, and that now it is the center of my life and the highlight of my week!"

Eileen continued her race toward the religious world. However, just as runners sometimes report "hitting the wall," a mental and physical barrier which limits their further exertion, there was one change that she had difficulty accepting — giving up wearing pants.

"I loved my jeans. They were comfortable. They gave me a sense of empowerment. It took a big internal change to commit to wearing skirts all the time. Like a wild horse, I had to tame myself."

She worked gradually to modify her wardrobe. Surprisingly she actually found that changing her external style of dress had a bigger impact — it actually helped her to mold her outsides to reflect the emotions she was feeling inside.

"It was such a deep transformation, going from a jock to taking on a more feminine role. The clothes help mold the personality. I did it because that is what Hashem wants. In the Torah, Hashem makes clear guidelines about how men and women should dress. We need those guidelines to make sure we are fully in the role that G-d has given us. I wanted to become more feminine and it worked.

"I was reading in Jewish books — when you cover the external, you let the *neshamah* shine through more and more. I wanted the Shechinah in me to shine through. Also I was meeting Rebbetzins, and they all had an aura of holiness around them. I wanted that aura to be around me."

As her outsides and insides began changing in line with the Torah's values, Eileen saw that she was having an impact on those around her as well.

For example, Eileen used to do private exercise coaching. A local Jewish but non-observant Russian woman once hired her to come to her house to give her children swimming lessons in the pool in their basement. Eileen came that week three mornings in a row. When the woman asked her to come the following day as well, on Saturday morning, she found no difficulty calling up the courage to decline.

"I told her, 'Shabbos is the only day I don't work. Hashem has given us the gift of Shabbos. I'm a queen on that day.'"

"Really?" *("I'll never forget how she said that.")*

The following week when Eileen came to teach the lessons, she gave the woman a book entitled *The Chassidic Approach to Joy*. During future weeks, she brought her cassette tapes on Jewish spirituality and other topics as well.

Several years later, Eileen received a phone call from the woman.

"She called me up, and said, 'I just wanted you to know — I became *shomer Shabbos* because of you!"

The tapes and books, along with conversations that Eileen had with the woman, made an impact on her and brought her back to her roots. Over time the woman influenced her family and people in the community around her as well.

"She eventually became the mikveh lady in Great Neck. She was a very holy woman and loved Shabbos."

In 1992, Eileen's father passed away. His death was very hard on her, but she was aided by the lessons she had learned in classes about how to accept our challenges and to remember the immense love that Hashem has for us.

"There is no question that by having Hashem with me, it helped me to see the bigger picture. It wasn't just about me and my loss. I could see that Hashem has a plan. Hashem has a program. He calls people to come back."

Six months later, the Handes moved to Boca Raton, Florida. Eileen, now Yocheved, describes the move as a *Lech Lecha* for the family — just as Avraham embarked on a mission that changed his life and affected the entire world, when Yocheved and her family moved to Florida, the relocation had a tremendous impact on them and the Boca community.

As soon as they moved to Boca, Bruce began accompanying Yocheved and their children to synagogue each Shabbos.

Also within a short time of their relocation, Yocheved joined the community's mikveh committee. The pressing issue was to build a local women's mikveh, as there was none within walking distance. A trip to the mikveh required a long drive to Hollywood or North Miami Beach.

Yocheved threw her considerable energy into the project. Even her previous experience was a perfect match for the project — she had worked as an operator of a swimming pool in New York for thirty years and was able to advise the mikveh committee on the optimal water equipment and heating systems.

"It's fabulous to think that I could be involved in building our very own community mikveh when on Masada, fifteen years before, I didn't even know what a Mikveh was!"

Within two years, the mikveh was built. Yocheved later became a mikveh attendant and its president.

Upon moving to Florida, Yocheved also joined the community's *Chevrah Kaddisha*, in great part due to seeing the tremendous care and concern that had been given to her father's body following his death six months earlier.

"Before my father was buried, I saw him wrapped in his tallis. He looked so much at peace. I could literally see the holiness that surrounded him. I asked who had prepared him like this and was told it was the *Chevrah Kaddisha*.

"'What is that?' I asked, and was told that it is the Holy Burial Society. So when I moved to Florida and was asked to join the local *Chevrah Kaddisha*, I immediately said yes!"

In 2003 at age fifty-six, Bruce was diagnosed with cancer. He battled the disease valiantly. His days were spent in chemotherapy treatments and attending cancer support groups. But more importantly, he began learning Torah. A local Kollel rabbi opened his schedule to accommodate him. Bruce told the rabbi that he wanted to "learn about where he was going."

"While his body was quickly losing the battle, his soul was soaring. He told me that he loved learning but only wished that he had started sooner," Yocheved recalled.

After a year-long battle, Bruce passed away and received a full Jewish burial.

Yocheved felt like the lessons she had learned over her three decades of becoming observant had prepared her for her husband's passing.

"When my husband died it was a very sad time. Thank G-d I did not let the feeling of depression last very long. Over the years I had developed the spiritual tools to know that Hashem orchestrates everything in my life, including my husband's passing.

"It was still the faith that I had, the relationship that I had with Hashem that pulled me through. I always knew that I had Hashem. I saw Bruce's passing as another opportunity to grow spiritually.

"Knowing that Hashem was with me helped me to live my life and pull myself back together. You can get depressed and be sad, but life goes on."

In the years since, Yocheved's spirit has been buoyed by the support of the Boca community, and the messages she continues to learn from those around her.

"I continue to try to do everything with the rabbis' approval. It gave me lot of strength to know I was doing everything according to what Hashem wanted. It helped me live my life, to pull myself back together. All of the spiritual tools I learned over the years helped prepare me and helped me be there for my kids."

Some of her biggest sources of inspiration continue to be the people around her. She says the highlight of her week has been visiting an elderly Holocaust survivor named Bella. She also gains strength from the people around her who are on their own similar journeys to return to their religious roots.

In the years since Bruce's passing, Yocheved has thrown her bountiful energy into many other community projects. She teaches women's *shiurim* and organizes local programs. She writes a monthly newsletter for community women. She continues to work as a teacher, and also became a Massage and CranioSacral Therapist, and in this role she helps other people deal with trauma, pain, and tragedy.

"Life is all about sharing, about taking the light of a candle and bringing it to other people. Since Hashem gifted me the understanding of how beautiful being a Jewish woman is, I've been on a journey to help others see it too."

That message has stayed with Yocheved through all of the events of her life. Over the years, first through meditation, and then also through classes, Shabbos, and holidays, she has felt Hashem's constant love and has seen the direction of His guiding Hand. She has realized just how beautiful her role as a truly empowered Jewish woman is, and she uses her talents and energy to help other women realize their beautiful roles too.

Seeing beyond the Question

While working in outreach in Norfolk, Virginia, Rabbi Aryeh Gibber taught young couples and college students. Much of his time was spent helping young Jewish women to appreciate their special, valued place in the world.

One day at the local JCC he met a recently married couple, Jason and Michelle Coopersmith*. Jason was in medical school in Virginia and had come from a Conservative background, while Michelle had grown up Reform. They quickly developed a strong bond with the Gibbers and came often for Shabbos and Yom Tov meals.

The Coopersmiths were fascinated by the rituals and beliefs of Jews in the Norfolk *frum* community. They began to grow and take on mitzvos. Initially Jason was more interested than Michelle, but eventually she caught up as well.

During a conversation a few months after they had first met, Michelle described the forces that had slowed the process for her. She had long heard misconceptions about the role of women in Judaism. Her mind had been locked into these perceptions, and everything that she saw was being filtered and questioned in her brain based on them.

However over time, seeing the beautiful way in which women were being treated and valued in the *frum* homes she visited, she was able to move beyond those stereotypes.

"She said that nowhere in her experience in the Jewish world or the business world has she seen women treated like queens like she was seeing in the *frum* households. She said she had realized that if that characterization of Orthodoxy was so off base, then maybe she had to re-examine other things that she had been told."

When teaching students at a nearby university, Rabbi Gibber

often had female students come to class armed with similar misunderstandings of the role of women in Judaism. They would sometimes even ask provoking questions simply to try to challenge him.

He learned how to respond to them from a story about the first Gerrer Rebbe, the Chiddushei HaRim. He was once teaching a class when a man who was clearly non-religious walked in. From his style of dress and demeanor, it was clear that he had been caught up in the Enlightenment and had strayed far from his Jewish roots.

The man began a barrage of questions. The entire time, the Rebbe just sat quietly and did not say a word. After a few minutes the man got bored and left. The Rebbe then calmly continued his *shiur* from precisely the place he had stopped.

After the *shiur* ended his students asked, "We're sure you knew the answers. Why didn't you respond?"

"Questions I can answer. Answers I cannot answer," the Rebbe said.

Rabbi Gibber explained: "The man knew what he wanted to do. He had already made up his mind and only wanted to challenge and ridicule the Rebbe. It's very difficult — if not impossible — to reach a person at that point."

He said that it's important to know when and how to best answer questions that are asked. Some questions need an immediate response, while others are better addressed only once the questioner has experienced the proper context to appreciate the answer. For example, when newcomers begin to understand topics such as the rules of modest dress, and they see the holiness and purity the rules create, they gain a greater appreciation for their own self-worth. Their previous misconceptions then shatter and their questions fall away.

"My wife spent many hours with Michelle going through issues together, learning the Torah perspective on these topics. I don't think she would have been ready on the first visit."

Rabbi Yehudah Silver suggests a similar key rule for anyone involved in outreach: for sensitive questions such as these, it's necessary to look beyond the question and see the bigger picture.

"You can never answer the question. You have to answer the questioner. You have to see where the guy is coming from."

For example, he was once teaching a class on Chanukah. As he was talking about latkes and dreidels, a woman raised her hand and asked a question completely off topic, about how Torah Judaism views women. Without batting an eyelash, Rabbi Silver said that her question was very important and detailed and he would like to discuss it with her in-depth afterward.

After the class he approached the woman and while speaking with her, he realized that the real source of her question was difficult issues that she was having in her marriage and in her personal life. Upon hearing this, Rabbi Silver framed his answer to her particular situation.

"If I would have said some nice offhanded answer to get back on track, I would have lost that lady. You have to know where the person is coming from before answering the question. Nine times out of ten, the question is not the real issue."

14

Seeing the Hand of Hashem

HASHEM CREATES MIRACLES EVERY DAY TO BRING HIS BEloved children home. People involved in Jewish outreach and education say they see this constantly, from unexplainable twists of "fate" to undeniable, open miracles.

In every area of life, a Jew needs *hishtadlus* — effort. It's necessary to perform the physical acts to make money or to achieve a particular goal. However, he needs to be aware that the actual results are only up to Hashem. Sometimes a person can try valiantly to succeed, only to see his efforts fail completely. At other times even the most unlikely chances can produce the greatest results. And while it's true that the harder one works, the more Divine assistance he receives to make him successful, in the end the outcome is dictated only by Hashem.

This process is clear for people involved in Jewish outreach. They do the physical acts of reaching out to Jews and teaching them, but Hashem decides the results.

And when they see the daily miracles that Hashem makes for them and the assistance that He provides in their work, they are reminded that their success in every other area of life is due solely to Him as well.

In the Driver's Seat

Over his decades-long career in *kiruv*, Rabbi David Silverman of the Atlanta Scholars Kollel has taught students of every age and spoken about nearly every imaginable subject matter. He has been asked the most challenging questions from his students.

Just as the great sages Hillel and Shammai were asked to teach the entire Torah to a student while standing on one foot (*Shabbos* 31a), Rabbi Silverman has routinely been asked the most important and complicated questions only at the very end of his classes, just as his audience is packing up to leave. It sounds something like this:

"There are just a few minutes left to our discussion group ...
Any questions?"

"Rabbi, how do you explain the Holocaust?"
"What is Kabbalah?"
"Do we believe in life after death?"

"As they're putting their coats on, I'm trying to explain *hashgachah pratis*!"

Delivering clear, concise answers to those questions takes extra help from Hashem.

Rabbi Silverman has answers ready for most of these complicated questions, as he has been asked the same key questions repeatedly over his decades of experience. However, at one class he was asked a completely new and challenging question on a specific topic related to the Holocaust. Without thinking, Rabbi Silverman delivered a perfect answer, and yet had no idea where it had come from.

A few days later while driving in his car, he was listening to a tape of a study group he had been part of seventeen years earlier with Rabbi Yaakov Weinberg, *zt"l*, the Rosh Yeshivah of Ner Israel. Rabbi Silverman slammed on his brakes and had to pull over when he heard someone ask the exact same question on the Holocaust! As he heard the Rosh Yeshivah's words, he realized he had delivered the identical answer in his class that week.

He rewound the tape to listen to the answer again and strained to try to identify which student had asked the question. To his astonishment he realized — it was himself!

"The answer was obviously inside me on a certain level, but I was not consciously aware of it," Rabbi Silverman said. "I clearly felt Hashem's Hand — I needed that experience to know how to answer the question. I felt that HaKadosh Baruch Hu wanted me to do it. It was so validating."

Another experience drove the message home to Rabbi Silverman of just how much Hashem guides his work. He once tried to arrange a Shabbaton for a group of young Atlanta Jewish singles. He identified the perfect target group, but weeks of effort had yielded only a handful of people committed to attending. Finally, on the Thursday night before the Shabbaton, despite Rabbi Silverman's dim hopes for success, the group finally coalesced by itself in front of his eyes.

That night as circumstances literally turned 180-degrees in front of his eyes, he ran out to a local supermarket to pick up some last-minute items. As he got back into his car, he began to cry tears of gratitude to Hashem.

"I felt the Hand of G-d was saying, 'I will make this happen, don't you worry. You just have to go through the motions,'" Rabbi Silverman said. "As I sat at the wheel I looked up to heaven and said, 'Do you want me to steer or do you want to?'"

The weekend turned out to be unbelievable, far better than he had expected.

"We make all of our efforts, and yet we never know where our *hatzlachah* will come from."

Politically Correct

Rabbi Avraham Jacobovitz has a similar tenure to Rabbi Silverman. Fondly known as "Rabbi J," he estimates that over one thousand Jews became observant during his three decades working in Michigan, and said that thousands others have become more positive about their Yiddishkeit and less likely to intermarry.

Rabbi J was also the founder of the Maimonides Jewish Leaders Fellowship program, which offers classes to college students throughout the United States to learn about their Judaism. In 2010 he returned to his birthplace of Eretz Yisrael, settling in Ramat Beit Shemesh Alef where he continues to do Jewish outreach work.

His experience with one student, Matt*, surprised even him and taught him never to give up on even a single *neshamah*. Matt was a student at Michigan State University and occasionally attended Rabbi J's classes. He was clearly not interested in the religious aspect, and freely admitted as much, but loved speaking about Israeli politics and found Rabbi J to be a willing partner.

Sometimes after an evening shiur, the two would speak until three in the morning about the latest elections and other happenings in the Israeli government. Rabbi J himself acknowledges that his goal in campus *kiruv* was not to speak about politics, but he found them a useful way to maintain a connection with Matt.

Many a night after Rabbi Jacobovitz returned home from his late-night discussions, his wife asked him if he really saw a value in them. Matt was clearly not interested in religious growth and was not accepting any Jewish observances, so was it truly worth the Rabbi's time (and missed sleep)?

Rabbi Jacobovitz always replied in the positive. He said Matt was a sweet young man and he hoped that through their connection, he would eventually decide to to take on positive changes. And after all, our success in this world is decided only by Hashem. It's up to us to do the efforts we believe will succeed and Hashem will make them work.

Matt continued attending classes, and he and Rabbi J continued speaking about politics each night. College graduation soon came and Matt left Michigan, his religious observances unchanged.

Under normal circumstances, the story should have ended there. However a few years later Rabbi Jacobovitz received a phone call from Vered*. She introduced herself — conversing in Hebrew — as an Israeli who had recently moved to America and had settled in Michigan. She had grown up in a non-observant family. A few months earlier she had attended a Jewish awareness seminar in Israel by Rabbi Ezriel Tauber which had touched her heart deeply.

She had approached Rabbi Tauber after that program and said she was very inspired by it and wanted to learn more. At the time, however, she was engaged to a young American man who was studying in graduate school in Israel, and he was completely uninterested in religion; in fact, he was suspicious of it. Rabbi Tauber gave her advice on how to balance her newfound interest in Judaism with her fiancé's dislike of it.

The other issue was that they had decided to move to America after their upcoming wedding, to Detroit, Michigan. Vered knew no one there, and lamented that she was interested in learning more about Judaism but knew no one in Detroit who could teach her. She shared this problem with Rabbi Tauber.

"I have a great idea," Rabbi Tauber said, "Here's the number of a rabbi who lives there, Rabbi Jacobovitz. When you get there, call him. I'm sure he'll be able to help you."

Vered married her fiancé Matt and soon after they moved to Detroit. One day she was at home feeling bored and remembered the excitement she had felt from the seminar and conversation with Rabbi Tauber. She was hesitant to tell Matt. However she couldn't quiet the nagging feeling inside her, and so she told Matt that she wanted to speak to someone to find out more about Judaism.

"No, don't do that; they'll brainwash you."

She then told Matt about her conversation with Rabbi Tauber months earlier, and said he had given her the name of a certain Rabbi Jacobovitz who lived nearby.

"Rabbi Jacobovitz? I know him! I used to schmooze with him for hours in college. I'm not afraid of him."

That conversation led to the phone call which Vered was presently having with Rabbi Jacobovitz. He was amazed at how the Hand of Hashem had arranged the pieces so intricately to lead to the call.

He immediately invited them over. The three chatted and he and Matt made up for the lost time together.

Vered was deeply impressed by Rabbi J's warmth and his ready answers to her questions. She began attending his classes and soon became a loyal student.

She eventually began taking on the mitzvos of family purity, Shabbos, and others. Matt eventually followed and has since become observant.

When Rabbi J told his wife the story and reminded her about his conversations with Matt years earlier, she said, "You're right. I was wrong."

Rabbi J himself admits his own surprise at the events. Schmoozing about politics, about as far from religion as one could get, led to Matt and Vered's return. In fact, it was specifically because they had spoken not about religion but only about politics, that Matt did not feel threatened by him and was therefore able to be open to the eventual reunion. Rabbi J acknowledges the events were clearly guided by Hashem at every step of the way.

The letters of the word מקרה, *mikreh*, meaning "coincidence," can be rearranged to spell two words: רק מה', *rak m'Hashem*, "only from G-d."

In his years of experience, Rabbi J said every success he has had has been led and planned the entire way by Hashem. However, for a story as improbable as Matt's, he knows it was due to none of his own efforts but only due to the Hand of Hashem.

Israeli politics themselves are greatly improbable and often lead to unexpected results. So it's not really surprising that Hashem would use them as the linchpin in His own machinations for an improbable journey back to Judaism.

STICKING TO HIS PRINCIPLES

RABBI JACOBOVITZ HAS been careful throughout his three decades of teaching to maintain stringent standards regarding particular halachic issues. In certain areas, he has chosen not to rely on leniencies. But instead of these issues being a deterrent to his work or being intimidating to students, he has found time and again that sticking to his principles has actually encouraged his students to grow. He has also seen many instances in which he received extra *siyatta d'Shemaya* specifically because he was careful in these topics.

A newcomer, a young woman named Nicole Shprintzer*, once came to his weekly class on the *parashah* at Michigan State University. Before the class she introduced herself and stuck out her hand in greeting.

This is one of the areas where Rabbi Jacobovitz is stringent — not shaking hands with women outside his immediate family. Such rules maintain proper boundaries between the genders and create greater respect between people. And while there may be leniencies, for example to shake hands in certain scenarios, Rabbi Jacobovitz has decided to be strict. He admits that it has been difficult to follow this rule at times, but he says he has never found it to be a deterrent to his outreach.

Rabbi Jacobovitz politely apologized to Nicole and said he does not shake hands with women. She seemed a bit offended, telling him, "Rabbi, I have never heard of anything like it! Why won't you shake my hand?"

He told her that he would be happy to explain the practice to her, but as the class was about to begin, it would have to wait until afterward. To her credit, Nicole agreed and sat down for the *shiur*.

Rabbi Jacobovitz admits that he was nervous throughout the entire *shiur*. Immediately afterward Nicole hurried over to him. They spoke for around forty-five minutes as he explained the Jewish ideals of respect and boundaries between the genders. As the conversation progressed, he could tell that her feelings about the incident were changing.

By the end she was actually very interested and excited by the conversation. She said to him as they finished speaking, "Rabbi, I'm so thankful now that you didn't shake my hand. I never knew all those things. You gave me so much to think about."

When Nicole had originally asked her question, Rabbi Jacobovitz could have given her a quick answer on the spot. However, he knew that it would not do justice to the question, and he thought that she would appreciate a longer, more in-depth response. Therefore he decided to wait until after the *shiur*. It was certainly a risk, because she could have left without waiting for an answer.

His decision to take that risk, combined with Nicole's strength and curiosity, led to three incredible outcomes.

First, the class and conversation made Nicole more open and eager to embrace Jewish practices. Second, at that class she met a young Jewish man, they began dating, and eventually decided to marry. They have since become *frum* together.

The third outcome was still developing. At Nicole's wedding, Rabbi Jacobovitz met her parents. Mr. Shprintzer was the president of a large company and the wedding was lavish. Rabbi

J formed a close rapport with them then and in the years to follow. They were very grateful to him for his work with their daughter and for his indirect role in helping Nicole to meet her husband.

Rabbi Jacobovitz's work in Michigan continued to grow, and he wanted to build his own building, the Jewish Resource Center, to host his programs. He found a piece of property in a central location on campus near the Hillel House, but needed the seed money to begin construction.

Rabbi Jacobovitz decided to speak to Nicole's parents to see if they would be able to participate in the project.

Normally he only asks money from people who are directly affected by his work. However because of the appreciation that Nicole's parents had shown, he decided to go against his own rules and approach them.

Rabbi Jacobovitz arranged a meeting. After explaining his ideas and the monetary needs of the construction, he said that he needed seed money of $100,000 and asked if they could contribute. Mr. Shprintzer turned to his wife and asked her what she thought.

"It sounds like a good cause," she replied.

On the spot, they gave him the $100,000 that he needed!

Rabbi Jacobovitz attributes the turn of events to the devotion he had to his principles.

"The interesting thing about the story is that I had my rules and never broke them, *baruch Hashem*. There were certain things I would never do," Rabbi Jacobovitz explained. "One would think that being *machmir* would turn people away. But no, I learned it's the other way — because I stuck to my principles, I was able to build the building."

With the family's contribution, Rabbi Jacobovitz was able to start the project and eventually build a beautiful, large edifice that has allowed thousands of students to experience Judaism.

The building was built not just on the family's contribution, but on the solid foundation of Rabbi Jacobovitz sticking to his principles.

Megillas Rus recounts the story of the entry of the righteous convert Ruth into the ranks of the Jewish people. At a decisive point in the story, her mother-in-law Naomi tried to dissuade her from converting, and from here we learn the practice of testing the sincerity of potential converts by attempting to discourage them.

The verse then records: "When she saw that she was determined to go with her, she stopped arguing with her" (1:18). Ruth here was *misametzes*, determined. This is the only place in Tanach that this word is used, and it indicates an extraordinarily high level of determination.

After seeing her sincerity, Naomi ceased any further attempts to dissuade her. For the remainder of the story the two woman not only walked together, but Naomi actually guided Ruth's process of joining the Jewish people and marrying.

Ruth's fate changed when she showed that she was determined, and this changed Naomi's mind as well. When a person shows a sincere desire, even seemingly insurmountable obstacles fall away.

For Rabbi Jacobovitz, sticking to his principles and being determined in his goals yielded success in the most beautiful way.

Getting Help in the Ring

People involved in outreach report regular incidents of seeing how Hashem guides their efforts. For example, speakers sometimes report being asked specific challenging questions, questions they thought they would not be able to answer. Yet, they say that often Hashem plants the exact answers into their mind at the moment they are asked, or that they had had just learned the answer to the question the day before.

Sometimes the Divine assistance comes in completely unexpected ways. For example, when a person tries to achieve a goal in a particular area, he will often see success in a completely different place. Why does this occur? Hashem takes note of the person's sincerity and directs it to where He knows it will have the greatest result.

The staff of the Lezion B'rina Institute, a school for Russian students in Israel, saw this firsthand in 2010.

The story begins twenty years earlier. Following the fall of the Iron Curtain, Jews streamed out of the Soviet Union. They headed to greener pastures, such as Israel and America. They succeeded in rebuilding their physical lives, but seven decades of religious persecution had left them ignorant of even the most fundamental tenets of their religion.

In December 1990, the Karliner Rebbe of Yerushalayim took note of the problem. One week on a Wednesday he called in Rabbi Moshe Weiss, the head of the Karliner Yeshivah. He gave him an ambitious mission — to start a high school for Russian Jewish boys. His deadline? That Sunday morning.

After picking himself up off of the floor, Rabbi Weiss launched himself to meet the challenge. He found a building in Bayit Vegan that was not being used, borrowed tables and chairs from a nearby school and put ads into Russian newspapers.

A trickle of students signed up, but it was just enough to begin the school.

The makeshift project has blossomed into a well-established institution that now has hundreds of students. It is based on a beautiful sprawling campus in Beitar. Its students study religious subjects in the morning and secular topics in the afternoon. They come from homes with little knowledge of Judaism and all graduate with a greater appreciation of their religion.

Hundreds of students have passed through the school's doors and have become more connected to their roots. An affiliated girls' school located in Yerushalayim, Bat Zion, has helped many Russian girls in similar ways.

In 2010 the entire student body of Lezion B'rina and every Russian home throughout the world had one name on their lips: Jewish boxer Yuri Foreman. He had grown up in Gomel, the second-largest Jewish community in Belarus. As a young boy he realized his fighting skills could keep anti-Semitic bullies away. He soon discovered that his agility and boxing prowess could become a career as well.

Yuri moved first to Israel and then to Brooklyn. He trained and entered the professional circuit in 2002. He quickly moved up the ranks, remaining undefeated in twenty-nine fights. At the same time he began becoming observant. Along the way he made a commitment to never fight on Shabbos. That personal pledge, combined with his Jewish pride that he literally wore (in the form of a Magen David on his boxing shorts), made him an inspiration for Jews around the world.

Rabbi Josh Friedman, the Director of Development of Lezion B'rina, saw Yuri as an amazing role model for the school's students and struck up a friendship with him.

On June 5, 2010 Yuri had his big fight in Yankee Stadium, for the Middleweight Division title. It made him a household name in Russian communities throughout the world. The fight was scheduled for later than usual on a Saturday night to accommodate Yuri's observance. He stayed for Shabbos in a nearby hotel.

The students of Lezion B'rina produced a video to wish Yuri success in his fight. On the Thursday before the match Rabbi Friedman emailed it to him.

Yuri emailed him back later that day to thank him for the encouragement. Though he lost the match that night, he has remained a favorite son to Russian Jews. He has continued on his own path of Jewish growth and has since become a rabbi.

In the outskirts of Moscow, a young Jewish Russian boy

named Sasha was following news of the fight as well. While he knew he was Jewish and was proud to be so, he knew very little about his religion. But when Yuri Foreman came on the scene, Sasha felt even more proud to be a Jew.

One day shortly after the big fight, Sasha was searching on the internet for any information he could find on Yuri. He stumbled across the video produced by the boys of Lezion B'rina on the school's website. He had never heard of the school, and the video touched him. At the end of the video was the contact information for Misha Ziloniy, the head of recruitment for the school. Sasha emailed him for more information about the video and Lezion B'rina.

Misha travels frequently throughout the former Soviet Union to meet potential students and their families and to run seminars about how Lezion B'rina and Bat Zion are providing students with a brighter future. During his next trip to Moscow he arranged a meeting with Sasha. Sasha jumped at the chance to travel to Israel to learn more about his heritage. He was accepted and became an eager student in the school.

Rabbi Friedman notes that Sasha was one of the only students to ever find the school on his own. Typically, the recruitment seminars target students who have been referred by local Jewish organizations. And yet Sasha had completely slipped under that radar and came to the school solely because of the video.

"This video was produced by boys who had themselves been saved from a dismal future in the former Soviet Union, and it was able to help save another Jewish child and bring him to a better life in Israel," Rabbi Friedman said. "We intended the video to give *chizuk* to Yuri Foreman, which it did, but it also gave tremendous *chizuk* to Sasha."

When Yuri heard about Sasha and the impact the video had on him, he was deeply touched. He even arranged to meet Sasha in person during a later trip to Israel.

"I am so honored that the video had a role in helping Sasha discover his heritage," Yuri said. "It's amazing how the one video could light such a spark in him."

Yuri Foreman continues to motivate and uplift the students of Lezion B'rina. Sasha himself has never forgotten how Yuri threw him into the ring to help him discover how to live a fully Jewish life. And for Rabbi Friedman, the most inspiring message of Sasha's journey is how unexpectedly it all began.

Igniting His Soul

For Robert Kolodetsky*, a simple question sent him off on a quest that helped him to not only discover his past, but also to blaze a clear path for his future.

During his freshman year at George Washington University in Washington, D.C., Robert began learning more about Judaism and growing in his religious observance. Toward the end of the year, he decided to start putting on tefillin everyday, and asked a local rabbi to order him a pair.

"How do you wrap your tefillin, in or out?" the rabbi asked him.

He was referring to two different traditions about how Jews wrap the strap of their arm tefillin. Depending on the place of origin of a person's family and their background, they either wrap their tefillin strap toward their body or away from it. The direction also affects the particular type of tefillin the rabbi would order for Robert.

Robert didn't know his family's tradition, but knew that his grandfather used to wear tefillin so decided to ask him.

Robert's grandfather said his own father had taught him to wrap the strap outward. He also said that even though many men wrap the remainder of the strap around their hand in the shape of the Hebrew letter *shin*, this was not their family's custom.

The answer was surprising, as Robert's family had lived in Minsk and these practices differed from the prevailing customs of the community. His grandfather was unsure as to the reason.

The only other family custom his grandfather remembered was that they had sung unique tunes at the Passover Seder. No one could identify the source of the tunes, and Robert began to wonder if both the tunes and the method of wrapping the straps had Chassidic origins.

Robert began researching his family and the community of Minsk in depth. Separately he started learning from Chassidic texts and was deeply drawn to their teachings. As he grew more observant, he was especially drawn toward the Chassidic world, though was still unsure if it had ever been a path in his family.

"I knew I had found the path for my soul. Chassidus spoke to me," Robert said.

Three years after beginning his search into his family tree, Robert made contact with a Chassidic rabbi in Monsey, New York who had lived previously in Minsk. Robert was hopeful that the rabbi could tell him more about the Jews of the city and possibly even had heard of his family.

During their phone conversation the rabbi gave him information about the Jews of Minsk. But even more significantly, he said the maiden name of his aunt's mother was Kolodetsky! Her family had come from Minsk and was followers of the Koidenover Chassidic dynasty. Robert later found out Koidenov had been a large group of Chassidim in White Russia and Lithuania before being decimated in the Holocaust.

Robert was overjoyed. He wondered if he had found a long-lost relative. Because of his own interest in Chassidism, the potential that his family could have been Chassidic made him further ecstatic.

Robert spent the spring break week of his senior year in Monsey. He met the Chassidic rabbi and heard more about the Jews of Minsk. The rabbi also gave Robert the phone number of his sister-in-law, who was the wife of a *rosh yeshivah* of a Chassidic yeshivah and knew even more about the family.

Robert called her. He introduced himself and said that his great-grandfather was named Chaim Noach and had lived in Baltimore.

"Uncle Chaim from Baltimore!" she exclaimed.

They realized that they were indeed direct relatives. The woman said her grandfather was named "Zeide Yosef," whom Robert had known as Uncle Joe.

Robert had heard about Uncle Joe from his grandfather, but the families had lost contact with each other. Robert then asked her about other family customs. He sang the tunes he knew for the Passover songs, and the Rebbetzin said her family had used the same tunes each year.

She began filling in more details of Robert's family. They were indeed members of the Koidenov Chassidic dynasty. She said that her grandmother, who was Robert's great-great-grandmother, had the coveted job of baking the twelve special challahs that were used at the Koidenover Rebbe's Shabbos table each week.

"I couldn't believe it. I thought maybe I would track down information linking us to a particular Chassidus, but to find *frum* cousins was beyond my imagination," Robert said.

Robert later heard that some survivors of the Koidnenov Chassidus had moved to Israel after the Holocaust. The current Koidenov Rebbe lives in Bnei Brak and has been rebuilding the Chassidus and its institutions. So when Robert went to Israel to study in yeshivah after graduating from college, he made it his mission to connect with the Rebbe and learn more about the practices of Koidenov.

Robert spent his first free Shabbos with observant cousins

in Bnei Brak. On Friday afternoon he went to meet the Rebbe. Robert told him about his family and that his great-grandfather had been a Koidenover Chassid. The Rebbe quoted the verse, "*V'dor revi'i yashuvu henah* — And the fourth generation will return here" (*Bereishis* 15:16).

Robert's soul felt complete. Here was a direct connection to his family and heritage. More than that, he had found his direction in life.

"I had come home and I received a royal welcome," Robert said.

Over Shabbos, Robert davened with the Rebbe and ate meals at his table. He felt at home. These were his family's customs and tunes. These were his origins.

To this day Robert remains a loyal Koidenover Chassid and helps the Rebbe in his quest to rebuild their lost dynasty. The Rebbe has been a guide and a light to him, helping Robert to reconnect to his family's traditions and to continue to grow in his service of Hashem.

Robert still reflects in amazement on the fact that his whole journey, which led him to find relatives and his family's heritage, was launched by a simple question from the rabbi in college.

"Imagine if the rabbi from college did not ask me how we wrapped tefillin. He could have ordered me a regular pair with an Ashkenaz [knot], yet his one question sparked a search which eventually ignited my soul," Robert said.

When we return a *sefer Torah* to the *aron kodesh*, we recite several verses from Tanach. We end with the words, "*Hasheveinu* — Bring us back to You, Hashem, and we shall return; renew our days as of old" (*Eichah* 5:21).

Robert's return to Judaism was a true return to his roots. He discovered the source of his family's traditions and has succeeded in maintaining them, adding one more family to the proud ranks of the Koidenov dynasty.

The *sefer Lechem Dim'ah* explains the verse: the Jewish people beseech G-d that He should take the initiative and draw us near. When He does that, we will return to Him wholeheartedly.

It was not by chance that the college rabbi asked Robert about the tefillin. Hashem planted the question in his mind, knowing that it would send Robert off on a quest of discovery.

The Ties That Bind

ELIAHU LEVENSON HAD his own inspiration from a pair of tefillin. But for him the message was that Hashem expects us to maintain our commitments to Him, even when we don't stand up to those commitments ourselves.

Eliahu began his journey to religious observance in 1984. Two years later, he purchased his first pair of tefillin. He knew little about tefillin and even felt uncomfortable wearing them, which surprised him because he felt great excitement when performing many other mitzvos.

This discomfort led him to avoid putting on tefillin altogether. However he realized he could only change the way he felt about the mitzvah if he jumped into it. Therefore he made a deadline for himself: by the time he turned thirty-five, he would begin putting on tefillin each morning when he prayed. He chose his Hebrew birthday, which was several months away, so he still had time to prepare.

Days, and then weeks passed and he still had not put them on. The day was clearly circled on his calendar and the commitment was clear in his mind, but he was trying to postpone it for as long as he could.

His birthday was on a Monday, and as the day approached, Eliahu decided his first day of tefillin would be one day earlier on Sunday morning.

At the time, he was a member of his Orthodox synagogue's baseball team. The games were held each Sunday morning. Eliahu planned to daven in shul in his tefillin and then head to the game afterward.

Unfortunately Eliahu overslept that morning and missed Shacharis! He was now faced with a difficult choice: he could stay home, put on his tefillin, and daven by himself, which would result in his missing the game. Or he could forget about his commitment, skip Shacharis, and head to the game.

The shul's baseball team was the only Orthodox team in the league and it was having a stellar season. They had a chance at the league championship, a first for the team. Eliahu worried that he would let his teammates down if he missed the game. He decided to go back on his promise to himself, skip putting on tefillin that day, and go to the game instead.

The game proved to be both exciting and close. Eliahu was playing catcher. During one of the final innings the opposing team had a runner on third base. Eliahu knew that if the batter hit a ground ball his teammates would throw the ball home to get out the runner.

The batter hit a low bouncer and the runner took off from third base like a shot. The shortstop snagged the ball bare-handed and immediately threw it to Eliahu. The throw was too high but Eliahu leapt for it. He missed the ball and fell back to earth just as the baseman slid into home. The runner collided with Eliahu's leg and Eliahu crumpled to the ground in pain.

People gathered around him. His teammates picked him up and carried him to a friend's car. They drove straight to the hospital, where X-rays showed that Eliahu's leg was broken in four places.

"I knew in my heart without any question that I was in the hospital because I had failed to honor one of the most important commitments of my life," Eliahu said.

Surgery was performed that afternoon and he spent the next two days in the hospital. Eliahu was clearly struck by the irony of being in the hospital on his birthday, the same hospital in which he had entered this world thirty-five years earlier. He later asked his rabbi if the confluence of events was significant.

"He told me without hesitation that the thirty-fifth birthday was the midpoint of life. I had just spent the first day of my second half of life in the identical place where I had spent the first day of the first half of my life."

Eliahu's birthday also marked a major transition in his religious commitment. Though he had missed the first day of his commitment, the event propelled him to take the mitzvah of tefillin seriously and soon afterward he began to wear them regularly.

"Today I own an exceptional pair of tefillin and they are one of the treasures of my life. How things can change when one changes his life."

For Eliahu the event truly was a birth, a new beginning for him in his journey toward observance.

The Gemara (*Chullin* 89a) teaches that tefillin are the sign of a Jew. As we wrap their straps around our arms and heads we are binding ourselves to Hashem, committing ourselves to following Him and observing His mitzvos.

The *sefer Beis Yosef* says further: there are two *shins* on the sides of the head tefillin. The numerical value of the letter *shin* is 300. Together they equal 600.

One of the *shins* on every pair of tefillin has an extra arm, which looks like a letter *vav*. The numerical value of *vav* equals six. Together these numbers equal 606, which are the number of extra mitzvos that Jews have.

Eliahu made a tremendous statement when he said he would begin wearing tefillin by the time of his thirty-fifth birthday. This was not only a commitment to this particular mitzvah, but was a sign of his overall religious growth and his allegiance to serving Hashem.

Therefore when he missed this important moment, Hashem reminded him of it in the clearest way. Thankfully Eliahu listened to the message and did not miss his commitment again.

A Long Time in Coming

THE PROCESS OF a Jew returning to his roots can take years — sometimes even decades — from the time of an initial inspiration to when he decides to begin observing mitzvos. The change happens slowly, deep below the surface, as ideas that have been heard are consciously or subconsciously considered and weighed.

For the individual becoming observant, it's important not to rush into commitment too quickly. Rabbi Yitzchok Lowenbraun of the Association of Jewish Outreach Programs had a frequent visitor at his family's Shabbos table. The Lowenbraun family nicknamed him Sudden Sam, after a famous baseball pitcher. On his first visit he was wearing a pair of coveralls with long hair flowing down his back. Just a few weeks later he arrived for a Shabbos meal in a short haircut, black hat, and dark suit, looking exactly the part of a well-established religious Jew. Unfortunately, within a short time, he reversed direction and threw off all of his new observances.

People who jump into the religious pool too quickly often jump back out of it just as fast.

"A tree grows at a natural rate. So too, a Jew needs to grow naturally," Rabbi Lowenbraun said.

Even that slow, deliberate growth is part of Hashem's plan. A teacher can plant the seeds of inspiration, but then it's up to Hashem and the student to decide just how and when those seeds will flower.

Rabbi Emanuel Feldman led Congregation Beth Jacob in Atlanta for forty years and inspired hundreds of families in the city to become observant. Someone once approached him and said that he had become religious because of something the rabbi had said in a sermon a decade earlier!

When he had first heard the idea it didn't immediately affect him, but the concept germinated inside him for those ten years until it finally inspired him to return home.

Why does real, internal change occur so slowly? Rabbi Elazar Meisels, who has been involved with *kiruv* in Michigan since 1999, explains this phenomenon from a term Hashem uses to describe the Jewish people. The Torah calls us "a stiff-necked people." The Maharal (*Gur Aryeh, Bamidbar* 31:19) explains that this description actually has a positive angle.

Every person is formed from a composite of a spiritual side and a physical side. The Maharal explains that it is very easy to make changes to items in the physical world. He said for example, the physical shape of a candle can be changed by simply applying heat to one side. But permanently changing the shape and direction of its flame is much harder.

Similarly, it's simple to change one's physical appearance and clothes, as we see that trends and fashions in the outside world ebb and flow very sporadically. But for a Jew to change his underlying spiritual direction takes hard work and much introspection.

Rabbi Meisels points out encouragingly that once a Jew sincerely changes his spiritual direction and becomes *frum*, it's rare for him to stray back from his commitment despite the challenges he faces.

Rabbi Baruch Price grew up in South Africa and became the director of the Jewish Learning Experience of New Jersey. He cites an incident that inspired his decision to enter *kiruv*. At age fifteen, long before becoming a rabbi, he visited Israel. While at the Kosel one day, he sat down on a stone wall at the back of the plaza. A young man around his age sat next to him and asked him for the time. The two began speaking.

The young man was very distant from Judaism and lived in

Los Angeles. He had an Italian last name but he said his mother was Jewish. Baruch told him that makes him Jewish too. The young man replied that he had thought that was the case, but didn't know what it meant to be Jewish.

There, at the back of the Kosel plaza, Baruch told him about the rudiments of Shabbos, Israel, and Yerushalayim. They spoke for a long time. When it was finally time to depart, they exchanged addresses.

Over the next few months, the two young men kept in touch via postal letters. Baruch told him more about Shabbos and Jewish observance. Unfortunately they eventually lost touch with each other. Baruch wondered what had become of him.

Nearly ten years later, Baruch returned to Israel to go to yeshivah. While checking out various options, he stopped by a yeshivah geared for *ba'alei teshuvah*. He noticed a familiar face there — the young man he had met years earlier at the Kosel! Over the few years since their meeting, the messages that Baruch told him had grown inside him until he eventually became observant.

"It was very inspiring for me, as a teenage kid having a conversation. You never know what a conversation and a few letters can lead to," Rabbi Price said.

⇨ ⇦

The Chafetz Chaim once called a meeting of the leading *roshei yeshivah* of Europe to encourage the establishment of new schools for young boys. He opened the gathering by quoting two verses which are read on fast days:

"For just as the rain and snow descend from heaven and will not return there, rather it waters the earth and causes it to produce and sprout and gives seed to the sower and food to the eater, so shall be My word that emanates from My mouth. It will not return to Me unfulfilled unless it will have accomplished what I desired and brought success where I sent it" (*Yeshayah* 55:10–11).

The Chafetz Chaim explained that just as the rain makes plants grow, every word of Torah that comes out of a person has an effect on his audience. He said the speaker can never give up. Every word leaves a mark on the listener's soul. Even if the impact is not immediately evident, the mark has still been made.

That is the Hand of Hashem. The words of a Torah class, the inspirations of a Shabbos meal, or simply seeing the courteous way that members of a *frum* family treat each other, can plant seeds inside a Jew's soul that will eventually lead him back to his roots.

Planting Seeds in Others and in Ourselves

People involved in *kiruv* see lives transformed every day. Often, it is their own lives which are transformed the most drastically.

Picture the scene: a *frum* family, the Cohens, are hosting newcomer Jonathan at their Shabbos table. Jonathan arrives shortly before Shabbos, drained by the pressures of his tumultuous week at work or school. For Jonathan, the gift of Shabbos is something he has never experienced before. It's a chance to relax, unwind, and connect to a new family and in a new way to his religion.

Jonathan's excitement for the newfound practices of Shabbos rubs off on the Cohen family. They see through his eyes a new vibrancy and appreciation for mitzvos they may have performed for years by rote. They come to better appreciate the gifts they have. Plus, when Jonathan asks Mr. and Mrs. Cohen or their children for the reasons for various mitzvos they are performing, it pushes them to investigate and find explanations for actions they have done for years but may never have fully understood.

Rabbi Eli Gewirtz, when asked how many Jews have become more observant through his Partners in Torah telephone learning program, quipped: "I can't answer that question, but I can assure you that one hundred percent of the mentors have become more observant. Virtually every mentor tells us that he gained more from the learning than his partner."

Perhaps the greatest impact is seen on young, *frum*-from-birth Jews who get involved with *kiruv*. They have been taught from birth by their parents, schools and society about the beauty and meaning of Judaism. Despite this religiously rich upbringing, sometimes they only come to appreciate what they have when they meet Jews from less observant backgrounds.

For many years, Project SEED in the United States has sent *frum*-from-birth male yeshivah students in their late teens to out-of-town Jewish communities during the summer. Their goal is to study with local residents, to help with outreach programs, and generally to act as role models of inspiration for local residents. The young men themselves come back at the end of each summer greatly inspired, with newfound excitement for their own learning.

In 2005 the parent organization, Torah Umesorah, launched a girls' division to do similar work. Each summer they send groups of young women to more than thirty out-of-town communities to run day camps for children and to learn with local residents.

The girls' division is staffed by post-seminary Bais Yaakov graduates from New York, New Jersey, Chicago, and other established Jewish communities. They're sent to communities far from home, to Seattle and Savannah, Phoenix and Boca Raton. These communities have far smaller religious populations than the locales where the SEED women grew up. When the young women arrive, they provide a refreshing new face to the local outreach programs.

When the SEED members arrive, they are placed on pedestals by local residents and become instant role models. The roles push them to grow in ways they never knew existed, said Hindy Ungar, the program director. She speaks to the counselors at the end of each summer. They all thank her, telling her how much their lives had been changed by their time away. Many of their life goals also change as a result of SEED; afterward, they are more likely to consider community-focused professions in which they can give back to others.

Leah Weinreb* grew up in Lakewood, New Jersey and spent four summers as a SEED counselor in Boca Raton, Florida. She said the experience opened her eyes even more to the beauty of her own religious upbringing.

"It was an amazing experience as a Bais Yaakov girl to help me appreciate what I have. Seeing how the laws of the Torah protected me from ... some situations that are dangerous or inappropriate — we'll never get into that because of the Torah's laws. I also saw a lot of families trying to figure out how to raise their kids. We don't have to brainstorm how to raise kids or what morals to teach kids. It's all there in the Torah. We don't have to go through life as a trial-and-error [experience]," Leah said.

Leah said the biggest impression the SEED counselors make is simply by showing that they are ordinary young women. They have many of the same feelings and challenges as everyone else, but with a different frame of reference for approaching them.

"In synagogue on Tishah B'Av we were crying, and the next day we were having a great time with [community members]. They see there's a time and place for everything. The adults were impressed that we have the maturity not to be laughing with friends in shul. This is a serious time in our lives. This makes sense to us. They wonder, 'Why don't our kids understand that this is a serious time in their lives?'"

After packing up their bags and heading back to New Jersey, Leah and the other counselors received a letter from one elderly woman in the community, thanking them for the tremendous impact they had on their family: "You are all shining examples of what parents and grandparents should *daven* for — for our daughters and granddaughters to be as kind, learned, lovely, and caring as all of you."

The Gemara (*Taanis* 7a) derives an important lesson from the fact that the Torah is called an *eitz chaim* — a tree of life. If someone wants to light a fire with large pieces of wood, the flames cannot catch by themselves onto the large piece. It's necessary to first light little twigs or other kindling material, and only then will the fire spread by itself to the larger pieces.

The same is true in the Torah world. The large branches — the teachers and the outreach workers — gain inspiration and excitement for their own religious observance by seeing the enthusiasm of their students. Enthusiasm is contagious.

Rashi explains that it's not only the excitement of the students that rouses the teachers, it's the learning itself. He explains that the students light the flame in their teachers by "asking questions all the time." It's the very questions and the curiosity of the students that inspire the teachers to grow themselves.

⇨ ⇦

Rabbi Baruch Price said his involvement in *kiruv* has had an unparalleled impact on his own beliefs and observances.

"Certainly it makes me think about things I did not necessarily think about before. ... You think you might be giving over to the other person, but even though it sounds like a cliché, anything you receive in turn is well beyond your wildest imagination.

"Delving into questions, you're forced to reevaluate. Someone confronts you with a question about halachah and suddenly you need to look up halachos you always took for granted. You really have to do your research. You come up with answers quite different from what you initially thought."

Rabbi Price said a person's involvement in outreach has a positive impact not only on him, but on his entire family.

"When kids see that their parents care about the world beyond themselves and other Jews, it's the most powerful *chinuch* they can receive. It's a tremendous educational opportunity for parents if someone asks questions that normally wouldn't be raised in their house. It's a great opportunity to answer questions, not just to their guests but to their children — why do we think like this? [Why do we] do these things?"

15 Becoming a *Mentsch*

WHEN A JEW BECOMES OBSERVANT, IT'S NOT ENOUGH TO simply alter his exterior appearance and behaviors, take on mitzvos, and change his style of dress. Doing so is easy. What Hashem truly desires is internal change, for a Jew to view the world from a Torah-driven perspective. This does not mean a person should reject his prior upbringing and his individual strengths. It means bringing his emotions, desires, and the way he approaches his relationships in line with the proper Torah way of life.

Becoming *frum* means trying to live as a *mentsch*. It means working to become a more refined individual and living a life of a higher purpose. It means leaving an indelible impression on those around us as we try to act according to the way Hashem expects of us.

A non-observant mother whose teenage son had decided to attend synagogue every morning and to grow in his observances described to me the beautiful changes she was seeing in his personality. She told me she could clearly see him becoming kinder and more patient with his brothers and more helpful at home. She also saw in him a greater self-confidence and personal conviction that she knew came directly from his new religious beliefs.

These are our goals as Jews, to polish both our insides and our outsides. It means dedicating ourselves to serving Hashem at all times.

"The Holy One Blessed is He said: 'If you give Me your heart and your eyes, I know that you are Mine" (*Yerushalmi*, *Berachos* 9a).

From the Super Bowl to the Shabbos Table

He's one of the few observant Jews to have ever played in the NFL and to own a Super Bowl ring. Alan Veingrad played for five years as an offensive lineman on the Green Bay Packers, and then joined the Dallas Cowboys in 1991. It was with the Cowboys that he became the proud recipient of a Super Bowl XXVII ring from their 1993 win.

However Alan's journey back to his roots, after his retirement from football, was more exciting than any game he ever played on the field. In the process he discovered what really matters in his life.

Alan grew up in New Jersey and Florida in a home with few Jewish observances. When his parents dropped him off at an afternoon Hebrew school, he didn't even go to class. On most days he could be found skipping rocks at a lake behind the synagogue.

Alan attended East Texas State University (now Texas A&M University-Commerce). Many of his fellow players on the football team had never met a Jew before. They often asked him questions about his religion.

"Occasionally, I had an answer, but sometimes I just made up an answer," he admitted.

Alan played in the NFL for seven years, traveling the country and basking in his momentary fame, especially after the Cowboys'

Super Bowl win. However, after retiring in 1993, he faced a problem common to former NFLers: he was at a complete loss of what to do with his life. Players in the NFL are constantly on the go and are always surrounded by teammates, so often have trouble filling their time when they retire.

"You go through this major void in your life," Alan said. "I know players twenty, twenty-five years out of the league who are still in the void. 'Where's my locker, my itinerary, who are we playing next?'"

During this period Alan and his wife received an invitation for a Shabbos dinner from a cousin who had become *frum*. It was their first authentic Shabbos experience, but it was not quite the life-changing moment one would expect.

"Throughout the meal he was talking about the *parashah* of the week. ... Each of his four kids were giving over *divrei Torah* that they learned in school that week," Alan said. "I was eating the teriyaki salmon, the brisket in large quantities. I was so focused on consuming food I wasn't involved at all in the discussion. Nothing inspired me."

After dinner, Alan's cousin asked him if he would be interested in attending a local class given by a rabbi. He accepted out a sense of obligation. The class was held the following week in a mansion close to the Veingrads' Florida home.

"For the first fifty-nine-and-a-half minutes of the sixty-minute class I was so consumed with the location, this beautiful mansion hosting the class. I had never seen a house like this! I kept thinking, 'Is this house worth four million or five million or six million?'" Alan said. Thirty seconds before the class ended, the rabbi suddenly began talking about envy and materialism. He said if you let yourself be consumed by jealousy, it will only lead to emptiness and a complete void in your life.

"How did this rabbi know what I've been thinking for the last fifty-nine-and-a-half minutes?" Alan thought to himself.

The class ended, and Alan ran up to the rabbi.

"Hey, I need more information about what you're talking about!" Alan said. The rabbi told him to come back the following week for the answers. He returned and was hooked. He began attending the class each week.

Over the next several years in the class, Alan began learning about Judaism's focus on self-improvement and ethics, and especially its practical lessons for becoming a better spouse and father. He had always looked for wisdom from motivational tapes and books, especially those from famous athletes and coaches. He never imagined that he would find these lessons in his own religion. He always thought the Torah was just a history book, but when he discovered its deep focus on personal change, he jumped at the chance to learn more.

During this time Alan and his family also decided to try out a local Chabad House in Fort Lauderdale for Shabbos. It was one of the few times Alan had been to synagogue since his bar mitzvah and he was nervous, but the warm welcome he and his family received by the rabbis and members of the community made them decide to begin coming every week.

On one of his first visits to the Chabad House, Alan received an *aliyah* to the Torah. He had not had an *aliyah* in decades and was uncomfortable when called up.

"After an *aliyah* it's customary for a man to bless the people in his family. A hundred people were looking at me. I was feeling a little nervous. The *gabbai* said, 'Who do you want to bless?' The guy in front of me had listed his wife and children so I did that too.

"'Anybody else?' the *gabbai* asked.

"'The rabbi and his family.'

"'Anybody else?'

("I felt like I was doing something wrong, I had to bless somebody else.)

"'Yeah, the soldiers in Israel.'

"'Anybody else?'

"'No.'

"The *gabbai* said in a soft voice, 'The Packers or the Cowboys?'

("I smiled widely. This was unbelievable, the real deal, I'm in shul and he asked me which one to bless. I said, 'Yeah, let's give the Packers a blessing. I spent five years there, they need the blessing.')

"He said quietly, 'Okay, a blessing for the Packers!'

"He was serious about the *berachah*, of course, but it showed that he had a sense of humor and it made me feel very welcome. After that I stopped sweating. I smiled and said, 'Okay, let's get someone else up here now.'"

The camaraderie in the synagogue helped Alan fill the void he felt in his post-NFL life, and it would soon play an even more important role.

Alan's father passed away a few months after he became observant, and Alan was at a complete loss of what to do. He didn't know how to organize a Jewish burial and mourning. The community rushed in and took care of all the arrangements, including providing meals for Alan and his family during *shivah*.

"In a time like that, you need support, community, an extended family. You need the Jewish community to help you," Alan said. "No teamwork I had ever seen in the NFL matched what I experienced in that little Chabad House in Fort Lauderdale."

While Alan's father was alive, his greatest source of pride was that his son had played football in the NFL. He carried Alan's football card in his wallet, and showed it to everyone he met.

And yet a few months before his death, he said something to Alan that would stay with him forever. He said he could really see amazing differences in his son and grandchildren since they had began becoming observant. They were becoming more refined, giving, and driven people. Because of this he had decided he was more proud to now see his son in a *kippah* than he had ever been to see him in his football helmet.

"That was so powerful to me," Alan said.

Back on the Field

Rabbi Eliyahu Dessler teaches in *Michtav M'Eliyahu* (Volume I, pp. 5–6) that every item in this world is given to us by Hashem solely so we can serve Him and make the world more holy.

He said the physical items of the world can be compared to the vessels of the Beis HaMikdash. Each bowl, spoon, and knife in the Beis HaMikdash had a specific role in the daily service. So, too, all of the physical items of this world were given to us to serve Hashem, to add glory to His name, and bring people closer to Him.

Alan, now Shlomo, realized that his experience in the NFL gave him a unique stage to reach out to other Jews and inspire them. He traded in his football jersey for a suit and tie, and now travels the world as an in-demand speaker, captivating Jewish and non-Jewish audiences with lessons from his football days and from his *teshuvah* journey.

When Shlomo speaks, he encourages his listeners to commit to little steps in their Jewish observance, such as taking on specific mitzvos. Sometimes, people will approach him and tell him they gained new courage in their own observance from hearing him speak.

"Someone will come up and say, "I've never been proud to wear *kippah* outside, but come Monday morning, I'm walking into work with my *kippah* on. Someone else will tell me: 'After hearing your speech, I'm going to try to keep Shabbos.' If someone tells me this after forty-five minutes of my speech, that's amazing. If it's because of my words, what I did, it's so worth it to travel and share my life with people."

Shlomo frequently uses experiences from his football days to teach important messages for living as a committed Jew. For example, he learned from the days of rigorous practice schedules to be extremely careful with his religious commitments.

"When Jimmy Johnson, the great football coach, called a meeting at 7:00 A.M., if someone walked in late, he would look at him and say: 'Is there something more important in your life than preparation for a football game?'"

Shlomo applies that lesson to his prayers.

"I have to get to shul before they start, with tallis and tefillin on, ready to go. If one takes those extra minutes to prepare oneself, arriving early to put on his tallis and tefillin, it gives a greater lift to his davening."

One of the main messages Shlomo tries to impart when speaking is our responsibility as Jews to constantly perform acts of *kiddush Hashem*.

"If we're going to go around this world with a *kippah* on our heads, regardless of who we are, we all have that responsibility. We can't act up at the security counter in the airport. If our order is wrong in Starbucks or the grocery store, we have to act in an extremely dignified way. We represent something extremely big. We should all focus on being a *mentsch*. We all report to the biggest Coach there is."

Alan's transition from football player to a Jew representing Hashem comes across in his speeches, and leaves a great mark on his audiences. In a nation which elevates sports players because of their physical prowess despite the imperfections they may have in their personal behaviors and relationships, his message of personal change is inspiring.

After speaking at a university in Florida, one student remarked on how much she had noticed this message in him:

"In contrast, the Torah way of life provides a spiritual path of healing and satisfaction that comes from following an ancient connection to Hashem and the fulfillment of mitzvos like Shabbos, *kashrus*, and the study of Torah and Gemara. Judaism provides the spiritual and intellectual nourishment and the family life that are lacking in professional sports."

Shlomo was once speaking to a group of eighty Jewish high school kids in New York. He had brought his own children with him. Throughout the speech, his daughter was sitting in the audience giggling and talking. His son was standing behind him. Shlomo began recounting a story about running the forty-yard dash, one of the measures of a football player's speed. Just at that moment, he sensed that his son was running dashes behind him!

Shlomo tried as hard as he could to maintain his focus and not to turn around. He was beginning to get frustrated, but tried hard not to show it. Suddenly his son fell and started screaming. One of the rabbis ran up to the stage, picked him up and brought him to the audience.

"I was boiling inside!" Shlomo said. "They brought me in to give an inspirational speech, and here it was getting ruined!"

A little while later his son calmed down and decided to bring his father a bottle of water. He approached from behind to hand him the open bottle. Shlomo was speaking animatedly and was waving his hands. He did not see his son approaching him from behind. Suddenly Shlomo jerked his arm back and hit the bottle out of his son's hand, splashing water everywhere! The speech had gone from bad to worse.

After the presentation, one of the rabbis approached Shlomo.

"I'm very impressed with how well you maintained your composure!"

Shlomo just smiled. He was boiling inside, but had gained a critical victory by not showing his frustration. Prior to his *teshuvah* journey, he notes, he might have not reacted as sanguinely.

Reporting to the Real Head Coach

Shlomo's trademark, other than his 6-foot-5-inch, 235-pound frame, is his Super Bowl ring. He wears it everywhere and it's often the first thing people want to see. Shlomo gained a new insight into the ring's message during a flight once to New York for an event.

"On the flight, I looked closer at the Super Bowl ring, closer than ever before. It carries a lot of info, and there's one thing I never noticed in twenty years of wearing it. The ring has the numbers 16 and 3, because the Dallas Cowboys that year won sixteen games and lost three. If you juggle it around it's 613, representative of the 613 mitzvos.

"Seeing that solidified all the traveling and schlepping I do. Why do I have that ring? It's not about the Super Bowl. It's about the 613. That's the real reason I have that ring."

Traveling the world teaching others has also taught Shlomo important messages about himself and his own service of Hashem.

Throughout his travels Shlomo has met a wide myriad of Jewish people from different backgrounds and experiences. He said the one common bond uniting them all is their sincere care and concern for other Jews.

"I've had friends, former teammates ask me, 'How do you fly from here to Panama? You don't know where you're going, where you're staying. You're going all the way to South Africa — isn't it weird staying in other people's homes?' I tell them, 'No, we're family. There's an immediate connection. When you land, it's like reconnecting with a long-lost friend or a family member.'

"In the business world, it takes time to build relationships. It's different in the Jewish world — you take a car ride from the airport with your host, and it takes just a few minutes for the relationship to cultivate. Once we arrive [they tell me], 'There's your bathroom, here's your bedroom, we have something for you to eat. If you're hungry at night, feel free to help yourself.' People are really sincere; they just want to make sure I'm comfortable."

Shlomo has even succeeded in being a source of inspiration to his former teammates. From time to time he'll run into former players and spend time catching up with them. Shlomo always marvels at the stark contrast at the divergent paths between their post-NFL lives. Even his former teammates admit this upon meeting him again. They marvel at the self-control and personal strength he now has. He is not ashamed to tell them that these come solely from his religious growth.

He once met a former teammate at a restaurant. After spending a half-hour catching up, Shlomo excused himself and returned home to his family.

His teammate called him the next day at two o'clock in the afternoon with a raspy voice.

"I just woke up," the man mumbled. "I really want to talk to you. I was drinking until the wee hours of morning, doing things I shouldn't have done. I want to know more about your dedication to your religion and your commitment to your values that you don't do those things."

Shlomo said the man calls him routinely with the same message.

"He still calls me once a month. Something always comes up and he references that he realizes he has to get back into the church, or spend more time with his family and kids. He knows he needs more structure. He watches the Jewish people. We know these things; we know that we have a real responsibility."

In addition to his speaking career, Shlomo also works in real estate in Florida. Once, a close associate asked him why he decided to grow a beard.

"Alan, you're a businessman, you're living in this world. This beard, it just doesn't fit," the man challenged him.

"I said, 'Let me ask you a question. If I won the lottery and bought a very expensive, all-chromed out Harley Davidson, put an earring in my ear, wore a leather vest, boots, grew my beard down to my stomach, and drove my Harley up and down the road along the water, what would you think?"

"It would be really cool," the man replied.

"But if I'm growing it for myself, to get closer to G-d, what's the problem with that?"

The man had no answer.

In 2013, Shlomo was invited by the Dallas Cowboys to the twenty-year reunion of Super Bowl XXVII. He and other teammates, as well as players from Super Bowl XXII, were honored in a special event on the field at halftime.

"I wanted to be there on the field with my *kippah* on. Being a football player, not observant, and now wearing a *kippah*, it gave me a great sense of pride."

After the game the previous and current players joined up for a party in a hall below the stadium. In the middle of the party, head coach Jason Garret entered the room. He ignored the people crowding around him wanting to speak to him, but instead scanned the room. His eyes met Shlomo's and he made a beeline to him. The two men had played together years earlier, but they had not seen each other in a long time.

"You are like a legend around here," Jason said.

("I thought, 'I wasn't such a great football player to be a legend around here.'")

"You're always welcome here, we're so happy that you came," the coach continued. "I can only imagine how much wisdom and knowledge you've gathered over the years."

The Dallas Cowboys' assistant public relations director standing behind him perked up. "But Coach, you went to Princeton!"

"Yes, but it's not the same as what he has learned."

Those words made a deep impression on Shlomo, and indeed they have been his objective throughout his speaking career: recognizing the personal growth and insight he has achieved through his religious development and using them to inspire others. He has learned that it's not athletic victories and physical prowess that the real Head Coach demands, but the level of one's internal strength and personal growth.

Rabbi Shimshon Raphael Hirsch said the root of the word "*Adam*" is the word "*domeh*," to be similar. To Whom are we similar? To the *Aleph*, the One — Hashem.

The core of our existence is to emulate Hashem, to go in His ways and to teach others to do so. We need to constantly remind ourselves and others that we are Hashem's emissaries in the world.

It's easy to achieve this focus on Hashem when we are in the "religious world" of synagogue and Shabbos. But to achieve this Hashem-centric focus constantly, whether we are on the street, in public, or at home, is a more challenging task. It takes constant work to keep Hashem in front of us at all times, in all situations.

For each of us, every day is a Super Bowl. The real test is not how we perform for thousands of adoring fans, but how we treat our spouses, our kids, and those around us.

A Doctor's Kindness

Mark Paris, MD, is a leading infectious disease specialist in Palm Beach, Florida. His official title is Senior Physician, but his real job is trying to bring light to some of the darkest areas that patients face in the scope of their illnesses. It's a message that he learned forty years ago as he witnessed an Orthodox doctor dispensing simple care and love for all people.

"[Patients] know that I'm treating them the way I would treat anyone else. These are very sick people. All they want is someone to give them respect," Mark said. "The whole way I deal with people is based on my religious attitude."

Mark grew up in a non-religious Jewish household in Brighton Beach, New York. He attended PS 253, where almost the entire school was like him.

"I only had three or four non-Jewish kids in my class from kindergarten to fifth grade," Mark said. "It was a very Jewish environment but I didn't know anyone religious."

He attended college at Tulane University and then went to the University of Tennessee in Memphis for medical school. During Mark's fourth year of medical school he worked in a local hospital. It was there that he met Manny.

Emmanuel Stadlan, MD, better known among his patients and fellow physicians as Manny, was a pathologist in the hospital and an observant Jew. He worked at a time when segregation was still rampant in the Deep South, and many doctors had separate waiting rooms. Manny stood out not only because of the *kippah* on his head, but because of the incredible respect and warmth that he showed to every person.

"He used to sit and drink tea with the black housekeeper. I noticed this guy treated everyone the same. He didn't treat the cleaning lady any differently than his boss. He told me it was because he was religious," Mark said. "He told me, 'Everyone was created in G-d's image, so you have to treat everyone with respect.'"

Mark shadowed Manny in the hospital, not just to learn from his deep medical knowledge, but to study his conduct and sincere concern for everyone he met. The more time he spent with Manny, the more Mark saw that this was the kind of doctor that he wanted to become.

"He was very intellectual, a really smart guy," Mark said. "He realized he could be a great professor and could still sit and drink tea with the black housekeeper."

For Mark's last three months of medical school, he did a Tropical Medicine Fellowship in Costa Rica. For Passover, he and his family were invited to a local rabbi's house for the Seders. During the Seders, Mark sat next to the Jewish caretaker of the synagogue. Between the little bit of English that the caretaker spoke, and Mark's minimal Spanish, the two men struck up a friendship.

When the caretaker found out that the Parises were staying in a hotel, he insisted that they move in with him and his family for the remaining few weeks. They accepted. The accommodations were beautiful and Mark and his family were deeply touched by the caretaker's hospitality.

"He basically said to me that it's really terrible that my grandfather may have come from same shtetl as his, and we have to communicate with my broken English and his broken Spanish," Mark recalled. "I thought it was amazing that he would do so much for me even though we're not related. I decided I have to go find out more what it's all about and why he would do so much for me."

Mark returned to Memphis for his medical internship and began looking for answers. He began spending more time with Manny, and realized that much of the behavior he admired came from Manny's Jewish roots.

In the autopsy room or over informal cups of tea, Manny began sharing some of the teachings that had influenced him. Manny introduced Mark to other Orthodox families in the local community. Mark began reading all the Jewish books he could get his hands on. Over time, Mark and his family became observant.

Since his early days in medical school, Mark has been on a charged mission to try to bring love and care to patients throughout the world.

In Florida, Mark now spends much of his time running clinics for people from third-world countries. Many of his patients experience strong cultural stigmas associated with disease and medication, and suffer from depression and other challenges. Mark's compassion helps them to cut through the gloom.

Patients and colleagues attest that Mark's empathy is some of the best medicine he prescribes.

"The real concern that Mark has for other people is one of the hallmarks of his life and it really shows. Whatever he has learned, I wish they could bottle it and send it out. It's really wonderful," said Jeffrey Reynolds, a social worker who works with

Mark. "Today we were having lunch and a nurse came in and said, 'There's a patient sitting up in bed crying. Can you help him?' Mark got up from the meal and only returned after helping the patient. I can assure you his meal was cold."

Mark's wife Deborrah, a social worker, runs a nonprofit organization called Multinational Service Center which provides free or low-cost eye exams, glasses, and social services for patients. Many of her patients are immigrants from Haiti or Latin America. Mark and Deborrah also now travel the world consulting on medical projects and treating patients in third world countries, from the Amazon Rain Forest to deep into the heart of Africa.

Mark spent time in Peru researching infectious causes of blindness and has helped identify quick, low-cost laboratory tests that can be best implemented in third-world counties. Mark said his most meaningful project was when the Global Medic Corps sent him and his wife to Lesotho, Africa to be on the first African team of clinical mentors for the Clinton Foundation in 2005. Mark and Deborrah helped local medical practitioners to implement treatments in hospitals and clinics and they developed a curriculum for the Lesotho Ministry of Health.

Rabbeinu Bachya says strikingly in *Chovos HaLevavos* (*Sha'ar HaBitachon*) that the only person who can be truly happy and live a fulfilled life, with solid, warm relationships with others, is a person who has solid faith in Hashem.

When a person trusts that all of his success in his personal and professional life is decided by Hashem, he has no reason to fear or be jealous of other people. He is even eager to help others, not out of a selfish desire for a favor in return, but out of a sincere interest to see them succeed. He knows that encouraging other people's success will not take away from his own.

Such a person truly loves others and is beloved by them. Other people trust him as well, knowing that he sincerely desires their benefit. They have no reason to fear that he will trick them or turn on them for his own benefit, for he has complete *bitachon* that only Hashem decides his future.

When a Jew returns to his roots and places his faith in Hashem, the results are far-reaching. His relationships with others improve. He becomes more content with his life and personal standing and feels less jealousy of others. He even learns how to better handle disappointments and challenges.

Becoming observant does not only mean changing one's outward appearance or taking on particular new observances. It means finding true happiness and fulfillment in life, and living a life of ultimate joy in serving Hashem.

The Principles of a Principal

SHIMON WARONKER IS a man on a mission. He is a *ba'al teshuvah* and a Chabadnik, and an experienced school principal. He turned around one of New York City's most dangerous, crime-laden public schools into a model of proper education. His secret? Teaching students to take responsibility for their actions and to live purpose-driven lives. He learned these ideals years ago during his first few days in yeshivah while becoming religious.

Waronker was born in Santiago, Chile and was raised in a Conservative Jewish home. He was eleven when his father passed away and his mother subsequently moved the family to the United States, settling in Rockville, Maryland.

Growing up, Waronker was far removed from most Jewish rituals. When a cousin gave him a pair of tefillin after his bar mitzvah, he didn't even know what to do with them.

"I asked our [Conservative] rabbi," Waronker recalled. "He said, 'Tefillin — that's an anachronism. We don't do that anymore.' I really didn't know much so I accepted it."

Years later when Waronker visited Israel for the first time, he had his first experience interacting with *frum* Jews. He was approached by a Chabadnik at the Kosel who asked him if he would like to put on tefillin.

"I looked at him and said, 'We don't do that anymore, right?' He said, 'No, we still do.'"

Waronker attended college at the University of Maryland, College Park. He was a member of the college's ROTC U.S. Army program, and after college served on active duty as a lieutenant in a military intelligence unit. For the next two years he served in many roles in the military, including as a training officer, an executive officer of an army company and an aide-to-camp for a general.

Following his army service, Waronker began questioning his purpose in life, his religious beliefs, and the order of the world.

"I though that either life has a purpose or it doesn't. Either someone endowed it with a purpose or there is none," Waronker explained. "It made more sense for me to believe that life did indeed have a purpose, and that G-d created the universe and that there was only one G-d, not multiple gods. I realized I needed to find out more about my roots."

At the same time, Waronker had a friend who had become observant and was attending the Rabbinical College of America, the Chabad yeshivah in Morristown, New Jersey. Waronker was deeply impressed with his friend's transformation and growth in the yeshivah. At that point, Waronker was just beginning to explore his Judaism, and upon seeing the changes in his friend's life, he decided to try out the yeshivah as well. He entered the yeshivah in May 1994.

Upon first stepping into the yeshivah, Waronker knew that this was the lifestyle for him.

"The energy level was so amazing. It was like a *chasunah*. Walking into the hall and hearing the roar of learning was incredible."

On his first day in the yeshivah, Waronker joined a class

learning from the *sefer Tanya*. In that class he heard a profound concept that has guided him ever since.

"Most of you are wondering why you are here. We're now going to find out," the rabbi said. "The world is a dwelling place for Hashem. You're here to make a heaven on earth for Hashem. You're here to make this a better world."

The words hit a deep chord in Waronker.

"It struck me as true and good and solid," Waronker said. "That lesson the first day there stuck with me. It helps one focus. Every action we take should make this a better world. It was really powerful."

Waronker spent three years in the yeshivah, during which he became observant and married a *ba'alas teshuvah* named Marisa. The couple then moved to Crown Heights, New York.

Putting Faith to the Test

The words that Waronker heard on that first day in yeshivah, compounded by many other ideas he learned during the three years, sent him on a mission to improve the world and positively impact the lives of others.

Waronker began working as a teacher of English and Math in a religious school in nearby Williamsburg. In 2001, he joined the New York City public school system to teach in an all-minority school in Crown Heights. He caught the attention of his superiors and was recommended for an elite program to train future Board of Education principals.

Following the program, he was appointed to be the principal of the Jordan L. Mott School in the South Bronx, also known as Middle School 22. It was one of the twelve most violent schools in the city and was on the New York State list of failing schools. Gangs ruled the school and used it as their headquarters for their drug trade. Six veteran principals had quit over the previous two years, and even the large police presence stationed in the school was unable to control the students.

To put it mildly, Waronker was absolutely terrified by the assignment.

"For three days [before I started the job] I prayed and didn't sleep," Waronker said. "I had a growing family then. I was very concerned for my life and for my children, but I felt like a soldier. This was my mission."

His first day arrived and Waronker boarded the subway and set off for his new assignment. As a principal he knew that his first task was to check the school's register to see the number of students in the school. He checked — and did a double take when he saw the number. The school had exactly 770 students. Waronker took the number, the same number as the street address of the Chabad central headquarters, as a direct sign from Hashem.

"I said, 'Yes Boss, I'm here by Divine providence,'" Waronker recounted. "It was with pure *bitachon*. I told myself, 'I'm not going to be intimidated. I'm not afraid. I'm here because I have 770 students on my registrar.' That's faith, crystal clear."

Implementing Changes

Waronker entered MS 22 with a keen sense of his mission, based deeply on the lessons of *tikkun olam* that he first heard in the Chabad yeshivah.

"There are three principles that schools need to follow — they need to focus on relationships, empowerment, and transparency," Waronker explained. "To the kids, they need to understand what their mission is and why they're here on this planet: to create a better world."

The student body was composed of a mix of minorities — African Americans and recent immigrants from Africa who spoke only French, but it was predominantly Hispanic. Waronker's native command of the Spanish language and South American culture helped him immensely to gain acceptance and to make his voice heard among the students.

Waronker instituted numerous changes to the school, which

included tackling the gang violence head-on and inst... school dress code to purge gang colors. He divided the schoo... eight mini-schools, and even brought in an etiquette expert ... teach proper manners. His changes led to several death threats, both from students and parents, but he continued with his mission.

But his biggest change in the school was bringing in a fresh perspective, one of believing in the potential of his students and helping them to see a brighter future for themselves.

The New York City Board of Education, as well as students and parents of MS 22, had initially doubted whether a suit-wearing, bearded Jewish man could run the minority, lower-class school. But after only a few months in the school, he had already received widespread approval from parents, faculty, and the Board of Education.

One year, in December, an endless line of parents came to his office in the school to give him holiday presents. The number of families bringing gifts was unprecedented. Waronker finally pulled one mother aside and asked the reason for all of the presents.

"It's because you're Jewish and we know that Jews value education," she said. "That's why we know our child will have a great education here."

Waronker said his goal was to help the students visualize a life outside the one of poverty and violence to which they were accustomed. In his goals, Waronker succeeded beyond his imagination.

The school was removed from the city's list of most violent schools, and its test scores rose so dramatically that it earned an "A" on its new school report card. Daily school attendance rose to more than ninety percent, an unprecedented number.

"It's an entirely different place," School Chancellor Joel Klein told the New York Times. "If I could clone Shimon Waronker, I would do that immediately."

.een Sense of Leadership

Waronker has a clear vision that we as Jews are responsible for the well-being of the world and have a Divine mission to improve it. Central to his educational and leadership approaches is paying attention to the needs of those around him. He points to Rabbi Menachem Mendel Schneerson *zt"l*, the Lubavitcher Rebbe, as a sterling example in this area, and recalls a story:

A rabbi in the IDF once came to New York to meet Rabbi Schneerson. They scheduled a meeting for 2:00 A.M. one morning. The IDF rabbi was staying with a friend who lived nearby, and who offered to drive him to the meeting in the Chabad Headquarters, at 770 Eastern Parkway.

The IDF rabbi entered the building for the meeting and returned to the car two minutes later. He told his friend that when he had entered, Rabbi Schneerson had immediately asked him how he had arrived. He told the Rebbe about the friend who had driven him and was waiting outside in the car. Rabbi Schneerson told him to invite the driver to come inside out of the cold.

When the driver entered the room, Rabbi Schneerson stretched out his hands in a warm welcome and offered him a cup of tea. The Rebbe's sensitivity left a deep impression on the two men, as well as on Waronker who heard the story later from the driver.

"It was 2:00 A.M. and he was thinking of the driver! That's leadership — how do we make sure the needs of others are taken care of," Waronker explained. "I think there are two pillars of Jewish leadership — a sense of mission and *bitachon*, and to do it through sensitivity to other people."

These two pillars of Jewish leadership are apparent in Waronker's daily life. He personally models the behavior he expects from his teachers and students, said Pepe Gutierrez. Pepe was a teacher under Waronker at MS 22 and later joined a new public school that Waronker subsequently founded. He said Waronker's deep moral compass is obvious.

"Honesty is the key with him. Over the years that I've known him, that has always been at the forefront. What he said has value and weight to it," Gutierrez explained. "Also from a personal perspective he's a strong family man. His kids are always involved. He believes in good values and teaches those values."

Those principles of leadership and morality have been developing in Waronker since his first day at the yeshivah in Morristown — a responsibility to improve the world through sensitivity and love for others.

"We're here to make this a better world," Waronker said. "That's our job."

Life in the Fast Lane

In a blur of colors and a roar of engines, the Formula Ford race cars sped around the race track at the Riverside International Raceway in California. Hitting 125 miles an hour, George Gottlieb* pulled his car away from the pack. Lap after lap, the other cars tried to keep up with him, but to no avail. After ten laps the checkered flag waved as he crossed the finish line, far ahead of his competitors. The thrill of his first victory filled his body as he jumped out of his car and ran to the winner's podium on an emotional and physical high.

Minutes later, George was standing atop the podium clutching his trophy. It was a moment he had waited for literally his entire life, wining his first race. This was just the beginning of his career and he could already picture himself on the podium many more times after future successful races.

However as he basked in his victory, a feeling nagged at him.

"I was very excited that I had just won, but as I was standing there holding the trophy I realized something was missing,"

George said. "I ended up feeling empty. I thought there had to be more to life than just this."

George stepped down from the platform and slowly walked away from the track. Since he was a young boy, he had dreamed about becoming a racecar driver. He had planned his whole life toward that goal, but now, just after his first victory, he realized it was not worth the years of effort and tremendous planning he had put into it.

"Being a professional race-car driver, it's like any athlete. It's totally consuming. You're always thinking, going over tracks. It's a 24-7 job," George explained. "If you're not completely 110 percent in it, you'll never make it. I realized at that moment it just wasn't what I wanted in life."

George grew up as a Reform Jew in California, surrounded by many other non-observant Jews. Even as a teenager he felt that there had to be an order to the world and a higher Divine purpose. He looked deeply into his Reform Judaism but felt that it lacked the answers he pursued. He investigated nearly every other religious system he could find. He explored parts of Christianity, looked into Native American beliefs and tried Eastern religions. Nothing rang true.

"I kept finding castles in the sky that didn't turn out to be anything," George said. "I was always searching for truth. I knew there was something out there."

George was at a loss for answers to his religious questions, but applied his energy toward his goal of racing. As a child he had constantly watched races on television and daydreamed about races. Once he learned to drive, he tried to race whenever he could. As a teenager he begged his parents to let him become a professional race-car driver, but they repeatedly refused.

But the years of nagging paid off. At age eighteen, when he was a freshman in college, he convinced his parents to let him attend the Bob Bondurant Driving School in California for one day of advanced driving training. George drove exceptionally well on the course. His instructors told him that if he was interested, he could have a successful career ahead of him. But again his parents refused.

"Over our dead bodies," they told him. But realizing that they could not limit his choices forever, they added, "But if you really still want it, when you graduate college you can do it."

After graduation, George found a job in commercial real estate. He saved up enough money to travel to France to attend a two-week session at an elite racing school. He raced Formula Renault Turbo Martinis and absolutely loved it.

George returned to America and started working for the Skip Barber Racing School in California. It was during his time at the school that he had his first winning race at the nearby Riverside International Raceway, followed by his epiphany on top of the winner's podium.

After his realization that he had spent his entire life working toward an empty goal, George began looking for other outlets for his energy and new paths to pursue in life. Soon after, a friend told him about a local class hosted by the Jewish outreach organization Aish HaTorah. He attended it and was hooked. In the class a rabbi discussed popular secular topics and solicited feedback and discussion from the attendees. At the end of the class he provided the Jewish outlook on the topics. Every answer hit home with George.

"Every time I noticed how right [the Jewish perspective] was. I knew I was going on the correct path."

With his interest kindled, George began attending more local classes and then decided to attend a six-week Aish HaTorah summer program in Israel. This program solidified his realization that Orthodox Judaism held the answers to his questions. He came back for another year to learn.

Throughout his religious growth, George shared some of what

he was learning with his sister and parents. During his year in Israel, George's sister graduated college, and he invited her to try an Aish program in Israel. She loved it and stayed on to learn. Their parents had retired at a young age, and they came to visit their two children in Israel. They attended a handful of classes at Aish, spent time in the Aish community, and decided that this was for them as well.

Today the entire Gottlieb family is observant, thanks to George's pursuit for meaning in his life. He took the fervor and dedication that he had applied toward his earlier goal of becoming a successful racecar driver, and reapplied it to his new direction. Like a successful racecar driver who knows when to pull ahead and lead the pack, George has been leading his family on the correct course on the racetrack of life.

The *mishnah* in *Taanis* (2:1) brings a surprising example of the *teshuvah* that Hashem desires from us. The prophet Yonah had traveled to the city of Nineveh to beseech its amoral residents to repent from their evil ways. The people responded positively and Hashem forgave them.

Why did Hashem forgive them? The *mishnah* says that Hashem did not look at the fact that they fasted or that they tore their clothing. These were only outward signs of their *teshuvah*. Hashem instead looked at the sincere commitment that the people made to change their actions. The prophet describes metaphorically that the city's residents tore their hearts in addition to their clothing.

The inhabitants of Nineveh heeded Yonah's call to repent and responded with genuine *teshuvah*, completely changing their ways. That is what Hashem desires from a person who is growing. He wants us to change our insides, our drives and our desires. He wants us to realize what matters in life, and to race full-throttle to get it.

The Long Road to Recovery

For Gail Schaeffer*, discovering Hashem and the love that He has for her, provided direction and purpose to her life. But it gave her something far greater. It literally gave her life itself.

To an unaware observer, Gail today is the perfect model of a well-adjusted, stable young religious woman. She is married with beautiful children and is completely put together. However, hidden deep below her calm exterior is a story of a troubled childhood, filled with abuse and addictions. For most of her childhood and adolescence, she felt completely lost in the world and as if she had no one to support or love her. However, when she began discovering Hashem and His love, she found the strength to pull herself up out of the mire and recover from her abuse. As it says in *Mishlei* (8:35), "Whoever finds Me finds life."

Gail grew up in New York, in a pathologically dysfunctional home. She was physically and emotionally abused. She felt unloved by her family, and Gail developed severe depression and psychosomatic ailments as a result. She said now that she cannot remember a time in her life when she was not depressed.

She was sent to psychiatrists but to no avail. Instead of helping her deal with the underlying causes of her depression, they instead diagnosed her with bipolar disorder and other illnesses. At one point in her life, Gail was taking twelve different psychiatric medications! The medicines affected her body and dragged her down into further depression. She found out later that she didn't have any of the diseases she was diagnosed with.

With seemingly no hope for recovery, in high school Gail found a way to escape, albeit only temporary. She heard about a high-school program in Israel. It was a secular program, designed to give students only a basic awareness of Judaism.

Gail went for a year, mostly as a chance to escape from her

unbearable life at home. The program gave her the respite she needed. But during the year, she also began developing an appreciation for Judaism and Israel, especially from seeing the emotional support system inherent in her own religion.

Gail came home after the year and tried to bring some of the inspirations and lessons into her life. She tried to keep kosher at home and to follow other practices. Though her religious observances gave her strength and meaning, soon she encountered the same abuse and again fell into her cycles of depression.

When her psychosomatic symptoms returned, Gail's doctors sent her for ECT, electroconvulsive therapy. ECT involves shocks administered to the brain for patients with severe depression that does not respond to treatment. Side effects can include confusion and memory loss. In a small number of patients the effects can be even worse.

Gail received ECT treatment numerous times over a single month. The treatment did not rid her of her illnesses, but instead left her with intense long-term memory loss and even personality changes. Family members visited her in the hospital and she was unable to identify them. She had to learn how to read and write again.

However, the ECT brought one new item to the surface. As the ECT made her forget almost everything that she knew, it began drawing out ideas that were stored up in her soul. She began recalling and connecting to Jewish truths and teachings. She had no Jewish education and few religious experiences while growing up, but somehow she began recalling specific Jewish concepts. She began remembering profound spiritual ideas about the existence of G-d, faith, truth, and the holiness of the Creator.

"The only thing I remembered was my religion — anything pertaining to G-d and religiosity," Gail said. "When I had ECT, everything was taken from me, but I had a very strong Jewish *neshamah* and I clung to it."

Gail was put under complete anesthesia before each procedure. She said that Hebrew words popped into her mind each time that she received the anesthesia. They were the words of the Shema prayer. She doesn't recall ever learning the Shema, but inexplicably she knew what the words were.

"I never had any formal training, that's why I thought it was so amazing," Gail said. "Clearly I must have learned this in the womb."

Indeed, the Rabbis write (*Niddah* 30b) that an angel teaches the Torah to a fetus while it is in its mother's womb. Gail said it was this Torah that she was now recalling.

The ECT treatments ended and Gail felt like she had an amazing opportunity to start her life over. She recalled little of her childhood abuse but now had clear knowledge of her religion and a burning desire to cling to it.

"At first I couldn't form sentences, I couldn't really speak, but I knew Hashem, I knew that Hashem loves me. He created me," Gail said. "I knew that Hashem loved me so deeply so I had all the reason to live and serve Him."

This newfound awareness of Hashem and His love helped Gail recover from the treatments and previous abuse and build a new life. She began reading whatever Jewish books she could get her hands on. Within six months of the treatments ending she had begun keeping Shabbos and kosher.

"I really feel like a total soldier of G-d. 'Here is your mission — do mitzvos.' It might be difficult sometimes, life might not always be easy, but that's what Hashem gives you. You have to use it to serve Him."

Over time as her memory returned, she became aware again of the abuse that she had received as a child. However, her new religious beliefs and awareness of Hashem's love helped her to overcome them and to avoid slipping again into the negative behaviors she once had followed.

It's now been several years since the ECT treatments. Gail is off the treatments and all of her psychiatric medications and other substances.

"For me now, there's no need to take medicine. I found all of these ways to become healthy. If I'm feeling a little down, I always know there's Torah. I can read the *parashah* or I can just daven and I'll feel better," Gail said. "I won't say the treatments have no value for other people, but for myself, I was diagnosed with many conditions that I did not have. I did not need medicine — I just needed a little bit of love from Hashem and His guidance."

⇨ ⇦

Postscript: After finishing her treatments and discovering Hashem, Gail moved from her parents' house to Manhattan. At a class at a Jewish outreach center she met a sweet young man named Ben Blatt*. He came from a well-adjusted family and was just becoming observant.

They spent a year together in the same class but never spoke. Finally, a matchmaker set them up. They dated for three weeks. Ben showered her with encouragement and support, and she felt emotionally complete with him.

They were considering becoming engaged. A rabbi who knew Gail's story told her that she must tell him about her past. She was nervous. She was terrified that he would be scared away.

But abiding by her rabbi's words, she decided to tell Ben her entire story during their next date.

Ben's mouth dropped as she told her story, and he turned white. "Oh my G-d," he kept saying. Once she finished, he stood up and walked out of the room to think things over.

Gail felt like she had just lost the only person in her life who deeply cared about her.

After a few minutes he returned to the room and sat back down across from her.

"I love you," he said. "I don't care about what you just told me. Over the past year that I've known you, you've given me no reason to think that there's anything wrong with you. I don't think any of this will affect you."

They were married soon after.

The Rambam writes in *Hilchos Teshuvah* (9:1): if a person fulfills the Torah with joy and lives a purpose-driven life, the Torah itself promises that Hashem will remove physical impediments from him and will give him the means to observe it completely.

Once Gail found Hashem and realized the love that He had for her, she was able to rebuild her life under His guiding care.

Achieving True Happiness

In 2011 the Skverer Rebbe of New Square, New York, met with a group of rabbis involved with outreach and education. He left them with an important lesson about the significance of their work.

He explained that every Jew, regardless of their level of observance, will have a place in the World to Come. But, he said, the true question is: how many Jews have a place in *this* world? How many appreciate the true joys of life?

"True *simchah* is a Shabbos meal where the father is the king, the wife is the queen and the children are like princes. True *simchah* can only be attained by performing mitzvos," the Rebbe explained.

What is true happiness and pleasure? Judaism does not believe in asceticism, and the daily life of an observant Jew is full of physical joy and happiness. But Judaism also does not believe in unrestrained physical pleasure without limit. Such desires and actions can end up being physically destructive and even demeaning to the person and others. Rather, Judaism teaches people how to achieve appropriate pleasure, each with its particular time, place, and amount.

For example, when a Jew celebrates the joy of the holiday of Sukkos, he is experiencing the true, lasting *simchah* of this world. The holiday is full of mitzvos and observances that leave an eternal impact. When a man and woman marry and raise a family of children who follow in their footsteps, raising future generations of Torah-observant Jews, they have achieved true success in life.

When a person learns Torah and performs mitzvos, he is binding himself to his Creator and receives rewards both in this world and the World to Come. And when he lives a life based on substantial goals and has worked on his character and his relationships with others, he has achieved greatness. This is the true joy of this world.

A COMPLETE *TESHUVAH*

THE TORAH IS compared to fire (*Yirmeyahu* 23:29). Sometimes, just coming into contact with it can completely transform a person. Its bright light shines deep inside a person to reveal his inner strengths. It uncovers and exposes the powers of conviction that are buried deep inside him, even if he is unaware of them.

Mordechai Stimlowitz* was once witness to such a personal transformation. He watched how a few rays of the Torah's light illuminated a man's potential and led him on a life-altering direction.

Mordechai is not a trained outreach professional; rather, he is an ordinary businessman who lives in Lakewood, New Jersey, and owns a small furniture manufacturing company.

One day he was asked to become a mentor in a new program being started in an Orthodox synagogue in Twin Rivers, New Jersey. The program matched up local residents to learn in-person with mentors from the Lakewood community. The program had been conceived by the rabbi of the synagogue, Rabbi Eli Gewirtz. The program eventually grew into a highly impactful, nationwide Torah learning network called Partners in Torah, which matches people to learn over the phone and in person.

Once a week, Mordechai drove up together with other men from Lakewood to Twin Rivers. He was paired up with Alan, an unobservant Jewish man in his late thirties. It was Alan's first exposure to true Jewish learning.

"We started with Chumash, the *parashah* of the week. We used it as a springboard for many topics — *Mesillas Yesharim*, other books, Jewish philosophy. We spoke mostly about what it means to be Jewish," Mordechai said.

As a young man twenty years earlier, Alan had joined the U.S. Army. One night during boot camp in the early winter, he was caught in a raging rain storm and came down with a serious cold. A doctor on the base examined him and performed a full physical exam. He detected serious and previously unknown problems in Alan's heart. His heart had a hole and a valve which had not fully developed. Alan received an immediate discharge from the military.

Over the next twenty years, Alan took good care of his heart, carefully following his doctors' orders. He had no outside signs of any difficulties.

However six months after he and Mordechai began studying together, Alan began suffering from symptoms of his heart problems. His cardiologist decided to replace his undeveloped heart valve with one from a pig's body. Unfortunately, the procedure was unsuccessful.

Alan's health began to deteriorate and he had open heart surgery.

Mordechai visited Alan in the hospital frequently during his recovery. He helped him to put on tefillin for the first time. Alan told him that he was deeply touched by the visits. They also continued their study sessions whenever possible, either in the synagogue or in his hospital room.

Mordechai invited Alan and his family to their son's *pidyon haben*, and over time the two families grew closer together.

Their learning continued. Alan soaked up everything he was hearing, and his appreciation for Jewish wisdom grew exponentially. People who sat near Alan and Mordechai in the synagogue said they were greatly inspired by Alan's excitement for everything he was learning. Over time, Mordechai started thinking that he wasn't accomplishing anything as Alan never seemed to be impacted by their learning.

Mordechai spoke about this issue with Rabbi Gewirtz.

"Rabbi Gewirtz told me that it's not our place to change people. You could, however, ask him if would be interested in taking on something small."

During their learning session the following week, Mordechai raised the idea.

"Alan, would you want to take on a small step to bring to action the things we've talked about? It might bring fulfillment to your life. Maybe consider making a small change in your kitchen, or perhaps your wife would like to light Shabbos candles in your home."

Alan's face lit up.

"You know, that's an amazing idea. Let me think about it."

Mordechai looked forward nervously to their learning session the following week.

"The next week I could tell something had changed. His face was lit up, he was jumping in his seat, really excited. He told me, 'I thought about what you said. I spoke to my wife and this is what we want to do. We're not about to *kasher* our home now, but every Thursday night we go out on a date to particular restaurant, because on the menu is our favorite dish made of pork. We decided we won't go to that restaurant any more.'"

Alan's face was glowing as he said these words. Mordechai could tell that it had not been an easy decision, but he and his wife had made a genuine commitment to grow Jewishly.

As they departed from each other that evening, Mordechai left him with words of encouragement and commended him for the decision that he and his wife had made. Alan again conveyed his own excitement at the decision, which he hoped would be the first of many to come.

A few days later at 6:00 A.M., Mordechai's phone rang. It was Alan's wife. Alan had passed away suddenly from his heart condition during the night.

"We were the first people she called. That's how close we were."

Mordechai told her that he would handle all of the funeral arrangements. He called a local funeral home. Alan's body was prepared according to halachah and buried that afternoon.

Mordechai drove to the funeral with several other men from Lakewood. The eulogy was delivered by a rabbi who knew Alan and was aware of his excitement for learning and his recent decision.

The rabbi quoted the Gemara in *Bava Kama* 3b which discusses the word "*maveh*" used in the opening *mishnah*. The Gemara says that one explanation of this word is that it may mean "man," and it comes from the root "to seek."

"The rabbi said the root of a human being is we're searchers. We're always looking to make ourselves better. This was Alan. He was able, in mid-life, to become a searcher, to accept new opportunities."

Mordechai and the other men from Lakewood escorted the body to its burial in a cemetery in North Jersey. They gave Alan the final respect that he deserved, for a man who was able to change midlife and accept a new path on himself.

Mordechai and the other men decided to personally bury the body in the grave and cover it with dirt themselves, instead of the impersonal dump truck used in other burials.

After they finished closing the hole, a woman came over to them. She was not observant and was crying hysterically.

"She said, 'I live in Staten Island. I'm Alan's first cousin. To see what I just saw, to see people like you burying him, he must have had done something special in his life.'

She was right.

Now, decades later, Mordechai is still inspired by the commitment to change that Alan made at the very end of his life.

"The thing that obviously jumps out at you, it's so unbelievable — this man, who wasn't brought up religious, but at end of his life, just days before passing way, he made a life-altering decision. Can you imagine when he went upstairs the welcome they made for him?""

The rabbis extol us to "repent one day before your death" (*Pirkei Avos* 2:15). Since no one knows when he will die, how can a person achieve this? If a person makes a sincere commitment to change his behaviors, even if it is in only a single action at a time, then he has shown a tremendous commitment to trying to get close to Hashem. Then when his time comes and he is called to ascend to heaven, he will bring with him a clear sign that he rededicated his life to serving Hashem (*Shabbos* 153a).

Alan left this world just after making a decision to make a dramatic change in his lifestyle. He was already rewarded in this world with having a proper burial. Certainly he was rewarded in the world above as well. There, a person is measured not by his external behaviors and appearances, but primarily according to the merits he brings with him and the unseen changes that occurred inside his heart.

Living among Heroes

People involved in Jewish outreach say they are inspired daily by the tremendous personal strength of their students.

"*Ba'alei teshuvah* are the real heroes," Rabbi Baruch Price explained. "One of the basic characteristics of human beings and animals in general is that we follow the path of least resistance. It's very easy for a person to be on a path and have a sense of inertia: 'This is my path, I'm going to stick with it, why should I change?'

"But when a Jew comes to a conclusion that so many of the things he's learned and lived until now are not one hundred percent true, it can be quite a startling and shocking conclusion. People who have intellectual honesty can face up to that, not to turn their backs on it and walk away, but rather to engage and make an effort to learn more and change not only their behavior but their value system. Doing so requires an incredible amount of energy and sincerity."

He cites the story of Barbara Klein*, a middle-aged woman who grew up in a home that was staunchly Reform. She had a strong Jewish identity, but a complete lack of any Jewish upbringing or knowledge. She got married, had two children, and got divorced.

Barbara stumbled upon the Jewish Learning Experience and began attending classes. She even convinced her mother, who was then in her eighties, to attend the classes with her. Twice a week, her mother drove the three hours from her home in upstate New York to hear Rabbi Price speak.

"For me it was inspiring to see a woman in her eighties who was open to hearing new things. She didn't become *frum* before she passed away, but just that she was coming to class was amazing."

Barbara was also very serious in her attendance, but she argued with every word that Rabbi Price taught.

"She used to air her views about Orthodoxy very openly, and they were not always that positive," Rabbi Price recalled.

However Rabbi Price has learned that when a person argues with a teacher, it's necessary to hear where the questions are coming from. Are they coming from a point of defiance, or from a serious desire to learn and hear the truth? Barbara constantly challenged Rabbi Price, but continued to come every week to hear more, so he knew that her desire was sincere.

"For me if someone is asking questions, especially difficult and challenging ones, they're taking it very seriously. They're not just being passive about it and saying, 'Yes, yes,' and then going home and doing their own thing. Rather they believe in what they're hearing and realize it will have major implications on their life, so they want to make sure what they're hearing makes sense. Therefore I welcomed it."

Rabbi Price introduced Barbara to several families in Teaneck and she began coming to the community for Shabbos. She began to grow religiously. Her mother eventually passed away, and in her will she left her palatial home to Barbara.

"It was a dream house — in the country, on a lake, surrounded by rolling hills — but she eventually reached a point, as much as she loved living there, that she realized she needed a connection and a community. She realized that living in that dream home was not the ideal.

"After a tremendous struggle, she felt at peace with the idea that she would sell her estate and move to Teaneck. She wanted to set an example to her two sons. She wanted them to marry Jews. She realized if she would not make a commitment, how could she expect her sons to do so?"

Rabbi Price said he is inspired everyday by Jews like Barbara, who can live their entire lives with a certain direction and focus.

Then when they are exposed to the truth of Judaism, they have the courage and strength to build their lives anew.

"I really feel so privileged every single day to be dealing with people who are real heroes, who have the courage to change their lives in so many ways."

Jews such as Barbara, and the others profiled in this book, are seekers of truth. They are Jews who embark on journeys of discovery, unafraid of the challenges. They are prepared to grow and change even when doing so is difficult, and even when it goes counter to the world around them. When the whole world is running in a single direction, they push themselves to go against the flow and follow the path home that they know is correct.

The *Mesillas Yesharim* compares the world to a garden maze. The maze is filled with many incorrect paths, all of which look the same. However, only a single one leads to the correct destination.

"The walker between the paths has no way of seeing or knowing whether he is on the true or the false path, for they are all similar, presenting no difference whatsoever to the observing eye," Rabbi Luzzatto writes.

So what is the solution? A garden maze often has a guide standing on a platform above it who can see the entire maze, and who calls to the players with helpful suggestions to help them navigate to the finish line. Only he, who can see all of the paths, can properly discriminate which is correct and which will only lead to further confusion. It is up to the people inside the maze to listen to his suggestions.

"He who is willing to believe [the guide] will reach the designated spot, but he who is not willing to believe, but would rather trust his eyes, will certainly remain lost and will fail to reach it."

Rabbi Luzzatto cautions all of us: It's necessary to listen to the advice of those more learned than ourselves. What do they tell us? To constantly reflect on our actions and choices in order to ascertain whether we are on the correct path in life. To see whether our chosen path conforms to the dictates of the Torah, and whether it will lead us to the destination that we desire. Only through this reflection can we be certain that we are walking on the proper road, the one that will lead to the achievement of our goals. (See *Mesillas Yesharim*, end of Chapter Three.)

Hashem plants in each of us an awareness of the truth of Judaism and the eternal validity of the Torah. He calls to us. Sadly, many Jews miss the call or choose to ignore it. They are then forced to grope blindly through the maze of life, trying to find their way via trial and error. They don't notice the precious gifts they have, a heritage and millennia-old teachings of how to live a rewarding life. Only those particular individuals who are prepared to listen to the call, and decide to adapt their lives to the rules of the Torah, will succeed in arriving home.

After years of struggling on many incorrect paths, which at first seemed fruitful but instead led them to dead-ends, they will finally navigate their way through the maze. Then they will see the endless rewards waiting for themselves and their families.

They are finally home.

Additional Resources

THERE ARE NUMEROUS RESOURCES available — both online and through local organizations — that can help Jews learn about their roots. These include:

aish.com – a wide-range of articles and videos about Judaism, and links to local outreach organizations and synagogues

chabad.org – a plethora of information on Jewish holidays and rituals from a Chassidic perspective, as well as links to hundreds of Chabad Houses around the world

meor.org – Jewish outreach programs on numerous college campuses worldwide that offer Jewish courses and trips to Israel

jinternship.com – a program that combines serious professional internships with stimulating Jewish classes, located in Israel and the United States

partnersintorah.org – an organization that sets up one-on-one phone study sessions

simpletoremember.org – a wide collection of captivating articles by numerous Jewish authors

Or email us at grospublishing@gmail.com to inquire about how to find learning opportunities and additional resources near you.

Glossary

The following glossary provides a partial explanation of some of the Hebrew and Yiddish (Y) words and phrases used in this book. The spellings and explanations reflect the way the specific word is used herein. Often, there are alternate spellings and meanings for the words.

ALEF-BEIS: Hebrew alphabet.

ALIYAH: being called up to read from the Torah; moving to Israel.

AL KIDDUSH HASHEM: sacrificing one's life for Hashem.

ARON KODESH: the location in which Torahs scrolls are stored at the front of a synagogue.

AVOS: the forefathers of the Jewish people.

BA'AL TESHUVAH: literally "one who returns"; refers to a Jew who has returned to his or her religious roots.

BA'ALEI TESHUVAH: Jews who have returned to their roots.

BAIS YAAKOV: school system for religious girls and young women.

BARUCH HASHEM: phrase meaning "Thank G-d."

BAR MITZVAH: the age (thirteen) at which a Jewish boy accepts and becomes responsible for performance of the mitzvos.

BAS MITZVAH: the age (twelve) at which a Jewish girl accepts and becomes responsible for performance of the mitzvos.

BASHERT (Y.): the person whom someone was destined to marry.

BEIS DIN: a Jewish religious court.

BEIS HAMIKDASH: the Temple in Jerusalem. Built twice and destroyed first by the Babylonians and then the Romans, Jews await its final rebuilding at the time of the Mashiach.

BENTCH (Y.): recitation of the prayer of thanksgiving after eating a meal, also called Birkas HaMazon.

BITACHON: living with a constant focus on Hashem.

BERACHAH: a blessing recited before the consumption of food or another action. Alternatively: a personal blessing from a rabbi or other prominent person.

BRIS MILAH: ritual circumcision ceremony performed on or after the eighth day of a baby boy's life.

BUBBY (Y.): grandmother.

CHABAD: a Chassidic religious and outreach organization with branches around the world.

CHABAD-LUBAVITCH: the full title of Chabad.

CHABADNIK: a follower of the Chabad movement.

CHAI: the Hebrew letters *ches-yud* which stand for life.

CHAMETZ: leavened food composed of flour, yeast and water which is prohibited from consumption during Passover.

CHANUKAH: an eight-day festival during the winter which recounts the victory of a small group of Jews over Greek domination and the Jews' rededication of the Beis HaMikdash.

CHASSID: a member of a Chassidic group.

CHASSIDIC: practices of a branch of Orthodoxy that focus on specific traditions, which are often based on mysticism. There are numerous groups within the movement, each which follows particular customs and adherence to the teachings of specific leaders.

CHASSIDUS: the Chassidic movement.

CHASAN: groom.

CHASUNAH: wedding.

CHAVRUSA: study partner.

CHAZAN: prayer leader.

CHESED: act of kindness.

CHESHBON: calculation.

CHEVRAH KADDISHA: Jewish burial society.

CHIZUK: encouragement.

CHUMASH: the five books of the Torah.

DAVEN (Y.): pray.

DAYEINU: Hebrew phrase meaning, "It's sufficient."

DERECH: path.

DAVID HAMELECH: King David.

DIVREI TORAH: Torah teachings.

DREIDEL (Y.): a four-sided top played during the holiday of Chanukah.

ELIYAHU HANAVI: a prominent Jewish prophet.

EMES: truth.

EMUNAH: living with an internalization of the fundamentals of Jewish faith.

ERUV: the string around a community which defines its borders to allow carrying of particular items between buildings on Shabbos. It also often serves as a marker of the end of the Jewish neighborhood.

ERETZ YISRAEL: the Land of Israel.

ESROG: a citron fruit which is shaken along with three other species as part of the religious observance of the holiday of Sukkos.

FRUM (Y.): observant of the religious rules of Judaism.

GABBAI: administrator of a synagogue prayer service who distributes honors; assistant to a prominent Rabbi.

GAM ZU LETOVAH: Hebrew phrase meaning, "This is also for the best."

GEMARA: the Talmud, a sixty-three-volume collection of legal and religious teachings which form the basis of Jewish observance.

GET (Y.): a divorce document.

HAFTORAH: a selection of prophetic writings read in synagogue on Shabbos.

HAKADOSH BARUCH HU: G-d.

HAKARAS HATOV: acknowledgment of a benefit performed toward a person.

HALACHAH: Jewish law.

HAMOTZI: a prayer recited over bread before beginning a meal.

HAR SINAI: Mt. Sinai, the location at which the Torah was given to the Jewish people.

HASHGACHAH PRATIS: Divine intervention in a person's life.

HASHEM: G-d.

HASHEM ECHAD: the words of the Shema prayer which proclaim the existence of only a single Divine force.

HATZLACHAH: success.

KABBALAS SHABBOS: the Friday night prayer service.

KADDISH: a prayer said in the memory of a deceased relative and as a standard part of every prayer service.

KADOSH: holy.

KASHER: prepare at item to be fit for use with kosher food.

KAVANAH: concentration during a prayer or religious observance.

KAVOD HATORAH: honor shown toward the Torah.

KAYIN: the son of Adam and Chavah, the first people on earth.

KEDUSHAH: holiness.

KIBUD AV VA'EIM: honor showed toward one's parents.

KIDDUSH HASHEM: sanctification of G-d's name achieved through proper actions.

KIPPAH: head covering worn by men.

KIRUV: Jewish outreach.

KITTEL (Y.): a white garment worn by men at their wedding and on certain holidays.

KNEIDLACH (Y.): a food composed of dough stuffed with meat.

KOL NIDREI: the emotional Yom Kippur evening prayer service.

KOLLEL: a Jewish outreach and study organization.

KORBANOS: sacrifices brought in the Beis HaMikdash, used colloquially to refer to Jews who were killed during the Holocaust.

KOSEL: Western Wall of the Temple Mount in Yerushalayim, a place for prayer and introspection.

KOSHER: food or practices which conform to Jewish law.

LATKE (Y.): potato-based food item eaten during Chanukah.

LEIN (Y.): read from the Torah.

L'CHAIM: a toast made over a drink of liquor.

LECH LECHA: the Torah portion which recounts the original journey of Avraham, the founder of the Jewish people, to Eretz Yisrael. As an expression, it is used to signify a new direction in one's life.

LUBAVITCH: see Chabad.

LULAV: the middle branch of a palm tree which is shaken along with three other species as part of the religious observance of the holiday of Sukkos.

MACHMIR: binding observance to particular beliefs.

MAGEN DAVID: Jewish star.

MANNA: bread-like food that was provided by Hashem for the Jews to eat during their travels through the desert.

MASHGIACH: overseer of students in a yeshivah; a food supervisor.

MASHIACH: "the anointed one," who will lead the Jewish people in the period of redemption.

MECHITZAH: a divider placed between the genders in a synagogue during a prayer service.

MEGILLAS ESTHER: a text recounting the story and miracles of the salvation of the Jews when they were threatened by their enemy Haman in the fourth-century BCE in Persia.

MELAVEH MALKAH: literally "escorting the Queen." It refers to a meal eaten after Shabbos.

MENORAH: nine-branched candelabrum lit during the holiday of Chanukah.

MENTSCH (Y.): a person noted for his/her exemplary interpersonal behavior.

MESIRAS NEFESH: personal strength in overcoming challenges.

MEZUZAH: a piece of parchment containing particular Torah verses which is placed in a case on the doorpost of a Jewish home.

MIDDOS: personal character traits.

MIKVEH: ritual bath.

MINCHAH: afternoon prayer service.

MINYAN: a quorum for a prayer service.

MITZVAH (pl. MITZVOS): an action commanded by Hashem.

MITZVAH GORERES MITZVAH: one mitzvah leads to the next.

MODEH ANI: prayer said each morning thanking Hashem for returning our soul to us for another day of life.

MODIM: paragraph of thanksgiving said in the Shemoneh Esreh prayer.

MUSSAR: ethical teachings; Torah ethics and values aimed at character improvement.

NACHAS: pride.

NCSY: a Jewish organization that organizes activities for teenagers.

NEILAH: concluding service of Yom Kippur.

NER: light.

NER TAMID: the eternal light situated above an *aron kodesh*.

NESHAMAH: soul.

NISAYON: personal test.

OLAM HABA: the World to Come.

PARASHAH: Torah portion.

PESACH: the weeklong holiday called of Passover in the springtime which recounts the Exodus of the Jewish people from slavery in Egypt.

PIDYON HABEN: redemption of a first-born male child after a month of life.

RABBI: Jewish religious leader and teacher.

REBBETZIN: the wife of a Rabbi who often functions as a leader and teacher.

ROSH HASHANAH: a holiday marking the beginning of the Jewish year, typically used for reflection and prayer.

ROSH HAYESHIVAH / ROSH YESHIVAH: rabbinic head of a yeshivah.

RUCHNIYUS: spirituality.

S'CHACH: the roof of a sukkah which must be made of a naturally-grown material.

SEDER: meal eaten during the holiday of Pesach during which we recount the story of the exodus from Egypt.

SEFER: religious book.

SEFER TORAH: Torah scroll.

SEFER (pl. SEFARIM): religious book.

SEMINARY: institution of Jewish study for women.

SEPHARDIC: Jew from a Spanish-speaking or Middle-Eastern country.

SHALOSH SEUDOS: the third meal eaten during Shabbos afternoon.

SHABBOS: the Sabbath/seventh day, typically spent in synagogue praying and at home with one's family eating and resting.

SHABBATON: a program with prayer services, classes, and other events to experience the beauty of Shabbos.

SHACHARIS: morning prayer service.

SHADCHAN (pl. SHADCHANIM): matchmaker.

SHALIACH TZIBUR: leader of a prayer service.

SHAMAYIM: heaven.

SHAS: Gemara.

SHECHINAH: Divine Presence of Hashem.

SHEMA / SHEMA YISRAEL: prayer proclaiming one's loyalty to Hashem which is recited each morning and evening.

SHEMINI ATZERES: eighth day of the holiday of Sukkos.

SHEMONEH ESREH: also known as the Amidah. A prayer composed of nineteen blessings recited three times a day.

SHEVA BERACHOS: weeklong celebration for a couple following their wedding.

SHIDDUCH: a match made between a man and woman.

SHIN: second-to-last letter of the Hebrew alphabet.

SHIUR: Torah class.

SHIVAH: week-long mourning process following the passing of a loved one.

SHLEMIEL (Y): Yiddish for fool.

SHLOMO HAMELECH: King Solomon, the son of King David who built the Beis HaMikdash.

SHMURAH MATZAH: matzah prepared with extra stringencies.

SHOMER SHABBOS: Sabbath-observant.

SHOCHET: ritual slaughterer.

SHUL: synagogue.

SIMCHAH: joy.

SIMCHAS TORAH: a single-day holiday which follows Sukkos and marks the beginning of the annual reading of the Torah.

SINAI: refers to the giving of the Torah on Mt. Sinai.

SIYATTA D'SHEMAYA: help from Heaven.

SMICHA: rabbinical ordination.

SUKKAH: a hut built outside one's house for the week-long holiday of Sukkos.

SUKKOS: a weeklong holiday in the fall, or the plural version of the word Sukkah.

TALLIS: prayer shawl.

TALMID CHACHAM: Torah sage.

TALMUD: Gemara.

TALMUD TORAH: Torah study.

TANACH: the books of Jewish scripture and prophecy, composed of the Torah, Neviim, and Kesuvim.

TEFILLAS HADERECH: prayer said during a trip to beseech Hashem for protection from the hazards of the way.

TEFILLAH: prayer.

TEFILLIN: black boxes which contains sections of the Torah which are worn by men during the weekday morning prayer service.

TEHILLIM: Psalms, written by King David and others which form the basis of many Jewish prayers and which are individually recited at times of need.

TESHUVAH: returning to one's roots or seeking forgiveness for one's sins.

TISHAH B'AV: a day of mourning in the summertime during which we remember the destruction of the Beis HaMikdash.

TIKKUN OLAM: repairing the world.

TREIF: non-kosher meat.

TORAH: the Five Books of Moses or the study of Jewish religious books.

TZADDIK (pl. TZADDIKIM): righteous person.

TZEDAKAH: charity.

TZIDKANIYOS: righteous women.

TZITZIS: four-cornered garment worn by men under their clothing. On its corners are tied strings which remind the wearer of the mitzvos and of Hashem.

YASHER KOACH: Hebrew greeting for "a job well done."

YEKKE: a Jew of German descent, normally known for punctuality and strict adherence to rules.

YERUSHALAYIM: Jerusalem.

YESHAYAH: prominent prophet.

YESHIVAH: institution of Jewish study for men.

YID (Y.): Yiddish for "Jew."

YIDDISH: language originally spoken by Jews of Eastern Europe which combined Hebrew and German.

YIDDISHKEIT: Judaism.

YOM KIPPUR: day of fasting and repentance in the autumn.

YOM TOV: Jewish holidays which are similar to Shabbos in many ways (includes Rosh Hashanah, Yom Kippur, Sukkos, Pesach, and Shavuos).

YONAH: a prophet who was sent by Hashem to tell the residents of the city of Nineveh to repent. He refused to go and tried to escape in a boat. Yonah was thrown overboard and was swallowed by a fish. He later completed his mission and was successful in encouraging the inhabitants to atone for their sins.

ZEMIROS: Songs sung at the Shabbos table.

ZT"L: In blessed memory.

Bibliography / Biography

ABARBANEL: Rabbi Don Isaac ben Yehudah Abarbanel (d. 1508), leader of Spanish Jewry and prolific Torah commentator.

ALSHICH: Rabbi Moshe Alshich (d. 1598), Tzefas kabbalist and commentator on the Tanach.

ARIZAL: Rabbi Yitzchak ben Shlomo Luria (d. 1572), eminent Tzefas kabbalist.

BEIS YOSEF: legal commentary by Rabbi Yosef Caro (d. 1575), the author of the *Shulchan Aruch*.

CHIDA: Rabbi Chaim Yosef David ben Yitzchak Zerachia Azulai (d. 1806), prolific writer and Torah scholar.

CHAFETZ CHAIM: Rabbi Yisrael Meir HaKohen of Radin (d. 1933), leader of Torah Jewry and author of many essential works including the *Mishnah Berurah*.

CHOVOS HALEVAVOS: "Duties of the Heart." Classic work of *mussar* by Rabbeinu Bachya (d. 1340).

HILCHOS TESHUVAH: laws of repentance by the Rambam.

KITZUR SHULCHAN ARUCH: halachic work by Rabbi Shlomo Ganzfried (d. 1886).

MAHARAL: Rabbi Yehudah Loewe ben Bezalel (d. 1609), chief rabbi in Prague, Torah commentator, and kabbalist.

MECHILTA: early halachic/midrashic commentary to the Book of Exodus (*Shemos*).

MESILLAS YESHARIM: central work of ethical teachings by Rabbi Moshe Chaim Luzatto (d. 1746).

MICHTAV M'ELIYAHU: collection of speeches and writings by Rabbi Eliyahu Eliezer Dessler (d. 1954).

MIDRASH TANCHUMA: midrashic commentary to the Torah.

MISHLEI: a book of Tanach, a collection of ethical teachings written down by Shlomo HaMelech.

MISHNAH BERURAH: contemporary work of Jewish law written by the Chafetz Chaim.

OLAS TAMID: contemporary book explaining the everyday prayers.

PELE YO'ETZ: a collection and elucidation of key tenets of Judaism, written by Rabbi Eliezer Papo (d. 1826).

PIRKEI AVOS: "Chapter of the Fathers," a collection of ethical teachings in the Mishnah.

RABBI AKIVA: one of the leading teachers of the Mishnah. Martyred around 138 CE.

RABBI MOSHE FEINSTEIN: (d. 1986) foremost modern halachic decider and Torah leader in Russia and America.

RABBI AHARON FELDMAN: Rosh Yeshivah of Yeshivas Ner Yisrael, Baltimore.

RABBI NACHMAN OF BRESLOV: (d. 1810) founder of the Breslov Chassidic movement.

RABBI MENACHEM SCHNEERSON: (d. 1994) leader of the Chabad-Lubavitch movement.

RABBI MEIR SHAPIRO: (d. 1932) founder of Daf Yomi program of study and Yeshivas Chachmei Lublin.

RABBI NOACH WEINBERG: (d. 2009) founder and Rosh Yeshivah of Yeshivas Aish HaTorah, Yerushalayim.

RABBI SHIMON SCHWAB: (d. 1995) Torah leader in Germany and America.

RABBI SHIMSHON RAPHAEL HIRSCH: (d. 1888) prominent nineteenth-century Torah leader of German Jewry and author of a number of important works.

RAMBAM: Rabbi Moshe ben Maimon (d. 1204), author of the halachic compilation *Mishneh Torah* and other seminal works. Lived in Spain and Egypt.

RASHI: Rabbi Shlomo Yitzchaki (d. 1105), pre-eminent commentator on Tanach, Gemara, and other works, in Provence, France.

SFAS EMES: Rabbi Yehudah Aryeh Leib Alter (d. 1905) second leader of the Gerrer Chassidic dynasty.

SFORNO: Torah commentary by Rabbi Ovadiah Sforno (d. 1550) of Italy.

SIFSEI CHAYIM: a collection of lectures delivered by Rabbi Chaim Friedlander, the Rosh Yeshivah of Yeshivas Ponevezh, Bnei Brak.

SKVERER REBBE: Rabbi David Twersky, contemporary Chassidic Rebbe from New Square, NY.

STEIPLER GAON: Rabbi Yaakov Yisrael Kanievsky (d. 1985), leading Talmudic scholar and author in Israel.

TANYA: Chassidic work written by Rabbi Shneur Zalman of Liadi (d. 1812), the founder of the Chabad-Lubavitch movement.

VILNA GAON: Rabbi Eliyahu ben Shlomo Zalman (d. 1797), brilliant Torah scholar and leader in Eastern Europe.

ZOHAR: kabbalistic work of the Mishnaic sage Rabbi Shimon bar Yochai.

Index

In honor of our mother

Isabel Gros

And in memory of our parents

Henri Gros
(Naftali ben Yaacov)

Lewis Case
(Label ben Moishe)

Mildred Case
(Malka bas Fischel)

ת.נ.צ.ב.ה

Bonnie and Jacques Gros

In honor of our beloved
children and grandchildren

Michoel and Shoshana Gros
and their children

Jennifer and Efraim Berenholz
and their children

Bonnie and Jacques Gros

In memory of

Zahava Goldwasser
(Zahava bas Moshe Abba a"h)

who inspired so many Jewish *neshamos* to become *ba'alei teshuvah* by showing them the beauty, wisdom, and warmth of Yiddishkeit.

ת.נ.צ.ב.ה

Shmuel Coleman

לעלוי נשמת

עליזה בת שמואל הערש

עודד בן שמואל הערש

זהבה בת פנחס

שמואל הערש בן לייזר לייב

ת.נ.צ.ב.ה

משפחת הייטנר

לעילוי נשמת

בנימין בן הרב **חיים פישל** הלוי ז״ל

פייגל בת הרב **יעקב מאיר** ז״ל

Norman and Fay Levitz

גרשון בן **דוב בער הלוי** ז״ל

משא צירל בת **שמואל ירוחם** ז״ל

Gerson and Martha Bernstein

ת.נ.צ.ב.ה

The Levitz Family

Ramat Beit Shemesh, Israel

וצדקתו עומדת לעד... זה הכותב ספרים...

Dedicated with love and respect in honor of our parents שיחיו

Jacques & Bonnie Gros
Heshy & Manya Berenholz

and our grandmother **Isabel Gros** who have instilled in us the values of our forefathers, and showed us the path of the righteous.

And in blessed memory of our grandparents, לזכרון עולם:

Naomi Berenholz
Nechama *bas* Rav Tzvi Aryeh

Henri Gros
Naftali *ben* Yaacov

Michel David Denholz
Dovid Aryeh *ben* Nechemia

Rabbi Moshe Berenholz
Rav Moshe *ben* Alter Shimon

Mildred Case
Malka *bas* Fischel

Lola Denholz
Leah *bas* Asher

Silvia Berenholz
Tzirel *bas* Yechiel

Lewis Case
Label *ben* Moishe

Paul Denholz
Pesach *ben* Nechemia

ת.נ.צ.ב.ה

DEDICATED BY

Efraim & Jennifer Berenholz and Family

In honor of

R. Michoel & Dr. Shoshana Gros

for all the amazing work you do for
the continuation of Klal Yisrael!
Also in honor of our *mechutan*

Dr. Mark Paris

whose amazing story is
chronicled in these pages!
We are inspired, and you are admired!

Matti & Beth Friedman
Hillcrest, NY

לע"נ

מרת **שושנה היימן גרינבוים** ע"ה

In memory of

Mrs. Shoshana Hayman Greenbaum

She brought her students closer to Torah,
mitzvos and their Creator.

ת.נ.צ.ב.ה

Mr. and Mrs. Eliyahu Dovid Hayman

Ramat Beit Shemesh, Eretz Yisrael

In memory of

Mireille Bloch

Myriam *bat hechaver* Binyamin Zeev

loving wife, caring mother, and dedicated grandmother, who taught us to always search for the good in everyone and everything. May we always follow her path.

FROM HER HUSBAND

Gerard Bloch

HER CHILDREN AND SPOUSES

Jean-Francois Bloch and Valerie Michel

Martine and Marc Weill

Jacques and Isabelle Bloch

Valerie and Laurent Cudkowicz

HER GRANDCHILDREN AND SPOUSES

Noemie and Gilad Alon

Elie and Odiya Cudkowicz

Tamar, Ben Cudkowicz

Simon, Judith Weill

Alexandra, Leah, Elsa Bloch

This book should be a *zechus*
for the *refuah sheleimah* of

Luba Baila bas Devorah

and is dedicated in memory of our dear cousin

Debbie Rosen O'Day

whose memory remains an inspiration for those
who knew her and continue to love her.

The Gros Family
Ramat Beit Shemesh, Israel

In memory of my beloved husband

Henri Gros
(Naftali ben Yaacov)

whose enthusiasm for life
and for Judaism was successfully
transmitted to his descendants.

Isabel Gros

In honor of

Michoel and Shoshana Gros

Mazel tov on the publication of
this beautiful book!

David and Jill Krischer

Atlanta, GA

לע"נ

בנינו בכורינו ואחינו היקר
ירא אלוקים עדין הנפש

הבחור שלמה ז"ל
ב"ר נחום דור בער שיבלחט"א
לורינג

נפטר ביום ט"ז באלול תשע"ה

ת.נ.צ.ב.ה

Robert and Jan Cohen

Moshe Chaim Golinski and Family

Dovid Nisenbaum

YS Venture Group

In memory of

Zeev** ben **David Arye

Ester** bas **Meyer Baruch

Arye** ben **Avraham

Raizel** bas **Chonoch

Avrum and Rita Epstein

Hatzlachah Rabbah!

May this book help many Jews come home!

The Kamionski Family

לע"נ

אריה בן **אליהו**

מרים בת **מרדכי**

פרידה בת **דויד**

מרדכי בן **אהרון**

מאת

אליהו ודניאלה ליבא

About the Author

MICHOEL GROS lives in Ramat Beit Shemesh, Israel with his wife and eight children where he learns Torah full-time and writes Jewish books and articles. He grew up in a Conservative Jewish home in New Jersey and Virginia, and became observant during college. He later studied at several *yeshivos* in the United States and Eretz Yisrael.

Prior to his *aliyah* in 2009, he worked as the Chief Operating Officer of the Atlanta Scholars Kollel outreach organization, and as a writer and editor for a technology magazine in New York.

In 2016, he self-published his first work, *70 Questions and Answers on Megillas Esther.* This is his second book.